WOMEN AND GLOBAL ECONOMIC ORDER

A Feminist Perspectives

WOMEN AND GLOBAL ECONOMIC ORDER

A Feminist Perspectives

S Rani

MD PUBLICATIONS PVT LTD
NEW DELHI
www.mdppl.com

Published by:

MD Publications Pvt Ltd
"MD House", 11, Darya Ganj,
New Delhi - 110 002
Phone : +91-11-45355555
E-mail : contact@mdppl.com
website : www.mdppl.com

ISBN: 978-81-7533-319-2

Published and Printed by Mr. Pranav Gupta on behalf of **MD Publications Pvt Ltd** at JJ offset Printers, Delhi.

PREFACE

Although there is a great deal of rhetoric about the evils of globalisation it is a very poorly defined concept. At one level, the term 'globalisation' refers to the processes by which the world is becoming more interdependent. Interdependence is a concept that is extremely well understood by indigenous peoples because it is embedded in our psyche. Globalisation also refers to other processes - for example the notion of the global village, to the way in which we are becoming politically and socially more and more interdependent. However it also and primarily these days, is used to refer to the creation of a single global economy.

Economic activity and the strengthening of the economy - a process that may include, but is not synonymous with, economic growth have a crucial role to play in achieving the material and spiritual prosperity of a region and its people. Humanity's growing appreciation of the economic interdependence among different regions of the world and the possibilities for global integration are also of great value. However, the narrowly materialistic worldview underpinning much of modern economics has contributed to the degradation of human conduct, the corruption and dissolution of important institutions, and the exploitation and marginalisation of large segments of the population - women and girls key amongst them.

Economic pressures, among other things, resulted in the disruption and dislocation of families and communities and the disappearance of diversified, ecologically sustainable small-scale agriculture, mostly in rural areas where it is often women who carry out the bulk of the work and who are disproportionately affected by these trends. Such pressures have also led to growing insecurity within local economies that have historically valued social ties and a collective sense of well-being over competition and individual advancement. To make these statements is not to romanticize the past or to promote a naïve ideal of the 'local' in reaction to the idea of a distant, all powerful 'global'. Rather, it is to recognize that diverse economic arrangements need to be explored and given space to develop.

It is widely recognized that the economic empowerment of women is an essential aspect of the advancement of the equality of women and men and necessary for assuring that women have options and the ability to make decisions conducive to their own well-being and that of their families. In light of the observations made above, those who wish to foster women's full and equal participation in society will also need to reflect on the nature of the economic arrangements within which this participation is to take place. We need to ask ourselves whether such arrangements should only be concerned with the accumulation of material wealth that enriches a few or whether they should aim to enhance collective prosperity and promote community well-being and environmental sustainability.

I am very grateful to Mr. Pranav Gupta, Director of MD Publications Pvt Ltd, New Delhi, for his kind cooperation and support for this book.

S Rani

CONTENTS

1

Analysing Global Governance

As one considers the different UN agencies and departments responsible for the global governance of its development efforts, it can be helpful to refer to the Organizational Chart of the United Nations System. The United Nations Development Group (UNDG) coordinates UN development efforts. UNDG is an instrument for UN reform, created by the Secretary General in 1997, to improve the effectiveness of UN development at the country level. UNDG brings together the operational agencies working on development. The Administrator of the United Nations Development Programme (UNDP) chairs UNDG on behalf of the UN Secretary General. UNDG develops policies and procedures that allow member agencies to work together and analyze country issues, plan support strategies, implement support programmes, monitor results and advocate for change. These initiatives increase UN impact in helping countries achieve the MDGs, including poverty reduction.

The full UNDG membership has grown to 28 agencies, plus five observers. The group meets at least three times yearly to decide on issues related to country level coordination to achieve the MDGs. UNDG's Executive Committee consists of the four funds and programs that report directly to the Secretary General: the United Nations Children's Fund (UNICEF), the United Nations Population Fund (UNFPA), the United Nations World Food Programme (WFP) and the United Nations Development Programme (UNDP). The United

Nations High Commissioner for Human Rights is an Ex-Officio member of the Committee. The Executive Committee focuses on reforming the work methods of the funds and programs and manages the mechanisms of UNDG. It meets every other month and is chaired by UNDP's Administrator. The United Nations Development Programme (UNDP) is the UN's global development network, an organization advocating for change and connecting countries to knowledge, experience and resources to help people build a better life.

UNDP is present in 166 countries, working with them on their own solutions to global and national development challenges. UNDP publishes annual Human Development Reports. According to UNDP, the Human Development Report was first launched in 1990 with the single goal of "putting people back at the center of the development process in terms of economic debate, policy and advocacy." Since the first Report, four new composite indices for human development have been developed — the Human Development Index, the Gender-related Development Index, the Gender Empowerment Measure, and the Human Poverty Index. Each Report also focuses on a highly topical theme in the current development debate, providing analysis and policy recommendations. National human development reports have been published at the country level in more than 120 nations.

The Human Development Report is an "independent" report in that it is commissioned by UNDP and is the product of a selected team of leading scholars, development practitioners and members of the Human Development Report Office of UNDP. While UNDP is responsible for the in-country development efforts of the United Nations, the UN Department of Economic and Social Affairs (DESA) engages in policy development. DESA serves as an interface between global policies in the economic, social and environmental spheres, and national action. DESA works in three main interlinked areas:

- It compiles, generates and analyses a wide range of economic, social and environmental data and information on which Member States of the United Nations draw to review common problems and to take stock of policy options;

- It facilitates the negotiations of Member States in many intergovernmental bodies on joint courses of action to address ongoing or emerging global challenges; and
- It advises interested Governments on the ways and means of translating policy frameworks developed in United Nations conferences and summits into programs at the country level and, through technical assistance, helps build national capacities.

Three DESA divisions are responsible for development policy: the Development Policy and Analysis Division, the Division for Social Policy and Development, and the Division for Sustainable Development. DESA's Development Policy and Analysis Division aims to contribute to a strengthening of international cooperation for the economic and social development of all countries, and to foster their effective integration into the world economy in the context of UN Development Agenda. The Division's core functions include. onal development agenda; and

- Monitoring and analyzing global economic trends and prospects and formulating advice for global macroeconomic policy coordination;
- Analyzing long-term development trends and preparing policy advice on the international development agenda; and
- Serving as the secretariat for the Committee for Development Policy.

Although managed by DESA's Development Policy and Analysis Division, the Committee for Development Policy was established in 1965 as a subsidiary body of the United Nations Economic and Social Council (ECOSOC). ECOSOC is an intergovernmental body responsible for formulating policy recommendations to Member States and to the United Nations system on matters pertaining to development. The Committee for Development Policy provides inputs and independent advice to ECOSOC on emerging cross-sectoral development issues and on international cooperation for development, focusing on medium- and long-term aspects. Each year, ECOSOC advises the Committee about the theme(s) that the Committee should consider at its annual session.

The General Assembly, the Secretary-General and the subsidiary bodies of ECOSOC can also propose, through the Council, issues for consideration by the Committee. In addition, based on its expertise, the Committee itself often provides more general advice to ECOSOC concerning critical issues and the international development agenda. The Committee is also responsible for undertaking, once every three years, a review of the list of least developed countries (LDCs), on the basis of which it advises ECOSOC regarding countries which should be added to the list and those that could be graduated from the list. In accordance with the Council's resolutions, the Secretary-General nominates 24 experts, in their personal capacity, as members of the Committee for three-year terms. ECOSOC has responsibility for deciding on appointments to the Committee. In making the nominations for the Committee, the Secretary-General takes into account the need to have a diversity of development experience, including ecologists, economists, and social scientists, as well as geographical balance, gender balance, and a balance between continuity and change in the membership of the Committee.

DESA's Division for Social Policy and Development has as its main objective the strengthening of international cooperation for social development in the context of the comprehensive and detailed framework of commitments and policies for action by Governments, intergovernmental and nongovernmental organizations provided by the Copenhagen Declaration on Social Development and Programme of Action of the World Summit for Social Development. The Division for Social Policy and Development focuses on the three core issues of poverty eradication, employment generation, and social integration. DESA's Division of Social Policy and Development is responsible for managing the United Nations

Commission for Social Development which is one of the ten functional commissions established by the United Nations Economic and Social Council (ECOSOC) since 1946 to advise and assist it in carrying out its work.

The Commission for Social Development consists of 46 members elected by ECOSOC. Since the convening of the World Summit for Social Development in Copenhagen in 1995, the Commission has been the key UN body in charge of the follow-up and implementation of the Copenhagen Declaration and Programme of Action. As a result of the Summit, the mandate of the Commission was reviewed and its membership expanded from 32 to 46 members in 1996. It meets once a year at the United Nations Headquarters in New York, usually in February for about two weeks. Each year since 1995, the Commission has taken up key social development themes as part of its follow-up to the outcome of the Copenhagen Summit. At the end of the Summit, Governments adopted the Copenhagen Declaration, the Ten Commitments, and the Programme of Action of the World Social Summit.

The Ten Commitments include:

- Create an economic, political, social, cultural and legal environment that will enable people to achieve social development;
- Eradicate absolute poverty by a target date to be set by each country;
- Support full employment as a basic policy goal;
- Promote social integration based on the enhancement and protection of all human rights;
- Achieve equality and equity between women and men;
- Attain universal and equitable access to education and primary health care;
- Accelerate the development of Africa and the least developed countries;
- Ensure that structural adjustment programmes include social development goals;
- Increase resources allocated to social development;

- Strengthen cooperation for social development through the UN.

Five years later, Governments reconvened in Geneva in June 2000 for the 24th special session of the United Nations General Assembly, to review what has been achieved, and to commit themselves to new initiatives. Since the Summit in 1995, the UN General Assembly has annually considered the issue of implementation of the outcome of the World Summit for Social Development, taking stock of follow-up activities undertaken at the national level and within the United Nations, including in its subsidiary bodies ECOSOC and the Commission for Social Development, as well as sharing experiences, lessons learned and obstacles encountered. Each year, the Assembly has held a general debate and adopted a resolution on the implementation.

DESA's Division for Sustainable Development provides leadership and is an authoritative source of expertise within the United Nations system on sustainable development. Sustainable development is defined as balancing the fulfilllment of human needs with the protection of the natural environment so that these needs can be met not only in the present, but also in the indefinite future. Sustainable development does not focus solely on environmental issues. More broadly, sustainable development policies encompass three general policy areas: economic, environmental and social. In support of this, several United Nations texts refer to "the interdependent and mutually reinforcing pillars" of sustainable development as economic development, social development, and environmental protection.

DESA's Division for Sustainable Development promotes sustainable development as the substantive secretariat to the UN Commission on Sustainable Development (CSD) and through technical cooperation and capacity building at international, regional and national levels. The CSD was created in December 1992 to ensure effective follow-up of the 1992 United Nations Conference on Environment and Development (UNCED - also known as the Earth Summit), in Rio de Janeiro, Brazil, where world leaders signed the Framework Convention on Climate Change and the Convention on Biological Diversity; endorsed the Rio Declaration and the Forest Principles; and adopted Agenda 21, a 300-page plan for achieving sustainable development in the 21st century. The CSD is composed of 53 members elected by the ECOSOC from amongst the Member States of the United Nations for terms of office of three years.

The CSD meets annually for a period of two to three weeks; and receives substantive and technical services from DESA's Division for Sustainable Development. The CSD reports to the Economic and Social Council and, through it, to the Second Committee of the General Assembly. In addition to administering the CSD, the context for the work of DESA's Division on Sustainable Development is the implementation of Agenda 21, the Johannesburg Plan of Implementation and the Barbados Programme of Action for Sustainable Development of Small Island Developing States.

The goals of the DESA Division on Sustainable Development are:

- Integration of the social, economic and environmental dimensions of sustainable development in policy-making at international, regional and national levels;
- Wide-spread adoption of an integrated, cross-sectoral and broadly participatory approach to sustainable development;
- Measurable progress in the implementation of the goals and targets of the Johannesburg Plan of Implementation.

The Division on Sustainable Development engages in the following activities to achieve its stated goals:

- Facilitate intergovernmental negotiations, consensus-building and decision-making through the provision of substantive support to the work of the CSD and other related bodies;
- Provide technical assistance, expert advice and capacity building to support developing countries and countries with economies in transition in their efforts to achieve sustainable development;
- Facilitate inter-agency and inter-organizational cooperation,

exchange and sharing of information, and catalyze joint activities and partnerships within the United Nations system and with other international organizations, governments and civil society groups in support of sustainable development;

- Promote and facilitate monitoring and evaluation of, and reporting on, the implementation of sustainable development at the national, regional and international levels;
- Undertake in-depth strategic analyses to provide policy advice to the USG/DESA, UN system and intergovernmental fora focusing on cross-cutting and emerging sustainable development issues.

The United Nations Research Institute for Social Development (UNRISD) is an autonomous UN agency engaging in multidisciplinary research on the social dimensions of contemporary problems affecting development. Through its research, UNRISD stimulates dialogue and contributes to policy debates on key issues of social development within and outside the United Nations system. UNRISD was created in 1963 as part of the first United Nations Development Decade. The Decade emphasized a "new approach to development," in which "purely economic indicators of progress were seen to provide only limited insight and might conceal as much as they indicate."

UNRISD thus became a pioneer in developing social indicators and broadened the development debate. Since then, the Institute has sought to promote a holistic and multidisciplinary approach to social development by focusing on decision-making processes, often conflicting social forces, and the question of who wins and who loses as economies grow or contract and societies change. The world economy grew 5.2% in 2007 powered by growth in China (11%), India (9%) and Russia (8%). The global economy faces a real risk of 1970s style stagflation however, with resource constraints tighter than ever before. Things could scarcely have looked rosier for the world economy at the start of 2007. The Emerging Markets, led by the giants of China, India, Russia and Brazil (the BRIC countries) had been posting 7%-10% grow rates for years. Property and stock market booms had brought consistent growth in North America and Europe. Investment was bringing economic development to much of the Middle East and Africa, and even Japan was recovering from its deflationary Lost Years.

Economic conditions within these countries play a major role in setting the economic atmosphere of less well-to-do nations and their economies. In many aspects, developing and less developed economies depend on the developed countries for their economic wellbeing. Theories were even circulating that thanks to the growth of the developing world, we might enjoy years of unfettered growth, as new markets would go through successive growth spurts and counter the effects of slowing growth elsewhere. It was suggested that Asia was decoupling from the US and able to grow under its own steam thanks to its two Awakening Giants.

What a difference a year makes. The global economy has been hit by a rapid one-two punch that may be setting the stage for stagflation to make a come-back. It started with the sub-prime crisis in the US, caused by loans to risky or sub-prime mortgagees who did not have strong credit histories. While house prices were rising there wasn't a problem. But as house prices slowed and then crashed to earth, default rates started to rise. To add fuel to the fire, sub-prime loans had been packaged and re-packaged in a range of derivative financial instruments such as Collateralized Debt Obligations (CDOs). It was not always clear what the contents CDOs consisted of, as they were combined, sliced and re-sold between financial institutions and funds, and which in some cases allowed risky debt such as sub-prime loans to be packaged as part of low-risk instruments.

Vast swathes of CDO investments had to be written off, and banks became suspicious of investment, borrowing and lending, since it was not always clear what the underlying security was. Once banks stopped lending the Credit Crunch hit. We then witnessed extraordinary scenes of government regulators in US and UK having to help save collapsing banks in order to avert a meltdown of the financial system, and to Sovereign Wealth Funds (SWFs) from the developing world taking large stakes in venerable western banks like Citibank and UBS in return for keeping them liquid. With house prices having fallen more than 20% in many areas of the United States, even prime mortgage holders now find themselves with negative equity. The federal government has been forced to step in and assume responsibility for both Fannie Mae and Freddie Mac, who between them back over half of all American mortgages.

The second part of the one-two punch has involved the rise of commodity prices. Just before the dawn of the 21st century, oil average $16 a barrel. By July 2008, less than 10 years later, oil hit a high of $146 a barrel a stunning rise of more than 800%. From early 2007 to mid 2008 alone the price has risen more than threefold from the mid $40s. During the Oil Crisis of the 1970s, oil spiked at a nominal peak of $38. In today's prices (adjusted for inflation), that is $106, a figure that we blew past in early 2008. The price of food has also started spiraling. Rice and other grain prices have doubled from 2007 - 2008, leading to food riots in a score of developing markets. Most agricultural and farm produce prices have been going through the roof. In fact almost all commodities, including those used for energy, construction and consumption, have been rising rapidly.

Price rises have been fueled by the demands of the emerging markets, particularly the BRIC nations, who together account for nearly 3 billion people. In order to maintain their high rates of growth and help lift more of their populace out of poverty, they require more and more commodities. A bigger worry for economists, however, is whether the natural resources exist to meet these burgeoning demands. A similar crisis was faced in the 1970s. After a period of strong global economic growth, when the world economy was averaging 5% a year GDP increases, the world hit supply constraints in oil and food. For the next fifteen years, global GDP growth slowed to an average of 3.2% per year. This became known as the stagflation era. Growth opportunities were limited, but prices continued to rise with a continued lack of supply.

A great debate ensued as to whether we had reached the limits of the earth ability to support our growth. In 1972 the Club of Rome famously argued exactly that, saying that the global economy would collapse. And yet the opposite happened. According to Jeffrey D. Sachs, Director of the Earth Institute at Columbia University, world crude oil production grew from 21 million barrels per day in 1960 to 56 mbd in 1973, a growth of 166%. The stagflation crisis also brought about a Green Revolution through fertilizer and irrigation development, and through the development of stronger seed strains. This led to much higher agricultural productivity levels. Since 1970 however, crude oil production has only grown 30% worldwide. More worrying still is that crude oil production in the Middle East has peaked at 21 mbd in 1974 and remained stagnant, while mature fields in the North Sea, Norway and Alaska are all in decline.

In fact there is a growing school of thought known as Peak Oil that believes we have " or will soon" reach peak oil production capabilities. In the 1950s Dr M. King Hubbert correctly predicted peak oil and decline rates for the mainland US oil industry. His model came to be known as The Hubbert Peak Theory. It predicts that world peak oil production will be reached sometime between 2000 and 2010, and will decline thereafter. This impending crisis has also helped to raise the price of food, since increasing amounts of land are being devoted to biodiesel crop development, and since higher oil prices raise the cost of fertilizer (for which petroleum is a key ingredient) and food transportation. It seems increasingly likely that a massive investment in renewable energy sources will be needed in order to avert another stagflationary period in the world economy, or even a global recession. The jury is still out as to how quickly oil supplies will decline or how fast alternative energy sources can be brought online.

2

Gender and the Making of Global Markets

The question which this chapter attempts to address is 'whether the international trade regime can be utilized to advance the objective of gender equality and if so, how?' The discussion on gender and trade regulation would raise a number of questions. First, should there be a linkage between gender concerns and international trade regulation? What do the facts on the ground indicate? How do the underlying policy considerations in the two fields relate to one another? In order to analyze these questions the framework of linkage within the trade regime is to be employed.

THE INTERNATIONAL TRADE REGIME

PRACTICE OF LINKAGE IN INTERNATIONAL TRADE REGULATION

A number of issues have been raised in connection with international trade regulation over the years. Among these, environment, labour and human rights issues top the list. A practice through which these issues have been linked to the regulation of international trade has been developed. For instance, the EU has included human rights, environmental and gender considerations in its trade agreements with ACP states. Similarly, in the generalized system of preferences the US has linked human rights and labour concerns as part of its trading arrangements. Linkages have also occurred in the multilateral trade regime of the WTO.

A typical example is the introduction of the significant flexibilities in the TRIPS agreement. It was considerations of the public health crisis associated with the HIV/AIDS pandemic that brought the health agenda to the WTO. Linkages in trade regulation come in different forms. An issue may be linked to trade regulation because it is substantively related to it. It may also occur to further other policies through the instrumentality of trade regulation. In this case, trade may be used as an incentive or alternatively as a sanction to bring about the desired change in other policies.

CONCEPTUALIZING LINKAGE IN THE TRADE REGIME

In whatever form it may come, linkage ultimately becomes a question as to the proper boundaries of the trade regime. Questions about the boundary of the trade regime came around the 1990s where the impacts of trade regulation on areas like environment and labour started to be articulated. With the expansion of subjects of trade regulation into trade in services and intellectual property rights under the Uruguay round, the boundary of the WTO became a major subject of analysis. Arguments regarding the boundary typically took a certain form reflected in terms of a contest between different values namely trade and non-trade values.

The 'trade and' and/or linkage debate became the characterising vocabulary for the discussions surrounding the boundaries of the international trade regime. However, international trade law scholars argue that understanding linkage as a contest of trade versus other policy issues is problematic. This is because; the focus on the contest between the different values will move one value forward only at the expense of the other. This inevitably brings us back to the starting point for determining which value should trump the other.

Instead, Jackson argues, the focus should be on how to maximize the goals in the contested fields. Similarly, Lang suggests that the focus should be on what the desired goals and purposes of the trade regime ought to be. According to Jackson, this will require some kind of balancing which for instance in the case of the WTO has led to the recognition that the WTO can focus on values such as environmental protection.

In this chapter too, the linkage of gender concerns and the trade regime is viewed in the same light. Is gender equality a value which falls under the (maximized) goals and purposes of the trade regime? What kind of intricate balancing is required for gender concerns to be considered within the trade regime? And to what end? Before turning to this central question, let's see the different literature on gender and trade so as to examine the some of the observations on the interaction between the two fields.

INTERACTIONS BETWEEN GENDER EQUALITY CONCERNS AND TRADE REGULATION

In an attempt to establish the relationship between gender and trade, the legal analysis in this section looks into the interactions between the governing legal instruments in both fields. Accordingly, the points of inquiry in analyzing the interactions between gender and trade take the following form.

A. Direct conflict between trade rules and human rights of women: Do trade commitments conflict with a country's domestic and international commitments that are relevant to women? Do trade commitments in any way contribute to promoting the human rights of women embodied in international commitments as well as domestic laws of states?

B. Trade norms undermining the effectiveness of norms on women: Trade and state capacity: There are different ways whereby one set of norms undermine the effectiveness of another. In the context of trade, what is often invoked in empirical research is the impact of trade rules on state capacity to implement its obligations in economic and social life of its people.

Capacity is looked at both from the perspective of economic capacity of a state and its policy space. So, the questions in relation to gender and trade are - do trade agreements diminish the capacity of a state to protect, promote and fulfill the human rights of women? For instance affecting financial or economic capacity of the state? Do trade agreements capacitate the state either by creating policy space or by financially enabling the state to adopt and implement policies aimed at advancing the human rights of women? Two trade agreements; the Agreement on Agriculture (AOA) and the General Agreement on Trade in Services (GATS) were selected for the purpose of analyzing the relationship between the governing legal instruments of the two fields. The findings of the analysis indicate the following.

AOA

In relation to the AOA, the interactions between the two legal norms show the potential of the AOA to undermine a state's capacity and therefore a state's commitments to progressively fulfill the conditions necessary for the realization of the right to food. This mainly emanates from the inadequate attention given to some of the important non-trade objectives like food security in the implementation and enforcement mechanisms of the agreement. The indeterminate status of the non-trade objectives in the AOA implies that states may not successfully invoke them to implement policies that may clash with their existing obligations under the AOA.

In effect state policy making space is adversely affected. States' financial capacity may also be affected in situations where states cannot implement policies designed to raise revenue for ensuring food security. It may thus be argued that the AOA may undermine the right to food contained in the various human rights instruments. The logical conclusion with respect to the human rights of women, in this particular case, the right to food and food security is this agreement poses as an obstacle to promoting the human rights women.

GATS

Important human rights considerations raised in relation to GATS include access to essential services such as health care services, energy and education. These relate to a whole range of socio-economic rights of women. It is argued that GATS does not clearly carve out those services which are immune from the scrutiny of the agreement thereby affecting the access to essential services for the poor of which women constitute the majority. The opposing argument is that the mere fact that essential services are not carved out as supplied in the exercise of governmental authority may not be problematic per se. The argument further goes on to assert that the consequences that flow from opening such services to commercial competition can be managed through appropriate government regulation.

This holds true in principle. It even goes in line with government obligations to ensure equitable access to essential services to its people. The problem arises when one examines the consequent obligations that arise when the service in question is not carved out as one that is supplied in the exercise of governmental authority. This relates to the second issue raised in relation to the interactions of GATS and human rights of women. The second claim against GATS is that it restricts the available policy instruments that can potentially be employed by states to promote social justice and thereby contribute to gender equality. Related to this is the nature of GATS obligations and negotiating structure.

The negotiating structure or mechanism coupled with the structure of the agreement itself is inherently in tension with the progressive realization of socio- economic rights which dominate the services sector. There are specific obligations that come into effect when a member country makes a specific commitment with regard to a particular service sector in its schedule. These include the important obligations of market access and national treatment. These specific commitments or obligations contained in members schedules are significant in that they determine the implications, both positive and adverse, flowing from GATS. When a member makes specific commitments on market access or national treatment for specific service sector, it is entitled to subject the commitments to certain conditions and qualifications which are sometimes referred to as limitations. It can do so by specifying these conditions and qualifications in its schedule of commitments.

Therefore, the obligations of a member on market access and national treatment with regard to a particular service sector very much depend on the contents of the specific commitments found in its schedule. A state can also introduce limitations at a later stage. However there are certain conditions that the state should fulfilll. The most controversial of such conditions is the introduction of new conditions in terms of laws or regulations should be accompanied by compensation for trading partners which may be affected by these introductions.

This stems from the unique approach or methodology employed in GATS which "locks in" sector specific commitments with a built in penalty for any "roll back" on commitments. From this one can conclude that there appears to be an inherent tension between the general principle of progressive realization of socio-economic rights on the one hand and the approach of locking in commitments with an in built penalty for modification. The problem is further compounded by the built in agenda of progressive liberalization. The International Covenant on Economic, Social and Cultural Rights obliges states to take steps with a view to achieving progressively the full realization of the rights recognized therein.

The requirement of progressive realization affords states the possibility of realizing these rights over time. This requirement must however be understood and read in the light of the overall objective of the covenant-to establish clear obligations for state parties in respect of the full realization of the rights. The obligations towards fulfillling these rights take the form of respect, protection and fulfilllment. Overall, through progressive realization the aim is to ensure incremental realization of socio-economic rights to citizens of a state. This may be achieved through for instance the right to protect; measures such freedom of action, protection from more powerful economic interests. State legislation giving preference to women owned services suppliers may possibly qualify as an example of protection from powerful economic interests. It can also be achieved through the obligation to fulfill.

This is particularly important for the vulnerable and poor sections of society where no other possibility exists for the realization of socio-economic rights. The obligation to fulfill may be carried out either by way of facilitation or by of direct provision. Direct provision for example could consist in making available what is required to satisfy basic needs. Such progressive actions may be associated with improvements in available resources of the state. A government with improved financial capacity for instance may replace the private supply of for example essential services like energy or water services with public provision. However, this sort of measure may constitute a quantitative restriction on market access.

In conclusion, while progressive realization aims to ensure incremental realization of socio-economic rights to citizens of a state, progressive liberalization in GATS and its approach aim to incrementally lock in limitations to market access and national treatment. This approach of locking in commitments imposes significant burden on governments to make sure that they list every conceivable limitations from the outset. However, some limitations may prove necessary after sometime. Similarly, limitations or conditions may be dictated by new developments including economic developments in the state in question.

This approach of GATT may thus possibly discourage states from taking new measures lest such measures may be followed by demands for some form of compensation. Most importantly, this approach has the potential to limit the policy space available to sates to implement various policy objectives including gender equality. Consequently, it undermines the human rights of women in particular the socio-economic rights of women.

In conclusion, it can be said that the legal analysis briefly carried out shows that trade agreements may have the potential to undermine state capacity to advance the human rights of women thereby undermining the effectiveness of the human rights framework. This is particularly evident in relation to the agreement on agriculture as well as the agreement on trade in services. Having established as to how the legal norms governing the two fields interact, the next step is to examine how the underlying principles in the two fields relate to one another.

PRINCIPLES OF INTERNATIONAL TRADE LAW AND GENDER EQUALITY

Feminist theorizing provides the bases for analyzing the underlying principles of gender equality. Accordingly, this section focuses on examining international trade law from feminist perspectives. The relationship between feminist theories and international economic law is a relatively an unexplored area. According to Childs, one reason for this is the fact that "both subjects are relatively youthful bodies of legal knowledge and debate."

Another explanation is that trade impact review has not focused so much on the social impacts of trade. Thirdly, the rather late engagement of the feminist legal critique of international law in general provides additional explanation. This however does not detract from the need for feminist examination which is both important and timely. Any discussion on feminist perspectives in international trade law deals with quite a number of lines of thought on the relationship between these two fields.

This is inevitably so due to the variety in feminist theories themselves. There are certain categories of analysis that are employed to explain the various forms of power imbalance that shape gender relations in societies. The most common analytical frameworks include, gender/sex, race, class, and geographical location. The question is what sort of analytical framework/s can adequately address the relationship or interactions between the everyday life of women on the ground and the macro level international trade regime?

The empirical studies on the effect of trade on gender relations so far may shade some light on the categories of analysis that can possibly be employed to carry out a feminist analysis of international trade law. Often times, these studies indicate that it is poor women located mostly in developing and less developed countries that shoulder the brunt of the dislodging effects of trade liberalization. In the developed economies where liberalization has resulted in adverse impacts, it is in the majority of cases poor women concentrated in low paying jobs that are dislocated from their livelihood.

And often these are women of colour and immigrants. From the empirical evidence, it may possible to discern gender/sex, class, race and geographical location as some of the analytical frameworks that may be used to do a feminist analysis of the trade regime. Let's briefly examine these frameworks in light of the rules, principles and the institutional framework of the WTO.

ABSENCE OF GENDER CONCERNS IN THE WTO

Gender as a category of analysis which is used in liberal as well radical feminist theories can be useful to engage in a feminist analysis of international trade law. Two issues that arise while using gender as a framework are the absence of gender concerns in the legal framework of the WTO agreements and the absence of women in the public sphere in particular in the institutional structure of the WTO.

ABSENCE OF GENDER IN WTO LEGAL FRAMEWORK

One theme, which perhaps may be characterized as a common thread in many feminist theories, is a critique of the normative presumption of the neutrality and objectivity of the law. Neutrality and objectivity are also established claims even more in international trade law. The presumed neutrality and objectivity of international trade law and the consequences that follow from such an assumption are reflected at least at two different levels. These are at the level of rule making and at the level of rule enforcement.

Trade policy making takes into account the overall flows at the macro level emphasising on the overall and the long term. This macro level economic analysis views the household and the domestic outside of the market. Feminist methodology on the other hand starts its analysis with women's livelihoods and experiences. In relation to the outcomes of trade processes, this essentially implies an emphasis on the micro level. If as feminist economists have convincingly showed trade indeed has differential impacts on women and men and therefore is not gender-neutral, a gender-blind rule making which focuses on the macro level is potentially problematic for the interests of women.

This is because international trade law may not take into account the lived experiences of women vis-à-vis their relation with international trade. As a result, the law is often designed without regard to the socio-structural disadvantages that bar some women from making use of the opportunities it creates as well as equal participation in trade. The potential effect of this is that not only the law operates to the determent of efforts that aim at affording equal socio-economic opportunities for women but it may also further perpetuate inequality.

Similar to rule making, at the level of rule enforcement, neutrality is attributed to the WTO Dispute Settlement Body (DSB). The DSB is said to be a rules-based system. It replaced the power-oriented dispute settlement structure under the GATT. It is claimed that a rules-based system entails neutrality in the interpretation, scope and application of the norms of international trade law.

This conclusion logically draws from the objectivity of the law and legal methods. According to feminist critique of law however, the law is itself value-laden. Hence, the decisions and findings of the rules based DSB will inevitably involve choices which may be value-laden. From the perspective of the WTO framework addressing the interests of women, this means no consideration of women's experiences and the differential impact of trade on women and men. This eventually may have the potential to perpetuate inequality and frustrate the measures that can be taken to address the socio-economic problems that women suffer.

ABSENCE OF WOMEN IN WTO STRUCTURES

Similar to the absence of gender in the legal framework, there is gender imbalance in the institutional structures of the

WTO. Although gender imbalance is rather a common feature in most international institutions, the extent of the imbalance is more so when it comes to the WTO. At the beginning, all seven members of the Appellate Body were men. Except for the introduction of one female member of the DSB, this figure has remained unchanged. Similarly, women are appointed only infrequently as members of WTO panels.

It has been pointed out repeatedly that the mere presence of women does not guarantee bringing gender perspectives to the work of any international institution including the WTO. Despite this, the absence of women on its own also has some undesirable consequences. For instance, male dominance in the structures of the WTO may make it far less likely that the WTO will be presented with women's diverse experiences. It is also in this context that Childs makes a case for more representation of women arguing additionally that international bodies have a professional development and training role for their employees and therefore it is critical that these bodies strive to ensure equitable access to such opportunities.

FEMINIZATION OF LABOUR AND TRADE LIBERALISATION

Class is another analytical category in feminist theorizing. But defining economic class as an analytical category as it relates to women is a difficult task. The commonalities in women's gendered work in productive as well as the reproductive sphere lead to the conceptualization of women's economic class. These commonalities are reflected among other things in terms of segregation of women's work, low pay and the unpaid labour in the reproductive sector.

The main claim is that women's crucial roles in production and reproduction are regarded as key to undermining women's social status and power. From the perspective of international trade, this analytical category becomes important in the face of the increasing feminization of the work force around the world. The competition brought about by increasing integration of economies has led to the growth of export-oriented production such as textile, electronics, horticulture etc in parts of the world which formerly relied on agriculture and import substitution industries. The combination of these factors has brought about changes in the labour force. One important face of this change is the feminisation of labour.

The search for cheap and flexible labour in the era of trade liberalization has led to the feminization of the work force. Thus, one interesting consequence of trade liberalization is the increase in the percentage of women entering in to the work force. In addition to many women entering the workforce, feminists argue that restructuring is also bringing about changes in women's work. This is seen in terms of the kind of work women do, the hours put in, the conditions of work and pay. Women are getting more and more into the productive economy where they get paid jobs. The hours required of women are increasing.

Part time work and informalisation of work is becoming a growing trend. There is an increase in female workers in the sexual, domestic as well as the service industries. Thus, trade liberalization is creating a new working class constituting women. Just as the productive sector of the economy has seen changes in women's work, similar changes are starting to appear in the reproductive sectors as well. Trade liberalization and economic restructuring are blamed for the re-privatization of women's labour through policies which advocate for less state in the provisioning of services and redistribution of resources in the economy.

The staunch support for minimal state shifts the responsibilities for social welfare from the hands of the state to the household and the women therein. This has added the burden on women as household managers and nurturers. Feminists argue that the rise in the number of women entering the workforce is not mere coincidence. The argument goes, it is in fact the particular nature or type of labour that the current global economic system requires that makes female labour the preferred form of labour. Informal, flexible, cheap and abundant labour characterise the ideal nature of labour demand in the market today.

These features, due to the intersection of various societal and structural factors, characterise female labour. It is thus no by coincidence that the changing demand in labour in the global economy is shaped in its current form. On the basis of this, it is possible to argue that the trade regime is not a neutral system rather it is a gendered and classed system and is affected by geographic location. It is important here to note that the feminization of labour can be analyzed from the perspective of liberal feminism and a completely different feminist perspective on the trade regime may be adopted.

For liberal feminists the feminization of labour at least in the productive sector is viewed as a positive outcome of the operations of trade. They claim that the increase in world trade has opened opportunities for women to be incorporated into paid labour force. For liberal feminists, paid work is believed to increase the status of women. It is believed to give women greater autonomy within the household.

However, this strand of feminist theory also acknowledges the adverse impacts of trade on women in general and women in the labour in force in particular. Harsh working conditions, low pay and job insecurity are among the important negative effects that these feminists point out. There is a call among liberal feminists to advocate for women's rights within the trade arena not only to address these adverse impacts but also to maximize the positive spill over from trade.

POVERTY, INEQUALITY AND TRADE

Location is another analytical framework that is used in feminist analysis. This category is important in post-modern and post-colonial feminist theorizing. One theme that emerges from postcolonial theorizing which is quite relevant for analysing the international trade regime is the examination of the currently discriminatory aspects of international action vis-à-vis third world states. This theme can accordingly be adapted to analyse the trade regime from a feminist perspective. The focus of analysis from a postcolonial feminist perspective would be the discriminatory aspects of international trade law vis-à-vis third world developing and least developed states and the possible effect on gender equality.

There are two features of the trade regime that epitomize the phenomenon of discriminatory practice of the regime against third world states. These are the underlying principle of non-discrimination and the requirement of single undertaking practiced in the WTO. The principle of non-discrimination relates to the discriminatory aspects of international trade law vis-à-vis developing and least developed third world states. Non-discrimination in international trade law has two components.

These are the Most Favoured Nation (MFN) and the National Treatment (NT) rules. These rules seek to enforce an important legal principle-equality before the law. While the MFN rule guarantees equal treatment to products from different countries, NT assures equal treatment for foreign products in relation to national products. These two rules create equal conditions of competition for all products in the market. The logical conclusion is that, these rules create equal pressures to reform and adjustment for all the participants in the market - nationals and non-nationals.

This is irrespective of the respective positions of the participants in the market as well as the relative positions of beneficiaries from the market. Some may be poor others may be rich. Unequals', namely developing and less developed countries on the one hand and developed countries on the other may thus end up getting equal treatment. Another manifestation of the discriminatory aspect of trade law vis-à-vis southern states is the practice of single undertaking. This is something that lies somewhere between the very rules and the institutional structure of the WTO.

The practice of single undertaking compels all members of the WTO to sign into all the WTO agreements at once. Single undertaking replaced the doctrine of variable geometry which allowed members of GATT to decide for themselves whether to sign up for the complementary agreements negotiated in the different trade rounds. With the formation of the WTO in the Uruguay round, the concept of single undertaking came into the picture.

A question has arisen as to whether single undertaking is indeed an appropriate mechanism to integrate countries into the trading regime. It is claimed that single undertaking disregards the broad range of conflicting economic and development interests which different members pursue within their respective trade policies. It will force developing and least developed countries to agree to agreements that will place them in unfair competition with the developed countries. Some countries may not have the capacity to implement some of the agreements. The agreement on intellectual property rights is a good example.

It may also be the case that the implementation of some of the agreements may be detrimental to national interests and development properties. Accordingly, single undertaking not only retards national development and redistribution efforts but also perpetuates poverty and inequity. Evidence suggests that some developing countries are accessing global markets for global markets, technology and goods which in turn is propelling their growth. On the other hand a greater number of developing countries are being left behind. In addition growing inequality in cross-country and in-country income distribution has been witnessed. Interestingly, this inequality is correlated with the deepening of market integration and openness that is propelling global growth.

This is where trade rules like non-discrimination and single undertaking may be implicated in the growing inequality and consequently poverty in many developing and less developed countries. This outcome significantly victimizes women. This is because women are more vulnerable to poverty due to of the operations of different layers or axes of power that result in gender inequality. Access to resources is conditioned upon established gender hierarchies in societies. As is evidenced by different studies women lack access and control over productive resources and property. Similar gendered hierarchies have placed the burden of reproductive functions on women. This has wide reaching implications.

Location also says a lot about who may be further marginalized by this outcome. Among the world's poor women, the majority are found within the developing and less developed world-third world/southern states. There are thus a number of factors such as gender division of labour, gendered access to resources, location based difference in extent of poverty, which result in a differential impact of poverty on women. These factors deepen the extent to which poverty is experienced by women.

Accordingly, if trade is correlated to the deepening inequality and poverty, those that are more vulnerable will further sink into the poverty trap. Hence, the combination of these factors imply that equal pressure for reform and equal adjustment to trade as predicted upon the non-discrimination principle of the WTO may be a fallacy.

MINIMUM/WEAK STATE

The main reference here is the weakening of the state which is underscored by the strengthening of trade regulation through the WTO. It emanates from the different rules and principles of international trade laws such as non-discrimination, liberalization of services, strengthening of intellectual property rights. The adverse effect of these norms is that they de-legitimize any form of state interventions such as redistribution, helping or transforming the economically weak sections of society.

Empirical research findings suggest that the global market has generated imbalances, inequalities as well as maldistribution of resources within and among countries. These studies paint a gloomy picture from a gender perspective. Global trade has in many cases increased the vulnerability of women. In the face of such consequences, state interventions become crucial for dealing with inequalities. Non-intervention will only perpetuate inequality and further may create new inequalities. Similarly, the push for minimal state appears to gives centrality to efficiency rather than people and social goals. This leads to the domination of economic interests over all aspects of political and social life.

According to Beveridge, it "positions social interest as somehow opposed to market interest." The prioritization of economic or market interests over other aspects of social and political life will disproportionately affect women. This is due to the value given to women's work in an economy. A larger proportion of populations in the world engage in an unpaid production. Around the world women are disproportionately represented in the unpaid work force. The unpaid production is only indirectly linked to the market.

As a result, this form of economic activity is not elevated to economic or market interests. The needs and interests of the majority of women will only come secondary to the demands of economic efficiency - the market. This implies that women's interests will be advanced provided that they do not come in the way of the parameters of market efficiency. This becomes very problematic when the market itself is producing undesirable distributive consequences in the social life of people.

A very good illustration of this outcome is the decline in the provision of social services. This is dictated by the market either through reducing government revenue or through shrinking policy space of nation states. Women heavily rely on social service provisions in order to properly carry out their reproductive functions. To conclude, the gender issues that may be raised in relation to international trade regulation are the following. First, there is stark absence of gender concerns in the legal framework of the WTO agreements and absence of women in the public sphere in particular in the institutional structure of the WTO as a result of the interests of women may not be adequately represented.

Second, trade liberalization has significantly contributed to the feminization of labour especially in developing countries and it has brought about changes in the nature and burden of women's work. While gainful employment is viewed positively, conditions of work and increasing burden on women's reproductive work may make the gains questionable. Third, the growing inequality among and within countries which is correlated with the deepening of market integration and openness that is propelling global growth may disproportionately victimize women. Similarly, the weakening of the state due to strengthening regulation of international trade would again have disproportionate adverse impact on women.

UNDERSTANDING GENDER EQUALITY IN THE CONNECTION WITH TRADE REGULATION

This exercise which was carried out both from theoretical and legal perspectives has shown certain patterns of interaction between the two fields. Based on these interactions, one can identify the dimensions of gender equality having direct relevance to the operations of the international trade regime.

The dimensions mainly relate to socio-economic rights of women. This is because the effects of trade are disadvantageous to poor women and secondly it is in their reproductive role that women experience the adverse impacts of trade liberalization. These in turn relate to the material conditions of women in their day to day lives which directly correspond to the pool of socio-economic rights. Based on this gender equality for the purpose of this discussion can be understood to refer to the fulfillment of socio-economic rights of women.

This directly resonates with substantive equality which is defined in terms of the promotion of substantive rights that is rights to the material preconditions necessary to live a decent and dignified life with meaningful choices. Accordingly, one measure of the possible role of the trade regime in promoting gender equality will therefore be its contribution towards the fulfillment of the socio-economic rights of women. If one can frame the issue of gender in/equality that arise in connection with trade regulation as adverse effects on socio-economic rights, then what are the necessary conditions that should be fulfillled to realize the socio-economic rights of women in and through trade regulation?

Two of the most determinant factors for the realization of socio-economic rights are equitable distribution of resources and proper regulation. One can derive these factors from the nature of the obligations that socio-economic rights entail. The obligations for fulfillling these rights are very much linked to 'available resources'. Further, these rights require positive actions for their realization through among other things, regulation. The logical question that follows is can the trade regime-the institutional and legal framework of the WTO - contribute positively towards the realization of socio-economic rights of women through equitable distribution of resources and proper regulation to this end? Can one locate these as part of the goals and purposes of the trade regime? What are the legal bases for this? What are the measures that can be taken?

UNDERSTANDING THE GOALS OF THE TRADE REGIME

How is the purpose of the trade regime to be established? What are the possible references? The purposes of the trade regime are to be determined by reference to power or competence allocations, objectives of the WTO as enshrined in the legal instruments and thirdly the legitimacy of the trade regime. These points of reference seek to re- examine and re-question the goals and purposes of the trade regime.

POWER ALLOCATION AND OBJECTIVES OF THE TRADE REGIME

Power or competence allocation is directly related to the relationship between the WTO and its member states. The WTO is an intergovernmental organization with nation states as the main right holders and duty bearers. The birth of intergovernmental organizations brings about rearrangements in the power relations between the centre-the organization and the constituting entities-the states. States transfer some of their competencies to the new organization.

The question is thus, what are the policy areas or competencies that states reserved for themselves and transferred to the new organization, in this case the WTO? This question determines what the purposes of the regime are. What is outside is what states have reserved for themselves, while what is with in is whatever states have transferred to the new entity, WTO.

OBJECTIVES OF THE TRADE REGIME

The purposes of the trade regime can be construed from the perspective of the objectives that the trade regime is meant to advance. The WTO system consists of multilaterally agreed rules and regulations. Rules and regulations perform the task of providing a mechanism for reconciling the behaviour of separately motivated actors so as to generate outcomes that are tolerable to all involved. Rules and regulations achieve this through pressuring, guiding, controlling or changing the behaviour of actors to constrain economic, social and political behaviour. The rules and regulations of the WTO system serve similar functions.

The rules play significant role in deciding on the objectives that are to be advanced by the trade regime. These objectives get their expression mainly in the economic and social behaviours of states. Accordingly, a question on the boundary of the WTO is in part a question as to the emphasis on the constraints that the rules place on the different behaviours of states for example, emphasis on social over economic objectives or economic over social objectives etc.

LEGITIMACY OF THE TRADE REGIME

The third point is the legitimacy of the trade regime. Legitimacy is understood to refer to different but at the same time related concepts in various contexts. In this study when legitimacy is relied upon as one focus to determine the purposes of the trade regime, the reference is to an assessment of the contributions of the trade regime to contemporary social, economic and political conditions of the world.

In this context, questions regarding the purposes of the trade regime in part attempt to respond to challenges to the authority of the regime. The challenge emanates from what is expected of the regime in contemporary social, economic and political conditions of the world. This directly probes into the purpose of the trade regime vis-à-vis socio-economic conditions of the world on the ground.

LOCATING GENDER EQUALITY AS PART OF THE GOALS OF TRADE

Earlier it has been established that one can frame the issue of gender in equality that arise in connection with trade regulation as adverse effects on socio-economic rights of women. Further, equitable distributions of resources and proper regulation have been identified as the most determinant factors for the realization of socio-economic rights of women. Now the questions is do the trade regime have rules and objectives geared towards redistribution and regulation?

Do these rules and objectives allow for redistribution of resources both at the global and national levels? Do the objectives and rules of the trade regime grant adequate space for global as well as national level regulation aimed at promoting socio-economic rights of people? The WTO charter recognizes important objectives which have strong distributive dimensions. These include, the objective of sustainable development, raising of standards of living for all, recognition of the needs for positive efforts to ensure that developing and least developed countries secure a share in the growth of in international trade commensurate with the needs of their economic development. Re/distribution is quite imperative for the fulfillment of these objectives.

These objectives can be implemented through different redistributive mechanisms. One such mechanism involves revisiting the single undertaking principle. Another mechanism is the newly adopted 'aid for trade' initiative. This initiative attempts to take into account distributive consequences of trade on different sections of society thereby broadening the reach of trade regulation. Some of the rules of the WTO play important role in re/distribution and regulation. The provisions on special and differential treatment, flexibilities such the one introduced in TRIPS also serve similar purposes.

They provide for transfer of resources from developed countries to the developing and least developed countries. They also open the room for adequate regulation at the national level. From a gender perspective, what more is required to ensure that redistribution and regulation in and through the trade regime will have positive impact on improving the socio-economic rights of women? Gender mainstreaming assesses the implications of all policies and measures on the respective situations of women and men at the planning, implementation, monitoring and evaluation stages.

Policies and measures in all political, social and economic spheres are made subjects of analysis. From this understanding, it becomes evident that gender mainstreaming from the outset recognizes that there are gender differences and inequalities. It then proceeds to examine how these differences and inequalities are relevant to the particular subject under discussion. Finally, it attempts to identify opportunities through which these inequalities can be narrowed. Mainstreaming is the ideal instrument to add a gender element to the redistribution and regulation goals which are crucial for addressing socio-economic rights.

Gender mainstreaming goes beyond adding a gender equality agenda; it also involves the need to introduce changes. This change may include the re-examination of general policies and measures at the negotiating, drafting and implementation stages by taking in to account their particular effect on women and men.

At first glance, although gender equality concerns appear to be far removed from the regulation of international trade, trade regulation may significantly affect gender equality both in positive and negative terms. Gender equality seen in terms of the advancement of the socio-economic rights of women may well be a value that the trade regime can help promote. One can gather this from a closer examination of the stated goals and purposes of the trade regime.

3

Global Governance as Neo-liberal Governmentality

NEO-LIBERAL GOVERNMENTALITY

The 'neo' in neo-liberalism functions as a device or heuristic, thereby opening a space within which to critically examine particular departures from a liberal, Keynesian welfarist state. Matthew Sothern (forthcoming), extending Wendy Larner, points to the performative work of the 'neo', which disjoins or precludes a liberal foundation; Sothern's research on disability sex manuals intends to demonstrate a certain "identity crisis" for particular hegemonic neo-liberal critiques. The 'neo', therefore, draws attention to these situated departures and is always-already involved in their reproduction.

Neo-liberalism as analytic describes particular changes in policies: state restructuring, public/private partnerships, devolution of power, increased bureaucracy, and the importance placed on market rationality. Larner terms these shifts as "neo-liberalism policy" and articulates distinctions from/among neo-liberalism as ideology and governmentality analytics. It is useful then to revisit her conceptualizations about various neo-liberal forms of governance. Neo-liberalism as ideology, Larner writes, is a broader approach incorporating "institutions and organizations and processes".

This analytic employs Gramscian notions of ideology and hegemony to interrogate how particular individual and group identities were constituted through neo-liberal ideology. This focus on ideology, Larner continues, counters a top-down approach (neo-liberalism as policy) by focusing on "new welfare state arrangements [which] emerge out of political struggle" and a disciplinary and hegemonic power which changes ideology, resulting in state restructuring. Neo-liberalism as governmentality looks to the ways in which power is enabling through discourse, in the formation of political identities and subjects.

Foucault's project on (bio)power, captured in History of Sexuality, allows him to show how discourses around sex and sexuality enabled particular political subjects, through normalizations. Normalizations are tactical expressions of the enabling and disabling notions of power. Power, for Foucault, "is not an institution, and not a structure; neither is it a certain strength we are endowed with; [rather] it is the name that one attributes to a complex strategically situation in a particular society."

Power, instead is co-productive with discourse. Derek Hook explains an aspect of this connection: Discursive rules are hence strongly linked to the exercise of power: discourse itself is both constituted by, and ensures the reproduction of, the social system, through forms of selection, exclusion and domination. ... These concerns with not underestimating the functioning of discourse lead also to his [Foucault's] emphasis of the fact that discourse is both that which constrains or enables, writing, speaking, thinking. Discourse enables the mobilization of power-the power to exclude and select, as Hook notes. Individuals and institutions become objects of power; through tactics of governmentality-the specializations of knowledge and the use of normalizations.

Governmentality as an "art of government" targets population, by the regulation of individuals and activities in place-a "conduct of conduct". Therefore, neo-liberal governmentality is power working on individuals and institutions to conduct themselves through market rationality, forming political subjects who are self-actualized, entrepreneurial, and responsibilised. It is the formation of these political identities through both discourse and ideology and the restructuring through state policies which complicates neo-liberalism as a "multi-vocal and contradictory phenomenon".

Peck further describes this conflict and struggle as altering or blurring the notion of the state, "as the clean lines that were once imagined to exist between, say, the national state and the offshore world, bureaucracy and civil society, and the local and the global have become increasingly blurred and porous." The notion of the state itself, through neo-liberal governmentality, has been shown to be dysfunctional and contradictory, and yet has also become so pervasive and strengthened. According to Brown (2003) and eluded to by Larner, neo-liberal governmentality critiques must be careful that they do not reproduce the conditions of neo-liberalism by giving neo-liberalism some ontological status, incapable of resistance (minding the productive work of the 'neo').

Rather, a focus on discourse demonstrates the very constitutive nature of this process and therefore positions resistance and response at the level of discourse, not necessarily policy or ideology. Brown's point, that neo-liberalism should be thought of as a set of normalizations and not necessarily having some ontological status, illustrates a difference in approaches for some neo-liberal governmentality critics. A neo-liberal analytic explores these idealized norms (of rational choice, market rationality) as they construct (racialised) citizens and states. As Brown writes, neo-liberalism "does not presume the ontological given ness of a thoroughgoing economic rationality for all domains of society", making suspect notions of citizenship located, as Hindess writes, within a "system of states", where the "citizen" has some pre-given condition.

Again, careful attention must be paid to the ways a neo-liberal critique constructs the original departure from the liberal, Keynesian state. Neo-liberal participation and technologies even still, these three perspectives on neo-liberalism (as policy, ideology, and governmentality) resonate in the various ways geographers write about this phenomenon.

With regards to participation projects, Elwood (2004) describes the "new localism" in collaborative planning and revitalization programs in the UK and the US.

Here, she analyzes the discourses of each state context in motivating particular participation initiatives and local scales. Additionally, Graham (2005) examines the resulting inequalities which come with a shift from Keynesian to neo-liberal governance, whereby "software-sorting" techniques present in technologies like online GIS create new inequalities. While little research places participatory GIS in confrontation with a neo- liberal governmentality analysis, an extrapolation of the arguments of Elwood and Graham can begin to imagine how this critique might take shape.

Elwood (2004) describes the shifting of responsibility for urban revitalization from the state to citizens and voluntary organizations. For her, neo-liberalism is revealed upon inspection of the discourse used to motivate a focus on participation for these institutions and organizations. By pointing to the rescaling toward community and neighborhood, Elwood examines how a new localism exists to motivate participation through "effective planning" and an "empowering" of local residents.

However, she writes, many of these participation-based processes do not transfer any real influence or autonomy to local residents. Elwood concludes by recognizing the need to look toward these new localisms and the discourses employed to motivate collaborative partnerships. A certain 'fine line' exists for those engaging in participatory projects, especially those caught in the intersection of government and citizen interests. Graham advances a somewhat different critique relevant to those interested in participatory GIS.

His context is urban and inequality studies; therefore, he examines how online GIS works to constitute identities and supports an unequal consumption of urban space. Technologies such as online GIS represent a particular sorting of people and places, by software-resonating with neo-liberal governmentality critiques of the targeting of particular populations and the development of knowledges, facilitated by discourse. Additionally, Graham advises against notions that these technologies are "limitless, completely integrated, and all-powerful" while recognizing the difficulty in pursuing critical policy and activist agendas otherwise.

'Participatory subject' formation Graham, in his critique of software-sorting techniques like online GIS and closed circuit television, describes contemporary phenomena of post-Keynesian societies where "code-based technologised environments continuously and invisibly classify, standardize, and demarcate rights, privileges, inclusions, exclusions, and mobilities and normative social judgements across vast, distanciated, domains."

These technologies work to sort specific people, constituting populations and political subjectivities. The 'participatory subject' emerges as a subject bound to government through responsibilisation and so-called empowerment. In actuality, as Elwood writes, these collaborative partnerships "grant participating actors relatively little autonomy or influence in processes of urban spatial change." 'Participatory subjects' are these actors or individuals imagined in neo-liberal discourse. They are subjects, in the sense that they are expressions of neo-liberalism, and yet, they are specifically 'participatory' because it is their involvement and partnering which motivates and completes the project of Participation.

In other words, it is these subject's perceptions that they are in fact empowered or participating which allows these projects to further extend governance into the lives of individuals-to more completely target populations and practices. Projects of empowerment or participation constitute well-formed neo-liberal subjects through responsibilising discourse, as Elwood has explored. These subjects are invested with choice, and the ability to rationalize (via market rationality) decisions placed before them. This investment of choice and ability is laced with the intent to empower-that these individuals should transform their private interests into that of a common.

These 'participatory subjects' are co-productive with a governmentalised state; invested with supposedly devolved state power and responsibilised to that of their neighbors, themselves, and the common. Of course, this devolvement of power to the individual is not fully actualized; the participating individual at the receiving end may not actually have any additional power or autonomy, as Elwood (2004) has noted. Still, it is this imaginary 'participatory subject' which discursively frames for projects of participation both the objective and the process of reaching this objective.

This discursive, participatory subject obtains emancipation through the practice of participation-their empowerment contingent upon their self-actualized, autonomous (market) rationality, entrepreneurialism, and responsibilisation. By examining the 'participatory subjects' which emerge from governmentalised and neo-liberal discourses, a new set of questions can be articulated for the projects of participatory GIS. This discursive subject formation unites participation-based projects, and inspection of this subject assists in the re-examining of the motivations for such future participatory projects.

Implications for PGIS Mitchell Dean, in his depiction of projects of empowerment, castigate such efforts as "clear examples of those contemporary liberal rationalities of government that endeavor to operationalise the self-governing capacities of the governed in the pursuit of governmental objectives."

While not all participatory GIS projects are necessarily empowerment-based, recognizing empowerment as a particular technology of government, like Dean, is one approach of exploring further what a neo-liberal governmentality analytic might provide. In this concluding section, I offer future research questions which address PGIS as a project of empowerment that constitutes a polity and the political in particular, neo-liberal governmental ways:

- How (through what discursive production) is PGIS motivated by the empowerment of participants to meet particular government-institutional objectives?
- What participatory practices are expected of the participant? How are these practices structured and regulated?

- What 'training' becomes necessary for the participant? What 'background knowledge' or 'contextualization' must be facilitated in order to support effective participation?
- Where (at what points in the process) are participants allowed to express a political identity, if ever? How is PGIS able to monitor/calculate/eradicate such politics? Why do so at all?
- Is PGIS fundamentally a political project? In what ways is PGIS eliding any such political status? For what ends, must PGIS remain a neutral intervention?

These questions are motivated by a neo-liberal governmentality analytic, which seeks to expose power relations and discursive formulations whereby a 'participatory subject' is imagined and operationalised. Elvin Wyly's (2006) remarks at the AAGs suggested a "critical genealogy of data systems" which positions these sorts of endeavors as "narratives with a history". This sort of contextualization situates PGIS as productive of discursive subjects who participate and are 'empowered', who are responsible and are 'given voice', who are self-actualizing and calculating and are given the ability to choose.

The main purpose of this piece is to challenge the way we see neo-liberalism and to argue for a more social and political understanding of the term. Neo-liberalism has come to be associated with the idea of free market capitalism, deregulation and the rolling back of the state. When looked at internationally, neo-liberalism is often perceived in terms of the export of such conditions to various parts of the world or that such conditions might be imposed upon poorer countries by leading international bodies.

Joseph Stiglitz's (2002) critique of the roles of the IMF and World Bank would seem to indicate a growing discontent with neo-liberal methods and it might be argued that recently neo-liberal approaches are being reined in or that there has been a shift to the notion of good governance. What will be argued here is that such shifts are entirely consistent with neo-liberalism if we view neo-liberalism in a broader sense. Indeed, the narrow view of neo-liberalism as deregulated free market capitalism is itself a product of neo-liberal ideology.

An essential part of neo-liberalism is the belief that it is nothing more than this. Such has long been the case with variants of liberalism which present themselves in apolitical or asocial terms. The ideology of neo-liberalism (and I use ideology in a pejorative sense throughout this piece) is that it opposes itself to the role of the state, that it stands against forms of regulation and that it is an economic process distinct form social and political affairs. To use a different framework to analyze neo-liberalism-the governmentality approach of Foucault. Seeing neo-liberalism though the governmentality lens gives quite a different impression.

It is proposed here that neo-liberalism should be seen as a form of social regulation, a set of arguments about social and personal conduct, something that rather than acting against state power and sovereignty, reinforces and rearticulates them. Furthermore, neo-liberalism is not something that should be narrowly defined. Rather, it is a broad and fairly adaptable approach, more adaptable to the social environment than earlier forms of liberalism, and compatible with a range of political projects from Third Way politics through to authoritarian conservatism.

It must be stressed from the start that the aim of this piece is simply to assess the relationship between neo-liberalism and governmentality and that therefore a number of significant and problematic issues are deliberately bracketed. Towards the end the question of the wider social context is raised, but not really explored. In particular, questions remain about underlying social context and the significance of processes like capital accumulation. Other issues that are ignored altogether here include whether or not Foucault's understanding of the state as essentially super- structural is adequate, whether Foucault's qualifications of sovereignty can be fully applied to the international arena, and matters relating to Foucault's concept of power.

What will be done here is simply to state the relationship between neo-liberalism and governmentality. As well as drawing on Foucault, this argument borrows heavily from

Dean and Burchell and does not pretend to be original. However, it does point us towards a number of critical questions that require further consideration. The first is the matter of the relationship between governmentality and social theories themselves. It is argued that the governmentality approach is one of the few contemporary theories that analyses rather than reproduces contemporary governmentality.

The second is that theories of governmentality do have limitations in terms of what they talk about and that they must therefore be seen in a wider context. Socially this would mean looking at underlying conditions such as the process of capital accumulation, internationally this means that governmentality cannot be applied evenly across the globe and that it will be more successful in those areas with more developed social and economic conditions. What is governmentality? To explain neo-liberalism is to explain how it represents an advanced form of governmentality.

In particular, governmentality is to do with the emergence of new issues and problems confronting modern society and ever more complex ways of dealing with them. Foucault advanced the idea of governmentality based on modern society's ability to employ more sophisticated methods of discipline and regulation, utilising new technologies of observation, calculation and administration. Governmentality is not tied to any one institution or practice.

It refers to the ensemble formed by the institutions, procedures, analyses, and reflections, the calculations and tactics that allow the exercise of this very specific albeit complex form of power, which has as its target population, as its principal form of knowledge political economy, and as its essential technical means apparatuses of security. The theory of governmentality goes beyond the limits of state power to look at more subtle methods of power exercised through a network of institutions, practices, procedures and techniques which act to regulate social conduct.

This is not a rejection of sovereignty but an attempt to think through the operation of power inside and outside sovereignty and law. Foucault talks not of the end of sovereignty or state power, but the emergence of a sovereignty-discipline-government axis with its new concerns for population and the optimisation of health, welfare, happiness and labour productivity. Foucault is concerned with how sovereignty is affected by modern developments in disciplinary techniques that regulate and order the behaviour of people within a given territory. This requires a shift in focus. As Foucault puts it, 'rather than asking ourselves what the sovereign looks like from on high, we should be trying to discover how multiple bodies, forces, energies, matters, desires, thoughts and so on are gradually, progressively, actually and materially constituted as subjects'.

Furthermore, governmentality is not just about how a state, government or institution behaves. It has as much to do with a way of thinking as the 'mentality' part of the term implies. Governmentality is a framework for thinking about the world and addressing what are considered as important issues. Mitchell Dean argues that mentalities of government are collective, relatively taken for granted and not particularly open to question by their practitioners.

We might say that neo-liberal governmentality is paradoxical in this respect since it instils a collective sense of individualism. We can look at an 'analytics of government' in terms of ways of perceiving, questioning, acting and directing. It is in this sense, it will later be argued, that contemporary social theory often helps contribute to forms of governmentality. When Foucault says that 'Maybe what is really important for our modernity-that is, for our present-is not so much the statisation of society as the "governmentalisation" of the state' we can see this in trends towards rolling back direct state involvement in particular social matters, or bringing the state into cooperation with a complex network of other social institutions and giving the state more of a managerial role as an overseer of certain social processes.

Theorists of neo-liberalism and globalisation go along with this reality in talking of the 'hollowing out of the state' which somewhat disguises the governmentalising of the state taking place and the complex political processes behind this. Foucault argues that the governmentalisation of the state is, at the same time, what has permitted the state to survive. It is possible to think that if the state is what it is today, this is so precisely thanks to this governmentality, which is at once internal and external to the state-since it is the tactics of government that make possible the continual definition and redefinition of what is within the competence of the state and what is not, the public versus the private, and so on.

We might add that this is precisely what theories of neo-liberalism and globalisation help to set out-matters of what is inside or outside the state, what is public or private, what is within the competence of the state, what can be managed and how. Dean writes that 'The distinguishing feature of reflexive government is that the point of the reform of the institutions and mechanism of government is to secure them in the face of processes that are deemed beyond governmental control'. In this case, it is neo-liberal and globalisation theory that does the 'deeming'.

Dean goes on to talk of how the social is redefined as a series of markets in services and provision which encourage rational choice calculation and individual decision making. Whereas disciplinary power involves the regulation of bodies within confined institutional spaces such as barracks and factories, governmentality is a matter of the constitution and management of populations at a distance-through monitoring and surveillance, statistical analysis and modelling, and interventions oriented to the welfare and productive efficiency of populations.

The discursive aspect of this is important because before power can be exercised, its objects need to be defined and boundaries established. To understand Foucault's comments on the discourse of political economy, for instance, we have to see how this relates to particular social problems and the need for government intervention; as he writes, '[t]he new science called "political economy" arises out of the perception of new networks of continuous and multiple relations between population, territory, and wealth; and this is accompanied by the formation of a type of intervention'.

That said, governmentality is not simply a matter of governmental discourses and practices; governmentality refers to something deeper or, as the term suggests, to a mentality as well as a way of governing (suggesting a link to the earlier notion of episteme within which institutions and practices develop). And this mentality is not limited to the state, but is dispersed also throughout 'civil society'. Foucault's account focuses on governmentality through political administration as a way of showing how state, government and civil society are interlinked. Government is seen as a network.

For this reason, the theory of governmentality rejects a general view of the modern state, and sees it, not as a unified apparatus, but as a network of different institutions and practices. Power operates, not from a single source, but through a diverse set of procedures and techniques. Foucault's studies move from centralised forms of power to the local and regional level. Foucault is not concerned with the possession of power but with its exercise, application and effects, and how it circulates through the social body. He argues that the methods of government are not invented by the ruling groups, rather, they utilise what already exists, adopting, adapting and developing them for their own purposes. This is the way in which we should understand Foucault's comment that the state as super-structural.

Power proceeds from the micro- to the macro-level. Micro-powers may then be appropriated by state, institutions or even social groups. But even though they may be utilised, techniques of power do not originate from a social group. This reverses the normal way we see this process. Domination is the result of a hegemony that articulates the effects of micro-powers. The exercise of and resistance to this hegemonic form of power becomes multiple and diverse.

FROM LIBERALISM TO NEO-LIBERALISM

In the early modern period political rule stated to concern itself with new issues relating to the health, welfare and prosperity of growing and changing populations. Foucault uses the term bio-politics to describe this new concern with subjects as part of the population. Some of Foucault's best known work concerns itself with such issues as health, sexuality and reproduction in relation to the administration and management of populations. It is important to stress how Foucault relates the development of these forms of bio-power to the development of the capitalist economy. He regards bio-power as 'an indispensable element in the development of capitalism'.

However, Foucault uses such notions as bio-power and governmentality to emphasise how the social process is more complex than just economic development and how it involves a multiplicity of different sources of power, technologies, strategies and effects. These techniques of power are utilised by a diverse array of social institutions including, in the nineteenth century, the state, the church, private charities, educational establishments and so on. Foucault believes there is a historical shift from the model based on sovereignty and law (which is coercive and relies on force) to the emergence of new more complex techniques operating through multiple institutions and bodies.

Modern governmentality is about the government of the self and government of others. Through the concept of bio-power, governmentality is connected to the welfare of the population and the improvement of its condition, its wealth and its health. It is through a bio-politics of the population that governmentality brings together a diverse range of social issues. It is this account of the emergence of bio-politics that helps us to understand and situate liberalism. Liberalism should not be seen as something in itself, but rather, as something that is dependent on bio-politics and critically responds to the issues bio-politics raises. In particular, liberalism responds to the emergence of social issues by arguing for a limitation of government role. For Dean liberalism operates as a critique 'concerned with the idea that "one always governs too much"'.

To do this, liberalism makes a strong link between government and individual liberty and what is considered inside and outside the political sphere. Liberalism should not be seen so much a coherent political ideology or philosophy of individual freedom, but as a justification for the rationalisation of government, a 'rationally reflected way of doing things that functions as the principle and method for the rationalization of governmental practices'. Liberalism, for Foucault, describes a problem-space of government, a particular way of defining the boundaries and spheres of social regulation that fixes limits to what governments can do and how political sovereignty should be exercised, and also contributes to the moralisation and normalisation of the population.

With liberalism, sovereignty is tied to law, and notions of right. Liberalism is concerned with the exercising of rights, but because of this, has a strong normative character as to how these rights should be properly exercised and guaranteed. Under liberalism, emphasis is placed on the role of the market and the private sphere as a way of imposing discipline, this 'market discipline' being legitimated by liberal discourse as natural and free from state interference. Moreover, under liberalism, individual subjects are constituted as autonomous and rational decision makers. But the freedom and liberty of the subject is a social construct, created through social practices that reinforce rational normalised conduct.

Order comes not just from the state but from the private micro-structures of a supposedly non-political private sphere that lies beyond the operation of state and politics. We can see how an account of liberalism developed from Foucault's work on governmentality relies on the three way relation between government, discipline and sovereignty. Neo-liberalism, if we follow Foucault, can be viewed in a similar light. David Harvey defines neo-liberalism as 'a theory of political economic practices that proposes that human well-being can best be advanced by liberating individual entrepreneurial freedoms and skills within an institutional framework characterized by strong private property rights, free markets, and free trade.'

He goes on to note that the 'role of the state is to create and preserve an institutional framework appropriate to such practices'. So although it criticises the role of the state and promotes the (global) free market, neo-liberalism is also a particular way of defining boundaries and maintaining social regulation and the discipline of subjects. The private sphere is legitimated by neo-liberal discourse as natural and free from the interference of the state. But in its actual practices, as Burchell argues, neo-liberalism defines positive tasks for government, constructing the legal, institutional and cultural conditions for artificial competitive game of entrepreneurial conduct.

This means giving an 'enterprise' form to types of conduct and organisations (like those concerned with health and welfare) that have hitherto been seen as non-economic. The governed are encouraged to adopt an entrepreneurial attitude towards themselves. Burchell calls this a new form of 'responsibilisation' where the governed are encouraged, freely and rationally, to conduct themselves in new ways. The subject of government is given new obligations and duties. Government may intervene to help certain targeted groups, but the main emphasis is on the 'rational subject' taking responsibility.

Neo-liberalism employs a particular style of reasoning with a new subject of government-the client as customer and consumer of various services, but also as responsible actor who, as Rose notes, must maximise quality of life through acts of choice, seeking to fulfill themselves within a variety of micro-domains (1996: 57). Neo-liberalism can be seen as distinct from classical liberalism because it is a specific reaction to the historical condition of post-war national state regulation.

Neo-liberal discourse problematises post-war solutions to the issues raised by the concept of bio-politics-the health, wealth and well-being of populations-by stressing the need to move away from centralised government activity through the welfare state and Keynesian forms of government intervention. As Harvey notes, the marked shift under neo-liberalism is from government (state power on its own) to governance, defined as 'a broader configuration of state and key elements in civil society'.

The state is still an active player in producing the legislation and regulatory framework. We can follow Dean here in examining this coincidence of historical context, individualisation and reflexivity: the neo-liberal critiques of the welfare state sought to redeploy the 'free subject' as a technical instrument in the achievement of governmental purposes and objectives. Contemporary liberal rule rediscovers freedom as a technical modality ... The notion of freedom and the free conduct of individuals once again becomes the principle by which government is to be rationalised and reformed.

Despite setting itself up as a neutral doctrine of non-intervention into market mechanisms, neo-liberalism, we have noted, is a political discourse concerned with the governing of individuals from a distance. People are told to take charge of their own well-being and take rational decisions to avoid social problems like unemployment and poverty. For example, people should take on training, learn new skills or find ways of enhancing their abilities and developing self-esteem. Today's language of governmentality tells us to become more enterprising people, more active citizens, more responsible beings.

This is discussed in terms of rights, obligations and moral responsibility, but the economic dimension still seems the dominant one. The shift from state mechanisms to self-regulation follows changes in work relations while the dominant discourse is of the risks and benefits of rational decision making and performance optimisation. This applies the logic of enterprise to our individual acts. These ideas appeal to us as active individuals like citizens or consumers but they also act as ways to form and shape new subjects, selves or agents. Power now gets exercised over 'free subjects' who are faced with various new possibilities in a globalising world.

The exercise of freedom takes the form of the behaviour of a consumer expected to follow competitive rules of conduct. With neo-liberal governmentality we see the extension of the norms and values of the market to other areas of social life, as reflected in the widespread application of such terms as competition, initiative, risk-taking and prudence across various social domains. A concept such as risk, for example, renders social life into calculable forms and thus facilitates governmentality.

As Dean notes, the ethos of neo-liberalism is both radical and conservative. It is conservative 'in its revival and restoration of the values (or "virtues") and rules of conduct associated with these orders, particularly those of the market. And it is radical because, by the process of reduplication and folding back, it multiplies and ramifies these values and rules into ever-new spheres including its own instruments and agencies'. Government may have become 'more multiple, diffuse, facilitative and empowering', but it is also 'more disciplinary, stringent and punitive'.

It is claimed that government takes place through support for individual freedom, but in reality the free subject is a construction of various social practices. What constitutes acceptable behaviour is specified through a range of exceptions and pathologies. Modern governmentality involves the surveillance of populations, and the administration and regulation of individual conduct, enforcing obligations backed up with the power of sanction. In other words, neo-liberalism gives the pretence of freedom while acting in a coercive way. As Dean says, 'in order to act freely, the subject must first be shaped, guided and molded into one capable of responsibly exercising that freedom'. Even Hayek admits that freedom is a more cultural conception of something that has evolved over time, establishing a set of rules with their disciplinary effects. Subjectificiation, we could say, is at the same time a form of subjection.

THEORIES

The above discussion will now be used to situate a range of contemporary social theories in relation to contemporary forms of governmentality. By contrast, governmentality theory does provide an analysis of contemporary forms of rule, but it will be argued that there are also some significant problems with governmentality theories in terms of scope and applicability.

Despite a vast array of different and diverse contemporary theories, there are more arguments in common than is often thought. All claim that society is becoming increasingly complex, increasingly fragmented, more uncertain, more diverse and more flexibleised. Big questions are raised about the status of boundaries, the organisation of time and space, and of their relationship to place and identity. Yet, looked at broadly, these theories seem to be saying two different things at the same time. On the one hand, they are saying that politics is becoming more fragmented, diverse, uncertain.

Collective agency is dispersed and instead politics becomes concerned with the micro level of personal choice, lifestyle, risk taking and so on. But the recklessness of this position is revealed when we consider the other main claim of these theories-that unstoppable forces are at play that are sweeping away the old world and ushering in the radically new. These macro level forces are beyond our control, they are described by Giddens as a runaway world that we might be able to help steer, but we cannot stop.

So on the one hand we have the end of collective action, the fragmentation of social life and the turn to a politics of the self, on the other, we have unstoppable social change-firstly in the shape of processes of modernisation, rationalisation and secularisation which transform into conditions of 'reflexive' or post-modernisation, pluralisation and diversification, and then we have the globalisation theories about unstoppable forces beyond our control. To put this more pessimistically, we have unstoppable global forces that are forcing us into a micro-level politics of the self. These theories no longer allow us to control our destiny, to act on the big stage, to take important decisions. Rather we must adapt ourselves to a world we cannot stop.

Acting collectively is a thing of the past. Instead, we must get ahead of each other by learning how to regulate ourselves better by taking responsibility for our lives (which have already been largely shaped for us), to manage the new risks we encounter and realize new possibilities (that have actually been forced upon us). These theories stress the importance of personal decision making and responsibility which must adapt itself to this new social context and make the best out of the opportunities it offers.

Because Giddens, Beck, Held and others still draw on the critical theory tradition, they maintain, unlike the postmodernists, a utopian streak to their theorising. Their arguments therefore can be used to legitimate the current social order in the sense that they encourage us to hold out some optimistic hope that global forces (over which we are told we have no real control) are creating the conditions for a better way of life. The more Habermasian version of this in Held goes so far as to posit a better, cosmopolitan world order. In the case of Giddens (1990) and Beck (1992, 1999), 'reflexive modernity' empowers us to take personal responsibility for our lives. But this is exactly what neo-liberalism wants us to believe.

These ideas reinforce the dominant neo-liberal view that we are rational subjects who should organise our lives in certain ways. Our reflexivity is, however, seen entirely at the personal and inter-personal level. Contemporary social theory is less keen to be reflective about the bigger picture since global processes tend to be regarded as too big for us to be able to do anything about them. Indeed, contemporary social theory asks us to limit the way that we think about the world and to take for granted such things as globalisation or even neo-liberalism as frameworks within which we must act.

We must consequently readjust our social activity from the macro level of collective politics and social change to the micro level of risk taking, personal responsibility and individual lifestyle choices. Contemporary social theory is overly concerned with the latter to the point of legitimating the former as a natural condition that we must leant to live with. Even if writers like Giddens see themselves as challenging neo-liberalism, we can see how some of their ideas fit comfortably within a neo-liberal framework of governmentality. The ideologies of neo-liberalism and globalisation today act to justify deliberate policies by suggesting that there is no alternative but to follow the flows of capital and the logic of the free market.

Today's theorists of globalisation and reflexive modernity are the first to criticise approaches such as Marxism for belonging to a certain period of time and having outdated notions of collective action and emancipatory politics, yet they appear uncritical of their own society and the dominant socio-economic processes they claim to be describing. Instead, they focus at the level of individual conduct. First, these theories tend to de-motivate the sort of (collective) action that might be able to change society and its dominant social structures.

Secondly, having taking the conditions of contemporary society as a given, they switch attention to the conduct of the individual subject, something that plays into the hands of neo-liberal forms of governance based on the rational conduct of individualised subjects. Perhaps it is the utopianism in critical theory-in the Habermasian version, certainly-that leads Giddens and others to accentuate the positive aspects of today's society, seeing the unfolding of late-capitalist modernity and the globalisation process as bringing individual liberation rather than enslavement. But this is a view of freedom tied to the market which becomes a 'quasi-natural reality whose laws must be respected by government'.

Choice is reduced to the optimising behaviour of workers, managers and consumers. These new regimes of government bring with them what Dean calls 'prudentialism' or risk rationality, technologies of citizenship (and the belief in empowerment and consultation), and technologies of performance. Because of this, most influential contemporary social theories contribute to the social order rather than criticising it. Rather than helping us to understand contemporary social developments, these theories often confuse things and make the contemporary social order more mystical than it actually is.

Yet at the same time, and in virtue of this, such theories may actually aid or help the very processes that they fail to describe. This is where the power of discourse becomes apparent. For if a wrong idea is used enough times it may become real in its effects and so begin to construct itself, even in thin air. So is the case with globalisation theories which can become real if enough people believe them and they start to shape actions and policies. Indeed, they may become real if they encourage-through confusion or whatever else-either action or indeed inaction (the idea that we can do little to change the wider social order and must adapt our behaviour accordingly).

And perhaps it is because such theories are so close to the processes that they describe or misdescribe, that they are unable to account for them for they are unable to account for their own role in contributing to them. In this sense, such theories are closer to being ideologies in the sense that Marx understood the classical political economy of his time as ideology-its closeness to the very economic processes it tried to describe meant it was never able to penetrate surface forms and explain the essential nature of the workings of the capitalist economy. But ideologies have a sinister side to them. In pretending to be something other than what they are, they reinforce relations of exploitation. In this case, they reinforce the very power relations they claim are no longer significant.

As Dean puts it: The 'dirty secret' of many contemporary liberal governmental discourses of globalisation, moral obligation, the new paternalism, social inclusion ... is that a story of the diminution or end of national state sovereignty is aligned with the deployment of sovereign and coercive powers over the lives of a substantial majority of the world's inhabitants. The advantage of the governmentality approach, then, is that we do not have to see such theories as consciously advocating the dominant mode of thinking, but as reinforcing this through their assumptions and what they take for granted.

In this way globalisation theory should be seen less as theory in the intellectual sense and more as theoretical practice or as theory that is inseparable from the dominant set of social practices either as directly secreted by them, or as inseparable from them, or as articulations based on taken for granted assumptions derived from dominant practices or as simply so caught up in this way of seeing things that it is unable to maintain a critical distance or throw anything into question. Explanatory social theory would look at how forms of governmentality are a feature of modern society and relate governmentality to the wider processes it engages with-processes like the discipline and regulation of populations, the process of capital accumulation and the capital-labour relationship.

Instead, globalisation theory-like many other contemporary social theories (or ideologies)-remains within the governmentality framework, failing to provide an explanation of the wider social causes (reverting instead to spatio-temporal metaphors). It is therefore a reproductive social theory rather than an explanatory one-or in Robert Cox's terms, a form of problem solving within a governmentality framework. By 'solving' problems within this framework, it in effect reinforces the framework as something given.

Globalisation theory is therefore ideological in the sense that it cannot step back from the social practices that it describes to look at the bigger picture. Indeed, it cannot look at the bigger picture except in meaningless terms of time and space or in terms of an awe of the very things it is meant to problematise, but makes no effort to socially explain. Instead such theories make most of their suggestions at the level of the micro politics of everyday life and it is because of this that they lend themselves so readily to forms of social regulation or governmentality.

THE SCOPE AND LIMITS OF GOVERNMENTALITY AND GOVERNMENTALITY THEORY

To conclude, some questions will be raised about the scope of governmentality. Firstly, we will look at the need to examine the social scope of the concept, secondly, the need to critically examine the international scope of governmentality. The reason why governmentality might be a fruitful concept here is twofold. First, it orients us to global trends stemming from social developments that reach right down to the everyday micro-practices of human life. It helps move the discussion away from an agent-centered approach that speculates on who might be doing what to whom by setting such activities within a particular set of practices, institutions and episteme (the frameworks for thinking about and addressing certain issues in a particular way).

Indeed the latter is indicated by the term governmentality itself which combines 'government' with 'mentality' in such a way that does not end up ushering in an intersubjective social ontology (governmentality is ontologically prior to the individuals who may enact it). There are of course neo-liberal and transnational actors, but to understand their actions, we have to look at how they draw upon already existing practices, strategies and institutions.

To give a case in point, Nikolas Rose looks at how the various tactics that emerged under Thatcher in Britain in the 1980s were not the realisation of any particular philosophy, but rather, were: contingent lash-ups of thought and action, in which various problems of governing were resolved through drawing upon instruments and procedures that happened to be available, in which new ways of governing were invented in a rather ad hoc way, as practical attempts to think about and act upon specific problems in particular locales, and various other techniques were merely dressed up in new clothes.

But in the course of this process, a certain rationality, call it neo-liberalism, came to provide a way of linking up these various tactics, integrating them in thought so that they appeared to partake in a coherent logic. Secondly, as this quote also suggests, the concept of governmentality focuses on institutions and practices in the plural. It therefore rejects the state-centric approach of much IR theory. This critical stance is important when it comes to assessing something like neo-liberalism. For neo-liberalism is something that is both social and international, which is connected to institutions including, most importantly, the state, but which goes beyond them and blurs the boundaries between state and civil society.

Neo-liberalism is also a mentality or a certain way of seeing things. It is more than just the dominant ideology of a particular set of agents, more than just the imposition of the power of the dominant states on the world stage, more than just a leading group's conception of the world, but is a framework, a set of practices, a way of seeing and doing things that transcends such boundaries. The advantage of governmentality theory is that it does not buy into the ontological aspects of the things it describes. It sees risk, globalisation, even neo-liberalism, as strategies, tactics, techniques and ways of governing rather than as ontological features of late, post-, or reflexive modernity.

The error of approaches like risk society or reflexive modernity is to see such things as ontological features of contemporary society which demand strategic responses rather than as strategic issues themselves. For example, the notion of risk is a strategic intervention to justify the retreat from welfare and social provision and the shift to the idea of the neo-liberal rational subject making their own provision. This is a strategy of governmentality wrongly seen by Beck and Giddens as an ontological condition.

These concepts are thus ideological in passing themselves off as conditions of modernity, rather than as responses to underlying social processes. The governmentality approach does not go along with this and throws such claims into doubt by questioning the naturalness of risk, security, competitiveness and so on. It shows them to be strategic interventions. But the price paid is the question, what then is the ontological basis for governmentality itself? Although Foucault hints at developments in the capitalist economy, this issue is not really answered by subsequent literature. Governmentality stresses that the subjects who engage in such activities are actually constructed by them.

Implicit in the Foucauldian approach is a non-instrumentality that implies underlying conditions that shape action and help to constitute actors. The problem with such a Foucauldian approach is the limitation of this to governmentality. To complete the picture, we need to move from agential strategies to conditions of governmentality to underlying social structures and processes. Although governmentality refers to a set of techniques, practices and institutions that pre-exist and shape agents' behaviour and in this sense can be seen as something underlying, we still need a deeper level that explains the shaping of governmentalities themselves.

For example, the concept of hegemony (understood in more structural rather than purely agential terms) might be better than the concept of governmentality at highlighting the underlying structural basis of government. Theories of such things as global governance, global regimes and global networks are now popular in international relations literature.

They reflect a liberal turn both within IR theory and perhaps within the international itself. But IR realists would argue that such theories mask the continued anarchy of international relations and the dominant structures and relations of power.

Neo-Gramscians would argue that this process depends on developing economic conditions allied to an emerging transnational ruling class. As mentioned, Foucault is useful in pointing us away from conscious intervention by highlighting techniques and practices of discipline and control (which may be more subtle than the realist focus on power as something exercised over people). But there is a danger of missing out on the macro implications of the above-of global power, inequality and the unevenness of the international system, issues that Marxists and realists are better at highlighting.

One way to deal with this potential danger is to remind ourselves that governmentality is primarily a matter of techniques, practices and strategies. It should thus be distinguished from actual regimes, networks, states and the wider question of hegemony in the international system. These are the entities through which governance takes place while governmentality is more to do with the techniques, procedures and tactics, through which governance is enacted. If governmentality is regarded more as a set of techniques and practices, then the issue to address becomes that of how the techniques of governmentality can best operate-in which societies, which instances and occasions, through which institutions and organisations-and how effective they can be in various different geo-political contexts.

This takes us to the next matter of problems inherent in translating Foucault into the international arena. Foucault's insights on governmentality are primarily concerned with liberal societies, and hence to the extent that international politics has been liberalised and socialised Foucault can be applied. Strategies of good governance are fully consistent with neo-liberal forms of governmentality. But can they be applied? The World Bank and IMF take a normative stance in their emphasis on the need for recipient states to implement privatisation, open up markets to competition, cut back on state involvement in economic processes and disperse such functions across civil society.

The problem with such a strategy is that it is not fully applicable in many places which lack the kind of developed economic, social and political institutions that neo-liberal governmentality requires. It is more the actual applicability, rather than the desirability of neo-liberalism that is currently being questioned. It is important, therefore, to be aware of the limits of governmentality.

While a Foucauldian approach might be able to tell us what is going on in Western societies, can it tell us much about what is going on in Iraq? Here it would seem to be exactly a case of how modern techniques of governmentality do not apply. A Foucauldian approach could go along with this. It could explain why neo-liberal governmentality, for example, cannot simply be imposed. Rather, this form of governmentality requires an already existing social base, a developed civil society, and mechanisms and means for implementing various complex strategies and techniques of governance.

But to go along with this, Foucauldians would have to accept a broadened ontology that recognises that governmentality itself is dependent on underlying social conditions which allow for neo-liberal forms to be implemented in some parts of the world, but not in others. A governmentality approach in and of itself cannot explain why populations in the United States are more complexly administered than those in Iraq. Nor can it really explain why it was that the United States went to war over Iraq and what it was trying to achieve.

Once we accept the theory of governmentality as part of a wider social ontology, we have to then address questions such as the conditions of possibility for governmentality, the applicability of its methods, the unevenness of the social terrain, and the irreducibility of the international to the social conditions that make it possible. The international is no doubt increasingly socialised, but it has distinctive properties and problems of its own which limit the utility of certain social theoretical concepts including Foucauldian ones.

There is not space here to go into the limits of Foucauldian theory, but in assessing the strengths of the governmentality approach, we have to also be aware that while Foucault can help us analyse the workings of advanced liberalism, he is less helpful in helping us analyse the illiberal, uneven, and irreducible character of much that goes on within international relations. Where to go from here is a complex question. Essentially it involves a dialectic of two issues.

The main thrust of this chapter has been to argue for a widened conception of neo-liberalism as a form of governmentality rather than as a narrow economic doctrine (although we are now in a position to say that the narrow economic doctrine might be an aspect of neo-liberal governmentality). However, to account for governmentality, we must pay attention to its conditions of possibility which in the case of neo-liberal governmentality, we might suggest, means looking at how it relates to underlying processes of capital accumulation.

So having argued against a narrow economic definition of neo-liberalism we are now suggesting an economic definition of its conditions of possibility. But the other part of this dialectic is that when examined internationally, we have to say that neo-liberalism and governmentality cannot be reduced to these conditions of possibility (for example capital accumulation) and that the international is a complex, stratified and over determined arena.

This helps us to better situate the governmentality approach within a wider social ontology, although ironically, it also shows why ontologically governmentality cannot always be embedded in society. In a 1995 review of Beilharz's book Johnson wonders if Beilharz's approach to the Hawke-Keating government and Labor tradition fails to take into account the possibility that the transformation of Labourism was less its exhaustion than its expansion to include social groups outside the white, male heterosexual wage earner (1995).

She also wonders "what use Beilharz might have made of more recent Foucauldian approaches to issues of political economy and governmentality". While Johnson's 1989 political history is based on the method of an ideology critique, which "concentrates on the dominant premises underlying government policies", her 2000 text is a more methodologically diverse approach to political science and, indeed, towards political culture.

In Governing Change: from Keating to Howard (2000) Johnson reaches back through the Howard Coalition Government into the Keating-led period of the long Labor decade and approaches this approximately nine year period through a range of analytic methods, which she applies and evaluates according to their interpretive and explanatory power and utility. While heuristics based on technology, gender and sexuality are placed over the period to draw out the causes and implications of changes in governing and government that these methodological grids enable, it is Johnson's use of theories that emerge out of the Foucauldian governmentalities school and use of the Habermas-based critique of economic rationalism that Michael Pusey makes which is her central and important contribution to an understanding of the long Labor decade.

Rather than seeing the rise of Australian Neo-liberalism solely in terms of an ideology which presents itself as the necessary withdrawal of the state through such practices as "privatisation, deregulation, free-markets and the increasing role of the private-sector" Johnson's use of a governmentalities-based approach to the long Labor decade leads her to argue that "other forms of state activity" accompany these practices, which include "shaping and influencing the behaviour of its citizens, encouraging new forms of self-managing and self-regulating behaviour by individuals and relying on the disciplinary power of the market to influence citizen behaviour."

Considering that it is only recently that the lectures in which Foucault most fully outlined his theories and critique of Neo-liberalism, were published in English it is not surprising to find that definitions of Neo-liberalism rarely countenance Foucault's concepts that it is also a political rationality rather than just an ideology about market freedom and that it is a form of governmentality that changes the techniques by which states and individuals govern and are governed. The advantage of this approach is that it sets aside the claims of an ideological focus and critique in order to track the reasoning or rationality upon which government practices are based.

Such an approach uncovers the view that contemporary forms of liberalism differ from earlier forms in that they do not see the market as already existing in some natural form but as something that government needs to actively construct through establishing particular political, legal and institutional conditions. The state is then faced with the additional dilemma of needing to encourage the development of the particular forms of 'autonomous' and 'free' individuals that neo-liberal styles of government depend upon, given that liberal sovereignty in general takes a less directly coercive form than more authoritarian forms of rule. This is an argument which seeks to explicate the 'Neo' in Neo-liberalism.

A complementary historical argument is that the target of Neo-liberalism in many countries is the practice of Social-liberal techniques that were instituted through Keynesian practices in the period after World War Two until the early 1970s. The 'Neo' prefix thereby refers to the specific nature of this historically recent object of critique; a critique which, as Foucault argues, projects itself along the well-worn Liberal path of "governing too much," but which because of its Keynesian and Social-liberal object can be called New.

Thus Johnson's application of the insights of the Foucauldian conception of Neo-liberalism to the long Labor decade leads to her depiction of it as a specific project of identity construction and thereby behavioural 'encouragement': "In the Keating government's practice, governmentality took the form of attempting to construct a range of identities in ways that are compatible with Labor's conceptions of reconstructing the Australian economy" (2000: 104). Johnson's use of Foucauldian methods is a cautious one as she finds them inadequate for dealing with forces exterior to the state-subject relationship, such as market power in a capitalist economy.

In order to better approach these forces she turns to Michael Pusey's application of Jürgen Habermas's theories in Pusey's Economic Rationalism in Canberra: A Nation Building State Changes its Mind (1991). For Johnson, Habermas's method relies on an opposition between a "lifeworld" of human subjects that contains "culturally secured meanings, and . . . social action," and "systems structures," forms of which are money and power and which threaten to mediatise and colonise the lifeworld.

To some extent Habermas's schema is a retooling of the concepts he employs in The Structural Transformation of the Public Sphere: An Inquiry into a Category of Bourgeois Society (1989) where he places the practices and institutions of rational-critical discourse as central to the democratic potentials of modern liberal political life. According to Habermas there is a form of rationality higher and more suited to the life world, the source of democracy, than to those forms embedded in 'money' and (bureaucratic-state) 'power'.

This is both an argument for the safeguarding of these higher and more democratic forms from 'colonisation' and a reiteration of the central thesis of his earlier work on the political public sphere. For Johnson, Pusey's research into changes in norms and practices amongst Canberra's Senior Public Servants and critique of economic rationalism go far in explaining how and why "the Canberra Bureaucracy itself became a site intimately implicated in the colonisation of the life world by the economic subsystem".

Indeed, Pusey's critique is a compelling one that has a sharp moral edge and is one drawn on a comprehensible spatial model which clearly demarcates the sources of economic rationalism against what must be protected from it: the life world and its practices of communicative rationality. In a sense Pusey's is form of immanent critique, taking the language of the object, turning it back on itself and thereby undoing its claims to any moral superiority or longevity: This doctrine and its sponsors will pay the price of casting society itself both as the object of business strategy and, just as negatively, as the generic source of all 'market failure'. It is an aggressive reduction that pretends not to see that in the West in the space of little more than a generation, extended family, church, and local community neighbourhood have all been burnt up as fuel in the engine of economic 'development'.

Yet the limits of Pusey's critique of economic rationalism are those that the governmentality 'school' treat as the central objects of their practice. Pusey's Habermasean schema makes assumptions about the nature of the life world and the human-subjects who populate it which are not held by those that practice with more Nietzschean-influenced ideas on the relation of truth-subject-power that Foucault wields. Specifically, Pusey's critique is, like aspects of Habermas's writings, caught in the paradox of thinking a modernity that ruptures historical time into a traditional past and new future.

The paradox is that 'tradition,' like heritage, doesn't pre-exist modernity so much as it is made in the moment of the modern. The concept of 'life world' and of a transparent communicative rationality would seem to be Janus-faced: the life world a condition or state of human community that is the projection of a temporalisation made in the cauldron of modernity, and facing another way, the dream of a pure communicative rationality seemingly a secular model of redemption without the violence or revolutionary desires that Benjamin's messianic time conjures.

While this thesis sides with the Foucauldian concept of Neo-liberalism as a form of governmentality which ascends in the long Labor decade, it follows Johnson's scepticism about its limits and thereby accepts the usefulness of Pusey's critique to explain aspects of the forces operating on the long Labor decade. One dimension of Neo-liberalism is its forming, or bildungs, and re-forming of citizen-subjects in terms of freedom and market rationalities. This process of what Mitchell Dean calls "culture-governance" is analogous to the Bildungs: a term denoting the formation of self through culture and a term more commonly known through its deployment in the anglo-linguistic world as the novel genre of the Bildungsroman: formation-novel.

Much of the thesis is concerned with formation novels, or Bildungsromane, that traverse or arise out of the long Labour decade, and it argues that the representations of subject-formation in realist novels of this period are ones that can be seen to engage with the forces, rationalities and technologies of Neo-liberal governmentalities working in and through the cultures and discourses of Australian Labourism and industrial citizenship.

There is ongoing debate over how to describe and theorise the political project that the long Labor decade both attempted to enact and in part succeeded in realizing. The key tension in this debate concerns the description of Neo-liberalism as the submission of the State to global corporations and markets by privatising formerly state-owned and run businesses and utilities, by deregulating formerly protected and state-controlled markets in finance and labour, and by adopting business techniques in the running of bureaucracies and state utilities. This conception of Neo-liberalism, shared by such global Left intellectuals as David Harvey (2007) and the late Pierre Bourdieu (1998), is firmly rejected by those theorists of Neo-liberalism influenced by Foucault's writings and lectures on the subject.

The terms of this debate will be explored in more depth throughout this thesis, in particular in Part 3. But the advantages of a literary history of the long Labor decade as a track running alongside the political history is that fiction is more conducive to investigating the representation of political forces as they form the self. This thesis's focus on formation novels aims to give an account of Australian literary-fictional responses to Neo-liberalism which complements and contests non-fictional accounts. With the Internet becoming the 21st century global infrastructure for commerce and communication, a new regime of governance is emerging in the international communications field.

This regime is sensitive to the medium's architectural characteristics, the users' norms of behaviour in Cyberspace, and the regulator's (namely, the US government's) potential to exert "soft power". In this regime's normative code, for the first time in international relations, inclusiveness, openness, transparency, and accountability are all attributes of authority. In this regime's lexicon, 'multi-stakeholderism' is identified as the only legitimate way to develop the Internet regulatory environment, and 'collaboration and consensus' stay for the, admittedly, awfully messy and frustratingly slow deliberations. Moreover, the policy-making process, through which this regime is designed, empowers previously marginalized voices and allows the stakeholders to build coalitions of a global scale.

The proliferation of fora discussing Internet governance issues makes it difficult to study this unconventional political process. For one thing, there are a large number of stakeholders (governments, international organizations, business corporations, non- governmental organizations, experts and individual activists). How, as researchers, do we detect power dynamics in the network-like global multi-stakeholder formations? How do we assess a process of decision-making where legitimacy is vested in the ability to reach consensus? How do we account for the generated transformative energy in open deliberations on Internet development issues? The common denominator of all these questions, I propose, is the way we conceive power in a multi-stakeholder collaborative political process.

Do we see power as anchored in structures (hence, power as domination and oppression), or as emanating from interactions in relational networks (hence, power as a 'productive' social environment)? This chapter reviews theories of power and develops a multilayered theoretical framework specifically developed for the study of the innovative multi-stakeholder collaborative process in Internet governance. Power and power dynamics are focal variables of the investigation. The theoretical framework proposed holds explanatory potential as it contains a comprehensive synthesis of theory pertaining to the contemporary political process; from inter-organizational to the global public policy level.

This approach is based on the fundamental Foucauldian understanding that, as a pervasive social dynamic, power animates the relationship of communication technologies and society. The communicative process in general, as well as each of its constitutive elements (communication technology and policy among others), cannot and should not be studied apart from the historically-specific power matrix. Indeed, in Foucault's understanding of the political process, shifting social practices are constructed in and by historically specific matrices of power relations. Consequently, it is imperative that the deepest mechanisms of the political process are accounted for regarding the Internet's emerging governance strategies and fluid practices. For this chapter, power is conceptualized by employing three frameworks from Political Philosophy, Political Science and International Relations, and Organization Studies.

As this chapter will demonstrate, each of these perspectives provides key ideas for conceptualizing and studying power in a multi-stakeholder collaborative formation. Thus, the postmodern ontology of power (Political Philosophy) directs our attention to the shifting governmentality - from government-centered rationalities of governance to experimenting with multi-stakeholder collaboration. By reflecting analytically on real-world social trends, the globalisation perspective on power (International Relations Studies) recognizes both the effectiveness and the legitimacy of a regime of 'shared power' global governance (national governments, businesses, and civil society advocates participate as equal in the policymaking process).

Finally, the organizational approach to power in multi-stakeholder formations, where the dynamics of consensus-reaching practices are investigated, allows for the 'instrumentalisation' of power. The dialogue among concepts from those three perspectives, initiated in this chapter , is an original contribution to the studies of power in multi-stakeholder collaboration. Instead of focusing exclusively on the most powerful stakeholders and their ability to influence the collaborative process, the suggested synergetic approach unfolds the process of consensus- building through mapping power dynamics and exploring the practices of learning and sharing of expertise and experiences. As an experiment in global governance through multi-stakeholder collaboration, the Internet governance constitutes a rich empirical field for applying the constructed power dynamics theoretical framework.

DEFINING INTERNET GOVERNANCE

Internet governance is a contested terrain in contemporary global politics, as the UN World Summit of the Information Society (WSIS) (2002-2005) demonstrated. The principal stakeholders - national governments and international organizations, private corporations, civil society representatives, and Internet developers and operators - compete for reformulating the existing balance of power.

Currently, the US government retains the unilateral control over the content of the Internet root zone that is at the core of the global Net, and a private corporation - ICANN-is mandated with the creation of a property rights regime in cyberspace. Yet, what is Internet Governance? Let's begin with the observation that there is not a consensus on the definition of the term. The WSIS Working Group on Internet Governance's (WGIG) formulation, developed after seven months of difficult negotiations, was deliberately simple and descriptive. Internet governance was defined as "the development and application by Governments, the private sector and civil society, in their respective roles, of shared principles, norms, rules, decision-making procedures, and programmes that shape the evolution and use of the Internet".

It was coupled with four clusters of issue areas, ranging from infrastructural issues and the management of critical Internet resources (admittedly, the most controversial area, because it pertained to the Internet addresses property rights in cyberspace), to the use of the Internet, and to the developmental aspects such as capacity building in developing countries. One could argue then that this first attempt to identify and define a new field of regulatory issues on a global level is more concerned with both making 'multi-stakeholderism' work and experimenting with consensus-reaching political process than with 'mapping' the emerging notion of Internet governance.

Indeed, at the inaugural IGF (2006), some participants confided that the definition had not grasped the multitude of stakeholder expectations and they felt uncomfortable with what governance meant when applied to Internet. Thus, the very possibility of competing for participation and influence in the process of creating a global commons regime is a decisive advancement in the notion of Internet global governance based on multi-stakeholder collaboration principles. Moreover, stakeholders 'sharing' power in developing global commons regulatory regimes is an important operational principle in the developing regimes of international relations in the 21st century. In light of those developments, investigating power in collaborative formations and the power dynamics of the consensus process emerges as a challenging methodological issue.

POST-MODERN ONTOLOGY OF POWER

Modern theories of power (i.e. the liberal, or judicial, theory, and Marxist theory) share a common epistemology: first, power is perceived as "enhancing the capacities of those who possess it and, consequently, in so far as it impinges on other persons, as an imposition on the freedom of those persons", and, second, there is a common focus on the State as being endowed with power or exercising power for particular economic gains, and, more generally, on institutions and the people who rule them.

Michel Foucault revolutionized the conventional view of power by proclaiming that a political power (sovereign) that rules on the basis of consent is simply one among a number of "rationalities of government", and "therefore needing to be accorded no special analytical privilege". As one of Foucault's critics stated, he "almost single- handedly... moved the discussion of that most elusive and illusive concept from its modern or state-centered understanding to a postmodern or decentered version".

Along with shifting the ontology of power, Foucault introduced a liberating imagery of flowing interactions, productive networks of force relations, and endless possibilities of resistance and productive outcomes. For

Foucault, power is omnipresent and pervasive, and it should be understood as a "multiplicity of force relations immanent in the sphere in which they operate and which constitute their organization...and...as the strategies in which they take effect". He hypothesized that power is "co-extensive with the social body"; that "relations of power are interwoven with other kinds of relations (production, kinship, family, sexuality); that "one should not assume a massive and primal condition of domination, a binary structure with 'dominators' on one side and 'dominated' on the other, but rather a multiform production of relations of domination which are partially susceptible to integration into overall strategies"; and that "there are no relations of power without resistances" which are "multiple and can be integrated in global strategies".

To study elusive power relations, Foucault invented the neologism 'governmentality', which referred in a narrow historical sense to the distinctly new approach to governing, emerging in Europe from the sixteenth century, "which has as its target population, as its principal form of knowledge political economy". In a more general way, though, 'governmentality' is conceived as "a way or system of thinking about the nature of the practice of government (who can govern; what governing is; what or who is governed)"; or, as the way in which thought both "operates within our organized ways of doing things" ('regimes of practices') and "is embedded within programs for the direction and reform of conduct".

Following Foucault, Mitchell Dean (1999) calls this particular approach to governmentality 'analytics of government' and explains that "to analyze mentalities of government is to analyze thought made practical and technical", and to assume that "government is accomplished through multiple actors and agencies rather than a centralized set of state apparatuses". From the 'analytics of government' perspective, to grasp the logic of a particular 'regime of government' is to map its governmentality; that is, to detect and identify the rationalities of government, which are embedded in dominant discursive and non-discursive practices.

In light of Foucault's 'analytics' of the liberal political

reason, a number of authors in Political Science and Sociology have begun unraveling the neo-liberal governmental rationalities and newly-invented techniques of governance. A consensus has emerged that the neo-liberal governmentality, which rose to prominence under conservative governments in the 1980s, places emphasis 'upon the lives and decisions of individuals. Mitchell Dean, for instance, suggests that "the government through processes is increasingly displaced by a government of government, a 'reflexive government'", whose imperative is "to render governmental institutions and mechanisms, including those of the social itself, efficient, accountable, transparent and democratic by the employment of technologies of performance".

The governmentality school of research has been criticized, though, for its exclusively "programmatic orientation", its emphasis on "broad governmental themes rather than specific neo-liberal projects". Yet, it has been recognized that the perspective of governmentality "deciphers the so-called 'end of politics' itself as a political programme". As Lemke comments, "the so-called 'retreat of the state' is in fact a prolongation of government, neo- liberalism is not the end but a transformation of politics, that restructures the power relations in society.

What we observe today is not a diminishment or a reduction of state sovereignty and planning capacities but a displacement from formal to informal techniques of government and the appearance of new actors on the scene of government (e.g. NGOs), that indicate fundamental transformations in statehood and a new relation between state and civil society actors. This encompasses on the one hand the displacement of forms of practices that were formerly defined in terms of nation state to supranational levels, and on the other hand the development of forms of sub-politics 'beneath' politics in its traditional meaning."

Coinciding with the commercialization of the Internet, this project is benefiting from both the global communication connectivity and the democratic instincts and aspirations of the so-called 'civil society'. As a result, locally created forms of community self- regulation are transplanted to the global level, and forums are inaugurated for collaboration on contentious issues in a diversity of problem-domains (Internet governance is one of them) with the participation of stakeholders from governments, businesses and non-governmental organizations.

INTERNATIONAL RELATIONS PERSPECTIVE

The Internet governance controversies are evocative of the 1990s' 'great globalisation debate'. This debate was concerned with the shifting matrix of power relations and the rearranging of the Industrial-age social organization in unstable hybrid configurations. Through the 'globalists' optics, the contemporary globalisation refers to the "entrenched and enduring patterns of worldwide interconnectedness", and "represents a significant shift in the spatial reach of social action and organization" towards supranational scale. To this interpretation of the contemporary trends, the 'sceptics' oppose the view that "the discourse on globalisation... is... an ideological construction" and argue that it provides "a convenient myth which, in part, helps justify and legitimize the Neo-liberal global project, that is, the creation of a global free market and the consolidation of Anglo-American capitalism within the world's major economic regimes".

Although exhibiting differing interpretations of contemporary social dynamics, the globalisation debate correctly detects the changing paradigm of structural power relations on the supranational level. Thus, it has been broadly accepted that the centre of gravity in world politics has shifted, during the last quarter century, from the public agencies of the state to private bodies of various kinds, and from states to markets and market operators. Thus, escaping the state-centered concept, the academic discourse is entering the broader, and largely still in flux, field of global governance.

In many respects, the notion of global governance draws upon the postmodern imagery of networks and flows as implying decentralization of power, proliferating connectivity, reconfiguration of relationships, and localization of resistance and empowerment (Manuel Castells' theory of Network Society is a prime example here). In this imagery, global information networks are seen as related to the networks of power relations in three significant ways. First, according to Castells, in a network society, access to essential social networks (the Internet among them) equals enfranchisement in the society. Second, information networks replace earlier organizational forms.

They are seen as changing both the quality of human experiences, and "the way power is exercised and governance is organized in global politics". Third, because of their interactive nature, information networks "reconfigure, constitute, or reconstitute identities, interests, and institutions". In the publications focused on the concept of global governance, the predominant concern is, though, with formal, established global institutions, and the challenges to their effectiveness and accountability mechanisms. In contrast, James N. Rosenau (2000) proposed a broader approach to the term 'global governance', influenced by the Foucauldian concept of governance and governmentality.

He conceived of global governance "to include systems of rule at all levels of human activity-from the family to the international organization-in which the pursuit of goals through the exercise of control has transnational repercussions" (emphasis added). From this the author concluded that "global governance is the sum of myriad-literally millions-of control mechanisms driven by different histories, goals, structures and processes... In terms of governance, the world is too disaggregated for grand logics that postulate a measure of global coherence".

Apparently, in this broad understanding 'global' refers to the scope of political practices and effects, where the notion of uniformity is rejected. Indeed, diversity of arrangements can be expected, which "are more likely to evolve out of bottom-up than top- down processes", because they are "steering arrangements" emerging "through the shared needs of groups" and striving for legitimacy.

Drawing on cases exhibiting the growing tension between globalisation and the state's ability to govern, Reinicke and Deng (2000) propose that the strategy of global governance via mobilizing networks on a sectorial/functional basis provides the only effective governance alternative. In their view, global public-policy (GPP) networks are "effective, often remarkably so, in bringing together diverse and sometimes opposing groups to discuss common problems that no one of them can resolve by itself", and they "represent a unique opportunity for governments to regain the initiative in the debate over the future of global governance".

To elaborate upon the global public-policy network model, Reinicke (1998) introduced the principle of horizontal subsidiarity. As a political instrument, this principle helps to transfer part of policymaking responsibility to non-state actors, usually business representatives and non-governmental organizations (NGOs). The rationale is that these actors, whose range of activity are not bound by a particular territory, "have direct stakes in the outcomes of a particular public policy".

In addition, they possess better knowledge and understanding of the "increasingly complex, technology-driven" public-policy issues, which, in turn, "will generate greater acceptability and legitimacy for global public policy". As a characteristic feature, stakeholder inclusiveness lends legitimacy to the process and increases the chances of successful implementation of the policy outcomes. Reinicke and Deng trace the potential long-term contribution of these entities to the formation of social capital and the constitution of a global public space. They notice that, by enabling shared knowledge and learning, these networks, in fact, engage in 'capacity building' for local communities, especially in developing countries, "to take democratic control over their destinies".

For Reinicke and Deng, though, networks only complement the existing global governance institutions, and do not contribute to a 'power shift' away from governments and international organizations toward civil society and the private sector". They have emerged "to address cutting-edge global challenges" and help the formal institutions to manage risk. In this light, national governments, international organizations, and especially the UN agencies are advised to take the leadership in supporting this 'quiet revolution'.

Reinicke's model provides valuable analytical support to the argument that alternative policy responses are needed, which are compatible with both, globalisation's scope and complexity, and the mechanics of the powerful global trend towards redistribution of power. Nonetheless, the global public policy network model does not account for the 'shared power' dynamics in a multi-stakeholder collaborative process.

As discussed next, the possibility of an inclusive, deliberative mode of policymaking in a problem domain, from the local and national to the global level, requires both a more insightful understanding of the power dynamics in a collaboration, and skilful managing of the consensus-oriented negotiations. A number of conceptual constructs developed by Organization Studies scholars have already been probing the incentives and the outcomes of collaboration, mainly in business settings, but in hybrid multi-stakeholder alliances, as well.

ORGANIZATIONAL PERSPECTIVE

So far, we have developed two layers of the conceptual model of power that the investigation of Internet Governance requires. First, in ontological terms, power emerges as a relational and ubiquitous phenomenon that is capable of producing effects/outcomes (i.e. discourses, institutions, knowledge, policies, structures, etc.). It is discernible in the webs of force relationships, where it produces both negative and positive outcomes. Second, in political terms, new socio-economic dynamics, grasped by such metaphors as Globalisation and Information/Knowledge/Network Society, have induced a significant shift in the perceived balance of power on both national and global levels, and between national governments (and international organizations) and private actors (the 'shared power' formula).

In response, new forms of alternative policymaking have

emerged, which are designated as 'global public policy networks', in Political Science, and 'collaborative formations', in Organization Studies. Since the 1970s, a multitude of collaborative formations, functioning on the principle of 'shared power', have been convened mainly in the USA, on local, regional, and national levels. Consequently, the phenomenon of 'collaborations' or 'collaborative alliances', or multi-stakeholder collaborative roundtables, in Canada have been an object of vigorous investigation by Organization Studies theorists.

In the process, conceptual constructs have been redefined or invented, all pertaining to the realization of organizational interdependencies and collaborative advantages. In response to the need for a more dynamic process-oriented mode of investigation in inter-organizational relations, Barbara Gray (1989) developed an empirical theory of (multi-stakeholder) collaboration. It combined perspectives of organizational behavior and political science, and departed from the traditional model of inter-organizational relations that had hitherto dominated the literature. Gray suggested that collaboration was enabling organizations to manage their increasing interconnectedness.

In a collaboration, stakeholders "constructively explore their differences". The aim is "to create a richer, more comprehensive appreciation [common understanding] of the problem… than any one of them could construct alone", and resolve conflicts, or advance shared visions on the collective good. As Gray noticed, dissatisfaction with the status quo, and the desire to avert unwanted costs that it induces, constitute a major motivation for the principal stakeholders to turn to collaboration. There are stakeholders, though, who would be prompted to join a collaboration because of the attractive cultural norms it embodies (consensus decision-making vs. top-down governmental regulation), or the credibility of the convening party(ies). Thus, the expectation that through collaborative efforts some positive outcomes would be produced is a powerful incentive for participation in a collaboration.

In a "comprehensive theory of collaboration", 'collaboration' was defined exclusively as a self-governance process: "Collaboration occurs when a group of autonomous stakeholders of a problem domain engage in an interactive process, using shared rules, norms and structures, to act or decide on issues related to that domain". The comprehensive theory of collaboration links success with the participation of "those stakeholders... that are most interested in working collaboratively to solve a problem"; "the most powerful or influential stakeholders"; "the best organized networks of stakeholders... so that social pressure may be brought to bear on non participants", and, in principle, "the majority of stakeholders in a problem domain so that social norms can be established that pressure others to participate eventually".

This theory is based on the assumption that collaboration, as a strategy for managing interdependencies, evokes political dynamics (stakeholders are anxious to advance their own interests), but operates in the mode of 'shared power' as accepted by all the participants. Power dynamics are observable in each phase of collaboration in multi-stakeholder deliberative formations. Still in the problem-setting stage, power dynamics are conditioned by the conveners, for they "define the nature of the problem", decide how to address it, "what actions will be taken with respect of solving it", and even who will participate and in what forum the deliberations will occur.

Conveners, themselves, derive power from both their ability to influence outcomes in the domain (through their expertise, resources, and links to legitimate authorities) and the credibility they have with other stakeholders ("perception of objectivity or bias"). As Gray infers, "[i]dentifying and selecting stakeholders to collaborate, in effect, circumscribes the boundaries of the domain and empowers a specific group to address the problem. The power of conveners, then, is the power to organize" (emphasis in the original). During the direction-setting phase, power dynamics emanate from control over both defining an agenda for the domain and determining the range of mutually acceptable solutions (power to strategize). The success of the consensus-building process in this stage depends exclusively on reaching agreement on how the stakeholders will interact with each other.

This must be achieved in advance to the discussion of substantive issues in order to create trust among the stakeholders, and foster the sense of efficiency and effectiveness. Consensus is recognized as the primary objective of a collaborative formation. In fact, the ability to achieve consensus justifies the multi-stakeholder collaborative process as a valuable power-sharing policy mechanism. Along with programs, regulative decisions or regimes (tangible outcomes), the multi-stakeholder collaborative process produces consensus, learning and innovation, which constitute its intangible outcomes.

This realization suggests would argue, that collaborations can be interpreted not only as power-sharing forums, but as power-generating entities as well. Indeed, outcomes are deposits of transformative social energy, since the aim of a collaboration is to reconstitute a number of social relations in a particular problem domain. I would argue further that, when cast as a power-generating process, multi-stakeholder collaboration exhibits long-term and large-scale societal implications. Thus, the cumulative effect of a collaboration radiates on a number of levels (e.g., individual participants, constituencies, participating organizations, the domain, global interdependencies).

It induces new structural relationships among a multitude of players (e.g., contractual and unofficial alliances), while stabilizing existing force relationships or engendering a network of new dependencies in a particular domain. In addition, learning and innovation enhance an organization's capability to adapt to constantly shifting power networks. As these outcomes are undefined and unstable, I contend that we can gain a better understanding of their transformative capacity by mobilizing the elements of the above- presented theoretical framework.

From the Neo-liberal governmentality of self-governance to the convener's strategizing power in a collaboration-all these concepts can be fused in a coherent framework despite the fact that they greatly differ in analytical abstractness and belong to diverse fields of Social Sciences. This possibility arises when their focus on power is understood as being about interactive networks of power, which allows for identifying both instances of power dynamics and strategies of influencing the process.

TOWARDS A SYNERGETIC THEORETICAL FRAMEWORK

From the presented overview of contemporary interpretations of power, it can be inferred that the adoption of perspectives foregrounding decentralized and fractured authority offers analytical possibilities for those interested in theorizing Internet governance. Sharing a common concern with the contemporary shifting dynamics in governance (at global or inter- organizational levels), the theories presented offer significant explanatory power when the focus of Internet governance is on metaphors of networks, flows, shared power, interdependencies, and collaboration. Firstly, through Foucault's optics of omnipresent power and government as action, the contemporary political rationalities and practices emerge as exemplifying a distinct trend towards fundamental redefining of statehood, of the relation between state, civil society, and the private sector.

The shift in governance practices from an emphasis on the nation-state to broadening civil-society participation is conceived as a mechanism of globalizing local techniques of government, because their effectiveness is appreciated. The Neo-liberal rationality of self-governance in local settings (e.g. resolving environmental contingencies at local, national, and supranational levels) is now transplanted to the field of global governance. Secondly, according to scholars using Foucault's perspective on power and government, contemporary globalisation, which represents a shift in social action and organization towards the supranational level, is a governance project, and not simply an outcome of technological development. The Neo-liberal rationalities of government that espoused this project are characterized by a concern with performance and efficiency in governance, which substitutes for a concern with legitimacy.

In Castells' network society, government shares decision-making power with a number of players who bring their distinct expertise to the process. Thirdly, the invention of new organizational and institutional forms (i.e. global public policy networks) in response to these dynamics exemplifies the emerging 'global governance' mentality and order, which are based on a shared realization of the increasing level of interconnectedness and interdependencies of the world community. Nonetheless, this constitutes a particular challenge for political scientists. Besides the novelty of these phenomena, there is no suitable conceptual apparatus for investigation of 'shared power' dynamics, when governments are only one of the policymaking authorities.

Fourthly, in this regard, Organization Studies marks a significant advancement in comprehending the collaborative nature of such formations and scrutinizing the power dynamics in a multi-stakeholder consensus process. Dealing with real-life inter-organizational initiatives, scholars in this field have accumulated knowledge about stakeholder interdependencies in an organizational domain, the phases in a collaborative process, power positions of different stakeholders, strategies for influencing the process and the outcomes. And, fifthly, the microanalysis of power dynamics in collaboration allows for tangible and intangible outcomes to be detected and envisioned, and, hence, an argument to be developed that the accumulated transformative energy would lead to restructuring the relations in an organizational domain.

It must be noted here, though, that not much evidence can be found that analytical and empirical results have been communicated across disciplinary borders, when collaborative governance processes are investigated at local (inter-organizational) or global (supra- organizational) levels. In this sense, the present chapter contributes to the initiation of such a cross-disciplinary dialogue. By combining the 'government rationalities' perspective, which insists on contextualizing the techniques of government, with power-dynamic patterns in multi-stakeholder collaborations that have been detected and raised in Organization Studies, we can successfully apply this enriched, layered theoretical framework to the political process of Internet governance formations.

The present chapter constitutes a journey through the territories of three social-science fields in order to investigate the conceptualization of 'power' in each of them and consider the explicit and potential conjunctions, which provide for the creation of a theoretical framework for the investigation of the Internet governance field. It can be concluded that the above presented conceptual developments were inspired by a real shift in the public-policy regime - from the kind of unequal distribution of power associated with representative democracy to a more accessible, inclusive and collaborative decision-making process.

It has been argued that the creation of hybrid public/private or purely private authorities for Internet governance (for the latter, consider ICANN) is an experiment in advancing a public-policy alternative to the global level-multi-stakeholder collaborative formations functioning on a consensus basis. To investigate this alternative form of governing global resource, a multidisciplinary conceptual matrix was presented, which allows for a sharper profile of the power dynamics of the process, for deeper insights into the transformative potential of the stakeholder collaboration, and, overall, for more conclusive results from the experiments in Internet governance.

4

Governing Intimacy

Institutions in the global development industry, which I define as including multilateral institutions, bilateral aid agencies, state agencies and non-governmental organizations (NGOs), play a pivotal role in governing people's sexual and familial lives. (Presumably heterosexual) women, as 'mothers', are often made hyper visible in development frameworks; people who do not fulfill prescribed gender roles, who identify as lesbian, gay, bisexual, transgender or otherwise 'queer' (LGBTQ), and people whose families are non-normative by western development standards, often remain invisible. Both of these strategies work, often in paradoxical ways, to govern intimacy and to reinforce the 'heterosexualisation' of nation-states and the global development industry.

For example, in liberal development discourse, a working class lesbian without children in a country such as Venezuela may appear as 'unproductive' because she does not fulfill a culturally and institutionally prescribed role in national development: She does not contribute to the reproductive imperative of development because she is not a mother; she is not seen as linked to 'the family', which is mostly defined in heteronormative and Eurocentric terms; she is often typically seen as asexual and therefore as not-in-need-of-intervention. She thus remains outside the project of development, through a strategy of invisibilisation. The Venezuelan state reproduces this narrative, even in its current 'radical populist' version of 'endogenous development'.

President Hugo Chávez (2000-present) has called on Venezuela's mothers to 'birth the revolutionary nation'. Poor (presumably heterosexual) mothers have been the primary targets of his oil revenue-funded anti-poverty policies, which comprise an important part of his goal to shift away from the global neo-liberal development model. Lesbian mothers, if visible at all, are visible through a heterosexual, maternalist lens. To date, sexual rights activists have largely failed to have their demands included in Venezuela's new constitution, and while many originally thought that they could play a significant role in Venezuela's 'new Left', those who choose to play a role must do so from within a conservative, heteronormative, traditional Leftist political framework.

In general, activists focusing on sexual rights and/or gender justice have become increasingly marginalized since the inception of the Bolivarian revolution in 2000, with the exception of those who directly follow Chávez's ideological, heteronormative line. Thus, the question of how intimacy is governed surpasses a traditional discussion of 'right' *vs.* 'left', as in cases such as Venezuela we are witnessing a form of hyper capitalism as central to socialist projects for sovereignty in the post-neo-liberal era. In this context, increasingly globalized hot button issues such as homosexuality and abortion continue to serve as battlegrounds on which these larger struggles over westernization, globalisation and sovereignty take place.

DEVELOPMENT AND THE GOVERNANCE OF INTIMACY

To begin, an important aspect of my understanding of development involves how people's intimate lives are tied up with state and global governance. By 'governance', I am referring to the ways in the global development industry (e.g., multilateral institutions, aid agencies, foundations, NGOs) has played a pivotal role in defining how communities or nations are planned, and how individuals are 'targeted' as citizens, workers and recipients of aid. For example, as has been pointed out in Latin America, through the privatization of state-owned industries and economic liberalization measures in the neo-liberal context, non-state institutions have increasingly played interpretive roles in defining 'community', 'family', 'the economy' and 'citizenship' itself as well as what constitutes proper citizen practices.

Drawing from Michel Foucault's (1979, 1980), original work on governmentality and from more recent insights, I refer to this broader notion of governance, or governmentalities, as a way to capture the layers of institutions that are involved in defining and regulating our intimate lives. Seen through this lens, development policies work as instruments of governance and as methods of constructing and legitimizing subjectivities. Struggles for 'interpretive power' over policy definitions are not trivial conversations that take place within governing institutions, rather, they represent broader struggles over cultural representation, the right to security in the realm of intimacy and access to material resources. Thus, when non-normative individuals or family units are left out of policies, their invisibility on paper translates into myriad forms of symbolic and material violence against them.

In this case, their invisibility on paper serves as a mechanism to control their sexual lives and/or discipline them as sexual subjects. Yet both invisibility and hyper visibility serve as mechanisms of control and governance, particularly in the realm of intimacy. For example, as feminist scholars and development practitioners have pointed out, heterosexual women's bodies have been central to narratives and practices of national development from the start. Since its emergence as a hegemonic discourse in the post World War II period, development theory has constructed the nation as an object of inquiry and site of intervention, with important gender implications, and both it and the economy have been constructed as heterosexual.

These economic representations, which have been institutionalized through various sets of policy frameworks, the most recent being neo-liberalism and in some cases post-neo-liberalism, have significantly affected the ways in which women and queers themselves have been represented, legally regulated and socially addressed as consumers, labourers, citizens and aid recipients in countries throughout the world; it has also influenced the particular forms of LGBTQ identity politics that have emerged in the global South. Historically, (presumably heterosexual) women have been targeted in their roles as mothers of families and by extension, as mothers of the nation, in development efforts to eradicate poor health, 'control' population growth, improve access to education and economic standards among poor families, as the opening Venezuelan example illustrates.

Non-normative individuals are rendered invisible in narratives of economic crisis because they do not fit within this representation of the heterosexual household as the foundation of family reproduction and survival. Whereas (presumably heterosexual) women are targeted in their traditional gender roles, thereby gaining some recognition and possibly some 'rights', queers are more often than not left out of citizenship and economic restructuring. Paradoxically, when they do acquire certain citizen rights (at least on paper), such as in the new constitutions of South Africa, Fiji or Ecuador, these achievements have been embraced by neo-liberal supporters as evidence of the successes of marketisation and more broadly speaking, of the country's perceived progress toward modernity.

And even in 'new Left' contexts such as in Chávez's self-proclaimed Bolivarian revolution, non-normative individuals are typically treated as 'outside the national family' and therefore outside the realm of intervention or citizenship. While millions of dollars have been spent on incorporating poor and working class families-and especially women-from 'popular' sectors into the Bolivarian revolution, the push to include sexual rights legislation in Venezuela's new constitution, which would benefit heterosexual women as well as sexual minorities as defined in the proposals, thus far has been blocked. In contrast to the 'poor women as mothers' narrative, non-normative individuals have been largely absent except when viewed as potential threats to the reproductive imperative embedded in the heteronormative social order.

How non-normative individuals are viewed has led to contrasting and contradictory forms of regulation and visibilisation in development narratives. For example, because lesbians are typically viewed as non-procreative and as 'non-mothers', they are mostly left out of the picture, except when targeted in their reproductive roles (e.g., a pregnant woman or mother who happens to be a lesbian). In this case, their queer identity is sidelined and they are viewed primarily as mothers or mothers-to-be. Because of the absence of a male in their lives, symbolically, at least, they pose a perceived threat to state-building projects and to the reproductive imperative of the heteronormative social order. They are seen as not 'in need' of development interventions, as they are represented either as unlikely-to-get-pregnant or unlikely-to-get-AIDS.

It is not coincidental that much less research has been conducted on lesbian health issues than on gay male health issues, given the paradox of lesbian invisibility in the HIV/AIDS crisis as discursively constructed in the context of poor (especially sub-Saharan African but also other southern countries). Despite their invisibility, studies have shown how lesbians have experienced violence and pathologisation in gender-specific ways. For example, one study in Ecuador found that a large percentage of middle-class lesbians (i.e., lesbians whose families could afford to send them to therapists and/or who could afford to do so on their own) interviewed had been forced or coerced to undergo electric shock therapy, a practice which the study author found to be more widespread than previously understood.

And in late 2007, two lesbian activists were assaulted and raped in their apartment in Quito, following a public appearance in support of LGBT rights that they had made only days earlier. In both of these cases, these acts of violence occurred within intimate spaces, that is, in spaces not considered 'public'. Whereas there have been numerous reports of violence against gay men, cross-dressers and *travestis* in public settings in Ecuador, most accounts of violence against lesbians have taken place either within an institutionally legal setting such as a psychiatrist's office or in the privacy of lesbians' homes.

Electric shock therapy is an accepted practice to 'cure homosexuality' among a significant contingency of therapists in Ecuador. In these ways, lesbian invisibility serves as a mechanism of control and discipline. Development policies, which do not address intimacy as an aspect of women's security (now a buzzword in the development industry), are gravely missing the mark on 'protecting' or 'securing' women's rights. Men's queer bodies, in contrast, have been widely subject to development interventions through the lens of public health and disease control, primarily as a result of the HIV/AIDS crisis but also because of racialised constructions of gay male sexuality and 'men who have sex with men' (MSM) as hypersexual beings.

Seen as potential carriers of disease, MSM are now seen as an important target for intervention because of their potential HIV status; as such, they are brought into the fold of development through health interventions, often implemented by NGOs, that in theory are predicated on pathologised notions of deviance and/or contamination. Of course, many NGOs have negotiated the terms of development funding and reclaimed the purpose of HIV/AIDS projects in their own terms, thereby transforming this type of disease discourse into one of empowerment or strength.

As Timothy Wright has pointed out in his research on the globalisation of gay identities in Bolivia, many gay rights groups have utilized this type of funding, much of which originally came from USAID, to institutionalize their rights-based struggles for sexual and/or gender diversity, expression and rights in their home countries. What these narratives share are an unintended or conscious complicity with heteronormativity, namely with reproductive heterosexuality and its central place in modernist conceptions of development, family life and the nation. As Gilles Kleitz warns us, although much 'development work...delivers safe benign packages of income generation and improved rights for women with the family institution...the truly liberating revolution of redefining identities outside reproduction and the family remains mostly untouched....'.

This narrative about heterosexual family life powerfully shapes a range of scales and representations of daily life, cultural practice, racial purity, national identity and global political economy. The challenge remains to address heterosexuality as a social institution within development frameworks, and to address the heterosexualisation of the state and global institutions as they frame notions of intimacy and citizenship.

STRUGGLING FOR SEXUAL RIGHTS

What, then, can development scholars and practitioners do to counter these narratives and work toward a more equitable future? To what extent is there potential for radical transformation in any project that queries development and globalisation, particularly if we simply 'add queers and stir' (akin to a liberal 'add women and stir' or 'gender mainstreaming' approach) rather than rethink the social organization of sex/gender systems? What kinds of advocacy networks and solidarity communities do we wish to construct? Several existing scholarly and advocacy examples point us in the direction of social change. Future research could address heteronormativity in development frameworks and institutions as well as in the forms of activism, which aim to obtain sexual rights in a more inclusive fashion. Below I outline some possibilities.

DEVELOPMENT FRAMEWORKS

Scholars could better assess how heteronormativity is central to the frameworks they use, and how the privileging of heterosexual norms and traditional gender norms may obscure the broader range of sexual and gender expression that people actually experience. In addition, research could be conducted to understand how non-normative genders and sexualities are understood, experienced and negotiated in specific cultural, geopolitical contexts. While some work has been done in this area, much more could be done to understand how notions of gayness and queerness circulate transnationally and intersect with, subsume or have no resonance to local expressions of identity or sexual practices.

Research could also be conducted to address how heterosexuality as a social institution works to limit women's and men's forms of expression. Research on masculinities and femininities has begun to do this but more could be done to understand and delink the social institution of marriage and gender from the social institution of heterosexuality, and to situate this analysis in specific contexts, rather than apply a universal framework of gayness/queerness-or of heterosexuality-to families everywhere. More precisely, research could be conducted to analyze how development practitioners themselves think about gender and sexuality, and how this translates (or not) into development policies in the global South. Initial research has been conducted on the impact of gay and lesbian employees in the United Nations and on how lesbian and gay World Bank employees have fought for their rights as employees yet generally failed to integrate insights from their own institutional struggle into broader development and restructuring initiatives in the global South.

Likewise, research could be conducted to assess how, in accounts of globalisation, 'the economic' rarely includes 'the sexual', despite the fact that clearly sexual identity is a matter of survival-and security-for those who face discrimination on the basis of their gender appearance or perceived sexual identity. Some economists have addressed the relationship between sexual subjectivities and globalisation, but more could be done to address how development projects themselves serve to regulate people's forms of expression, define or reinforce the contours of 'appropriate' and 'inappropriate' sexual practices and govern intimacy.

SITES OF DEVELOPMENT

Scholars could intervene in debates on organizational planning within development institutions, state development planning, immigration and citizenship practices, family and household economics and labour market participation, to name only a few. Some research has been conducted on World Bank policies which confirms that the Bank's 'tightly spun heteronormative script' places individuals and families who do not fulfill western gender and familial expectations outside the scope of the development intervention. This type of scholarship points to the urgent political task of addressing recent family initiatives promoted by development institutions, and to the urgent intellectual task of delinking compulsory heterosexuality from gender roles and expectations and from western narratives of family life.

Another example concerns research on households and household survival strategies. Given the emphasis on economies of scale (e.g., household, community, local, regional, national, global economy) in economic development discourse, it is imperative that scholars contextualize their research on families and households within dominant cultural framings of heteronormativity, including addressing what non-normative families and households look like and how they open the possibility for re-imagining 'the family' from a non-normative perspective. For example, research could be conducted to more accurately analyze non-normative households and their locations in broader restructuring processes.

Scholars and practitioners could provide empirical data-'thick' rather than 'thin' ethnographic descriptions-of LGBTQ or other non-normative households, which take into account not only heteronormativity but also processes of racialisation and colonization as they are tied up with state and global development processes and with people's senses of national belonging. Attempts could be made to rethink heteronormativity in household bargaining models and other feminist frameworks of family structure and household survival strategies, a project already begun by feminist economists. The goal of this research is to liberate us all from repressive gendered and sexual scripts, rather than assume that heterosexuality is inevitable, omnipresent, merely 'western' or an imperialist imposition.

In addition, research could be conducted to address the differential impacts of restructuring processes on non-normative individuals, particularly those who face discriminatory barriers in the labour market and/or have little or no family support system. To my knowledge, only one systematic, comparative study has been conducted on lesbians and barriers to employment in developing countries, a collaborative report published by six NGOs in the Americas.

In the study, which addresses employment discrimination against lesbians in Bolivia, Brazil, Colombia, Honduras and Mexico, the authors argue that lesbians face 'double discrimination' in the workplace: as women and because of their sexual identities. While this type of research is normative in that it places lesbians in traditional development discourse by aiming to better 'integrate them into development', it is nonetheless important for making visible the verbal and physical discrimination faced by lesbians and for making a legal case for their human rights.

FORMS OF RESISTANCE

In terms of advocacy, two approaches which challenge heteronormativity in the global development industry include what I will refer to as the 'pleasure approach' and the 'sexual rights and gender justice' approach. The Institute of Development Studies (IDS) previously has sponsored research on the topic of sexuality as pleasure, as have other NGOs around the world that work in the area of women's rights and/or LGBT rights. The emphasis on pleasure rather than merely pain, suffering or exploitation is one way to invert development discourse in order to address people's agency with respect to their sexual autonomy, and to complicate how non-normative individuals face both choices as well as restricted mobility with respect to their sexual and gender forms of expression.

This approach can be potentially empowering for some individuals or groups but also limiting in its liberal scope. Other groups have challenged heteronormativity in development by introducing combining a justice and rights-based framework. Rather than focus on essential identities such as 'lesbians', 'gay men' or MSM, global justice activists have adopted a sexual rights and gender justice framework with the aim of repositioning the overall liberal rights-based framework. For example, activists who have worked at New York-based IGLHRC (International Gay and Lesbian Human Rights Commission) have argued that the 'persistent conflation of sexual orientation and gender expression' in legal, human rights, feminist, LGBT activist and other accounts of gender and sexually variant individuals has only exacerbated the problem of securing LGBT rights around the world.

They argue that part of the problem concerns the fact that even LGBT rights activists situate their advocacy work in traditional models of identity politics and 'minority rights' or 'civil rights' frameworks. Because many individuals do not necessarily define themselves in relation to heteronormativity or gender binaries, their identities are often misunderstood, misrepresented or erased in normative legal and policy accounts: As a movement, the LGBT platform has yet to adequately address the intersections of sexuality and gender and articulate, in explicit terms, the convergence and especially divergence of the separate but related agendas of lesbian, gay and bisexual organizing and transgender (and intersex) organizing. Instead, mainstream LGBT advocacy has, in practice, implicitly posited that 'LGBs' have sex, while 'T&Is' have gender.

Taking this advocacy trend into account, these scholar-activists call for a multi-faceted 'sexual rights and gender justice' approach that de-conflates sexuality and gender in conventional narratives of rights; a strategy that development scholars and practitioners could borrow from. Part of this project might include de-pathologising sexuality and gender as well, as in institutional strategies to rethink sexuality in terms of pleasure and recreation merely than in terms of procreation, violence, oppression and/or duty. Because these projects operate at the nexus of advocacy and scholarship, they necessarily focus on normative reform even if they recognize its limitations.

These examples of rethinking heteronormativity in the global development industry point us in the direction of denaturalizing and delinking gender/sex/sexuality in analyses of development and globalisation, a project increasingly being undertaken by scholars and advocates alike. Queer activists and scholars understand the effects of normativity in shaping, regulating and disciplining their lives, through the pathologisation and governance of intimacy and through their paradoxical hyper visibility (e.g., gay male visibility in HIV/AIDS discourse) and invisibility (e.g., claims that lesbians 'do not exist' in non-western countries) in discourses and processes of nation-building, national security, westernization and globalisation.

In light of the recent reassertion of homophobic discourse in global and national arenas, it is especially urgent that we place lesbian, gay, bisexual and transgender and otherwise non-normative lives at the centre of rights-based development frameworks-as establishing a normative set of rights is important-yet also, that we shift the dialogue from a liberal discourse of rights, which frames identity primarily in binary terms, to a discourse critical of liberalism, which frames processes of identification as multiply-mediated and constructed through forms of agency as well as through the various external interventions that frame who we are as the subjects of development.

When Paul Wolfowitz took over as head of the World Bank, he faced a delicate problem: Shaha Ali Riza, the woman with whom he had been maintaining an intimate relationship, was a World Bank official. For her to remain in place would sound conflict-of-interest alarms, but he could not simply fire her. So, following the informal advice of the bank's ethics committee, Wolfowitz arranged his companion's transfer to the US State Department. The problem was the terms of the transfer that Wolfowitz negotiated. According to the World Bank Staff Association's expression of "concern, dismay and outrage," Riza's transfer involved several unacceptable features, namely undue promotion, excessive pay raise, and unwarranted sharp annual pay increases.

The employees complained that Ms. Riza had received special treatment because of her relationship to Mr. Wolfowitz, thus violating the Bank's orderly rules for promotion, transfer, and compensation. Four days after a special investigative World Bank committee concluded that he had "violated his contract by breaking ethical and governing rules in arranging the generous pay and promotion for Shaha Ali Riza," Wolfowitz resigned, effective June 30, 2007. Consider a very different story from MedAptus, a small Boston medical technology firm. When its marketing director, Jennifer Crowley, faced the tragedy of Cian, her 7-month-old baby's imminent death from a rare pediatric cancer, project manager Andrea Berte Bellemare asked Dennis Mitchell, the company's chief executive, for permission to donate three of her leave days to Crowley.

Mitchell not only agreed but went further, creating a staff donation bank. As a result, Crowley received 33 additional leave days from her co-workers which allowed her to keep her job and care for her child. "We felt so helpless," Mitchell reported, "It's really pulled the company closer together to be able to donate time". Intimacy in economic organizations: threat or boon? The Wolfowitz mishap portrays intimacy as a threat to organizational effectiveness, but the leave bank story suggests that it is a boon. Two apparently contradictory principles come into play: disruption and solidarity. In the disruption view, intimacy disrupts organizational effort, and therefore requires inhibition and damage control.

In the solidarity view, on the contrary, intimacy builds solidarity and trust, thus enhancing organizational effectiveness. We might resolve the apparent contradiction by discovering that different kinds of intimacy have different effects on organizational life, that intimacy's effects don't depend on its sheer presence or intensity, and that they do depend on the location of intimate relations within an organization's interpersonal networks. When it comes to the positive or negative impact of intimacy, the crucial fact is not the sheer presence of intimate relations, but the type of relation and its location within the larger web of connections within the organization.

Intimacy consists of privileged access to another person's attention, information, and trust, all of which would damage the person if widely available to other people. Thus defined, intimate relations vary in breadth (from one narrow sort of attention to access that crosses a whole existence), in duration (from a fleeting rendezvous to a lifetime connection), and in intensity (from casual sharing to emotionally charged secrets). At one extreme-very broad, durable, and intense relationships-the case for disruption becomes compelling. Short of that extreme, however, many different combinations appear to be compatible with organizational effectiveness, or even to enhance it.

This chapter's main task is to survey and synthesize the scattered evidence for such a view. But before arriving at the evidence, we must clear some cluttered ground. Let us first look more closely at the disruption and solidarity views, noticing which sorts of intimacy and which features of organizational life advocates of those opposing views most often treat, and seeing in what ways they are plausible or implausible.

Then we can move on to available evidence concerning intimacy's impact on economic organizations and from there to tentative conclusions. I will discipline an unruly subject by narrowing it in four ways: fixing attention on formal economic organizations, thus leaving the informal economy, household production, and market transactions for treatment elsewhere restricting attention to relationships occurring within economic organizations, thus excluding questions about how outside intimate ties (for example, close outside friendships with competitors, relationships with spouses, and notorious love affairs) affect organizational performance concentrating on just three varieties of intimacy: sexual, friendship, and kinship, thus neglecting confidential relationships, management of organizational secrets, and formal mentoring or apprenticeship programs asking four main questions about such intimate ties:

1. How prevalent are intimate ties in economic organizations?
2. how do organizations respond to such ties?
3. What are the overall impacts of intimate ties' prevalence, intensity, and organizational location on aggregate organizational effectiveness?
4. How does the presence of an intimate tie affect the organizational performance of the pair and their relations to third parties within the organization?

Sexual intimacy, friendship, and kinship sometimes do disrupt organizations. But they often coexist with organizational effectiveness, or even contribute to it. I single out these three forms of intimacy not because they are interchangeable or because they mark degrees on some scale of intensity, but on the contrary because differences among them allow us to see more clearly how the presence of intimacy within economic organizations affects organizational performance. While lawsuits and scandals break into headlines much more often in cases of sexual intimacy, we will see that intimacy based on friendship and kinship can likewise have profound effects on how organizations perform.

Although they differ significantly in other regards, sexual intimacy, friendship, and kinship within economic organizations pose similar empirical, analytical, and policy problems for organizational analysts. Empirically, under what conditions do they proliferate, and to what extent does their presence coincide with disruption of organizational performance? Analytically, how extensively and how does the existence of such intimate relations within organizations alter adjacent relations (for example, with fellow workers or supervisors)? In a policy perspective, are these effects sufficiently large and deleterious to recommend blanket bans on intimacy — or at least its more intense forms — within economic organizations? This said, the three sorts of intimacy vary in contrasting ways.

Consider breadth and duration. Sexual relations range from fleeting and narrow-the one-night stand in which the parties hardly get to know each other-to broad and lasting. On the average, friendships last longer and cover a wider range of interactions. Kinship generally lasts even longer, but can run from quite narrow (the annual family reunion) to extremely broad (the shared household). The extent to which the three sorts of relations begin and remain within economic organizations also varies dramatically.

As we will soon see, sexual relationships often start on the job. Friendships split between those generated in the workplace and those carried over from elsewhere. Kinship almost always precedes and overflows organizational membership. Eventually any fine analysis of intimacy's organizational impact must recognize these distinctions. We turn now to the cases for disruption and solidarity. What are the organizational effects of intimacy, according to these two different arguments?

THE THREAT OF INTIMISATION

To move ahead analytically, we must look directly at the supposed organizational threat posed by the three forms of workplace intimacy discussed here: sexual, friendship, kin ties. In general, how do analysts and observers of economic life treat the intersection between intimacy and economic activity? Although earlier theorists had often allowed for the coexistence of solidarity and self-interest, from the 19th century onward theorists of economic processes have adopted two closely related theories. We can call them the theories of separate spheres and of hostile worlds. Separate spheres theories identify two distinct domains of social life that operate according to different principles: rationality, efficiency, and planning on one side, solidarity, sentiment, and impulse on the other.

As Max Weber put it in his analysis of the erotic sphere: "[the lover] knows himself to be freed from the cold skeleton hands of rational orders, just as completely as from the banality of everyday routine". In Weber's view, and many like it, intimacy generates and depends on warm sentiment, while efficiency requires rationality and therefore suppression of sentiment. Pioneer organizational analyst Donald Roy says this about the standard view of workplace sex: Sex is considered not only functionally inappropriate for industrial activity but also out of place, in a literal sense, in regard to general layout and material furnishings of the typical factory.

Industrial management may here and there show a diffuse sort of indulgence toward the premarital or extra-marital achievements of employees, but it is unlikely that benignity extends to approval of mating maneuvers on company time. Indeed, workplaces, as James Woods has shown, are typically designed as asexual spheres where sexuality looms as "an external threat to an organization . . . something that must be regulated, prohibited, or otherwise held at the company gates." What Woods calls the "asexual imperative" goes beyond protecting vulnerable workers, typically women, from sexual harassment.

It supports organizational prohibitions against the use of sexuality to determine matters of workers' hire, pay, promotion, or dismissal. One of the worst aspersions one can cast against a rising company official is that he or she slept the way to the top. Equally damning is the accusation of having put a lover on the company payroll. In the separate spheres account, a sharp divide exists between intimate social relations and economic transactions. Left to itself, goes the doctrine, each sphere works more or less automatically and well. Markets run themselves, and so do families and other intimate settings. But the two spheres remain alien to each other. Worse yet, contact between them produces moral contamination.

Monetization of personal care, for example, corrupts that care into self-interested sale of services. Thus emerges a view of the separate spheres as dangerously hostile worlds, properly segregated domains whose sanitary management requires well-maintained boundaries. The feared contamination cuts both ways. Generations of scholars and social critics have warned about the devastating effects of commodification on personal relations. Analysts of economic organizations, however, have implicitly adopted a precisely opposite doctrine: that a process we can call "intimisation" undermines organizational performance.

The dangers of "intimisation" constitute the mirror image of commodification threats. Here the introduction of sentiment and interpersonal solidarity into rational transactions produces inefficiency, favoritism, cronyism, and other forms of corruption. Indeed, organizational analysts and managers tend to think of intimacy as inefficient noise or worse, as a threat to organizational efficiency and productivity. Only markets cleansed of sentiment, in this view, can generate true efficiency. Corruption thus runs in both directions. Critiques of intimacy in organizations actually follow three somewhat different paths, but they end up in the same place.

The first variant argues that intimate relations distract their participants from an organization's main goals, and thus undermine organizational performance. A loving couple, in this view, is likely to make love on company time, or even to appropriate crucial company resources for their private use. A pair of old friends, runs the same line of reasoning, may well service their friendship instead of following orders that reach them from their superiors. Collusion among workers, whether based on kinship, friendship, or sexual relations, can likewise subvert organizational programs. Call this the distraction thesis.

The second variant argues that matching of persons with jobs on the basis of intimate relations instead of appropriate human capital produces inferior work. Thus the boss's daughter who takes an important job presumably blocks better qualified candidates from the post. Again the common practice of letting present employees recruit fellow members of their immigration network to new vacancies in a firm presumably excludes more talented potential workers outside that migration network. In either case, intimacy causes suboptimal organizational performance.

Call this the human capital thesis. In a third variant, intimacy creates unfairness by disrupting organizational systems of reward, as when promotion and salary are determined by favoritism rather than merit. Finally, intimacy can undermine organizational life becoming exploitative, as in sexual harassment. Call this the disorder thesis. The distraction, human capital, and disorder theses are not simple fantasies. Sometimes each of these processes does undermine organizational effectiveness. World Bank employees were not fantasizing with their fear of organizational disorder. The question is how regularly and how the presence of intimacy disrupts organizational effectiveness.

THE CASE FOR SOLIDARITY

Despite the plausible fears that cronyism, nepotism, on-the-job romances, and favoritism disrupt organizational performance, we can also make the case that intimacy often enhances solidarity, and thus actually promotes organizational performance. The case for solidarity builds on very different beliefs from separate spheres and hostile worlds. On the whole, goes the reasoning, a measure of intimacy within an organization fosters job satisfaction, enhances commitment of workers to the organization, facilitates communication among workers, and supports mutual aid in the performance of essential organizational tasks. We might call this view the sociable satisfaction theory.

Savvy managers themselves implicitly recognize the case for solidarity. They bend the rules as they encounter circumstances in which mentoring, trust, friendship, shared secrets, and mutual aid actually contribute to organizational ends. More exactly, they regularly choose among four different strategies for dealing with intimate relations on the job: ban, contain, regulate, and integrate. At the extreme, sexual misconduct and nepotism codes simply ban certain relationships from organizations on the ground that in general they produce more trouble than they are worth. Containment works more subtly through such devices as permitting flirtation, gossip, gift exchanges, or mutual aid at office parties and coffee breaks but not on the job. Regulation, in contrast, directly recognizes the presence of an intimate relationship but subjects it to scrutiny by means of conflict-of-interest declarations and disclaimer contracts.

Organizations also integrate intimate relations as they foster mentoring, reward secretaries who manage their bosses' personal affairs, or promote pairs known to work well together. Managers who seek to contain, regulate, or integrate intimate relations within their organizations could draw support from a decades-old literature on human relations in industry back to F. J. Roethlisberger and William J. Dickson or George Homans. The literature certainly sees dangers that close friendships among workers promote resistance to management directives, but it also declares that workers draw much of their job satisfaction from relations with other workers, and that job satisfaction leads to superior performance by individuals and work groups.

Although the classic industrial relations studies paid little attention to kinship and sexual relations, at least they raise the possibility that those forms of intimacy, properly managed, contribute to solidarity and thereby to organizational performance. More recently, a surprising array of literatures have confirmed this possibility. From disparate academic perspectives and often distinctive policy agendas, scholars — ranging from economic sociology to sexual studies — coincide in identifying positive features of workplace intimacy. Economic sociologists, for instance, have gestured in that direction by demonstrating the positive effects of certain kinds of personal ties for the overall effectiveness and efficiency of at least some kinds of economic organizations.

Such analysts as Ronald Burt, Asaf Darr (2006), Paul Ingram and Peter Roberts (2000), Brian Uzzi and Ryon Lancaster (2004) have pinpointed the reliance of agents in presumably impersonal markets on ties of friendship among contractors and even putative competitors. Quite independently, organizational analysts have discovered the importance of some kinds of emotions to organizational performance, challenging the idea that rationality requires the suppression of feelings. They have insisted that such emotions as anger sometimes activate and enhance organizational effectiveness.

In 1992, Dennis Mumby and Linda Putnam, for example, introduced the concept of "bounded emotionality" to signal the contributions that emotions make to organizational effectiveness. But so far no one has effectively connected the analysis of emotions within organizations to different kinds of relations among their members. Some of the most provocative statements about workplace intimacy come from scholars in sociology and the law, many of them feminists. Some voice complaints about scholarly neglect of what they call "organisation sexuality", but others go much further.

In a pioneer 1999 Annual Review of Sociology essay about sexuality in the workplace, Christine Williams, Patti Giuffre, and Kirsten Dellinger (1999) called for greater attention to consensual relationships, defined as those "reflecting positive and autonomous expressions of workers' sexual desire".

Acknowledging that some forms of workplace sexuality can be oppressive and exploitative, especially towards women, they insist that we should also recognize that sexuality may enhance "job satisfaction, self-esteem, and happiness". Similarly, Kari Lerum argues that under certain conditions, "sexualized interactions can communicate and construct a sense of worker camaraderie."

Other scholars have emphasized the solidarity-generating place of non- sexual intimate relations. Specialists in work and occupations, for instance, draw attention to the crucial yet little understood significance of co-worker intimacy, ranging from close friendships and companionship to more tangible forms of social support. Meanwhile, legal experts voice impatience with what they see as the disruptive impact of "intimisation" fears. Most emphatically, Vicki Schultz argues against what she calls the "sanitized workplace" where workers' sexuality is banished in order to prevent its potential deterioration into sexual harassment.

Paradoxically, Schultz notes, by focusing on sexual oppression, organizations neglect the more crucial discriminatory impact of sex segregation and inequality which, in her view, breed harassment. Equally significant, Schultz worries that sexual sanitization blunts the "role of open expression in promoting employees' shared sense of solidarity, intimacy, and humanity" (2006:103). Employers, Schultz insists, "should foster atmospheres of sexual tolerance and understanding and should recognize that sexual expression doesn't inherently undermine equality or organizational goals".

Even when it comes to sexual harassment, for example, Schultz argues that "sexual harassment policies now provide an added incentive and an increased legitimacy for management to control and discipline relatively harmless sexual behavior without even inquiring into whether that behavior undermines gender equality on the job". Schultz concludes that instead of banning sexually tinged relations, organizations would serve their own purposes much better by concentrating on the reduction of gender inequality and segregation.

Schultz is not alone. Equally concerned about the undermining of consensual workplace sexuality, legal scholar Sharon Rabin-Margalioth (2006:251) calls for more studies of "how and to what extent intimate sexual relations affect productivity, organizational efficiency, morale of co-workers." Rabin- Margalioth, furthermore, takes on anti-nepotism policies, in particular no- spouse rules. Countering "intimisation" fears that joint employment of spouses will create "organizational strife, favoritism, jealousy and tension among other co-workers" Rabin-Margalioth argues that anti- nepotism rules in fact have a discriminatory effect on women, who are more likely to be denied employment or fired as a result.

The needed confrontation between disruption and solidarity views of intimacy has not yet occurred. Organizational analysts must stage the confrontation on both theoretical and empirical levels. How should we join the debate, and search for a synthesis? How Intimacy Really Works Despite their obvious contradictions, advocates of the cases for disruption and for solidarity have not joined a coherent debate, made a serious effort to synthesize their views, or organized a comprehensive research program concerning the impact of intimacy on organizational performance.

As a cautious step toward those three goals, let me offer a selective review of empirical work bearing on four relevant questions:

1. How prevalent within economic organizations are intimate relations based on sexuality, kinship and/or friendship?
2. How do organizational managers respond to the presence of different sorts of intimate ties?
3. How do the prevalence, intensity, and location of intimate ties within an organization affect the organization's overall performance?
4. How does the existence of an intimate tie affect the individual and joint job performance of the pair, and their relations to third parties within the organization?

Although my review will differentiate among sexual, kinship, and friendship ties as well as intensities of intimacy where possible, in this survey it will be enough to draw tentative empirical conclusions from a highly disparate set of literatures. After the survey I will offer a series of conjectures in hopes of stimulating new work-both theoretical and empirical-on intimacy's impact within economic organizations. How prevalent are intimate ties within organizations? Sexual, kinship, and friendship relations are all impressively prevalent in workplaces. In a controversial book, Deirdre McCloskey rightly observes: Markets and even the much-maligned corporations encourage friendships wider and deeper than the atomism of a full-blown socialist regime or the claustrophobic, murderous atmosphere of a "traditional" village. Modern capitalist life is love-saturated.

With increasing entrance of women into the paid labor force, furthermore, increasing shares of love-saturated relationships cross gender lines. Although we lack a coherent literature documenting intimacy's prevalence and variety, a number of scattered but revealing studies provide valuable glimpses into workplace intimacies. We get some early glimmers of workplace friendships, for instance, from Susan Porter Benson's study of department store saleswomen in the first decades of the 20th century: In one department, women contributed to the support of Aggie, a particularly destitute co-worker; they paid her insurance and sick- benefit premiums, bought extra food for her lunch, and helped her to stretch her meager clothing budget.

But their actions went beyond self-help within the department to confront management on Aggie's behalf. When a manager halted their yearly collection to send Aggie on vacation and made them return the money, they ostentatiously collected it again outside the employees' entrance. They knew, however, that the only real solution to Aggie's problems was a higher salary, and their most impressive victory was in backing up her successful quest for a raise. More recent evidence comes from Randy Hodson. Despite giving more attention to resistance than to mutual aid, Hodson has advanced our knowledge of co-workers' intimate ties by combing and cataloguing more than a hundred ethnographies of workplace interaction.

The ethnographies report such practices as gift-giving in a chemical factory and mutual covering among sleeping car porters. "Coworkers," concludes Hodson: help provide meaning in work through the sharing of work life experiences and through friendships. Coworkers can also provide a basis for group solidarity and mutual support in the face of denials of dignity at work. Hodson identifies friendship and mutual aid as major compensations for physical hardship, tedious work routines, tyrannical managers, and even low wages. Without such close personal ties, we can infer, many workplaces, far from operating more efficiently, would actually collapse. Hodson reports a striking study of Washington, D.C. firefighters. A firefighter recalled: It's hard to describe the closeness that you felt with the guys in the fire house. Firemen then were a great bunch and a rough bunch . . . They played hard and rough. But when the bells hit, nobody would do any more good for you than a fireman. It's a group of men with a unique brotherhood feeling-they'll never let you down. Gail McGuire's (2007) interviews with 40 employees of a large female- dominated financial services company about what she calls "intimate work" provide even more specific evidence about the prevalence and variety of workplace intimacy.

Based on her respondents' reports of the types of social support they offered their network members, McGuire identified a broad range of assistance, including sharing, listening, counseling, caretaking, and non work services such as providing information about "managing finances, home improvements, church activities, real estate, weddings, weight loss, and pregnancy". Employees also reported offering co-workers help with a variety of tasks, including "residential moves, filing taxes, doing home improvements, babysitting, and giving help with transportation". Some provided straightforward material assistance, such as money or used furniture. Drawing on her evidence, McGuire argues for the significance of the workplace as "an important site for the development and expression of intimacy".

McGuire's findings echo Stephen Marks' 1994 attempt to gauge workplace intimacy. To do so, Marks analyzed 1986

General Social Survey data on close friendships among co-workers, plus Claude Fischer's 1982 Northern California Community Study. Based on his own analysis of these surveys, Marks concludes that: "at workplaces, intimacy appears to be a rather pervasive phenomenon". "For millions of American workers," Marks finds "close friendships are formed among co-workers, "important matters" are discussed with them, and such discussions are associated with greater job satisfaction". Intimacy within corporations, of course, often goes beyond platonic friendships.

As Roy colorfully reported: When the situation is one of men and women working side by side or sharing a task that calls for team work, Eros may infiltrate the production line to evoke attachments of various qualities and durations of affection, ranging from the protracted attentions of true love to ephemeral ardencies of the opportune moment. Likewise, Williams, Giuffre, and Dellinger (1999) point to a wide range of workplace sexual interactions, including "flirting with coworkers or clients (in person or via email); consuming pornography; sexual joking, bantering and touching; and coworker dating, sexual affairs, cohabitation and marriage". More concretely, the 2005 Society for Human Resource Management's (SHRM) survey of almost 500 human resource professionals and 400 employees, found that about 40% of employees had been involved in a workplace romance sometime in their careers.

Likewise, a 2007 Annual Office Romance Survey conducted by career publisher Vault among 575 employees in various industries around the U.S. confirms the importance of office romances: 47 % of respondents reported having been involved in an office romance. One researcher estimates a current total of about 10 million workplace romantic relationships. Not surprisingly, self-help books now offer advice for workplace romance. The authors of a book called Office Mate advise that "the greatest pool of potential mates is not online, not in a bar, and not on a blind date. It's in the office".

To what extent same-sex relationships originate in parallel ways remain uncertain in the present state of the literature.

The Vault survey reveals a surge in an intriguing adjacent phenomenon of male-female non-sexual office "marriages." Twenty-three percent of employees reported a platonic office "husband" or "wife," with whom they "hang out" regularly, spending a great deal of time together, sharing breaks or lunch. Available evidence, then, documents the widespread prevalence of intimate relations-both sexual and otherwise-within economic organizations. For our inquiry, that prevalence of intimacy has two strong implications.

First, no valid theory of organizational interactions can assume that interpersonal relations are normally impersonal within firms, that intimate relations are ipso facto anomalous and risky. Second, no practical policy of banning or radically containing intimacy is likely to work within economic organizations. Managers' response to workplace intimacy How, then, do managers actually react to the presence of intimacy within their organizations? Managers' practical responses to the perceived threat of intimisation vary so widely as to baffle any confident detection of trends in actual organizational practices.

The existing literature on workplaces from the 1990s onward so thoroughly mixes anecdotes, complaints, prescriptions, and reports on the prevalence and management control over intimate relations that we lack the essential evidence. Is there, as some suggest, a rising tide of prohibitions on sexual intimacy? What about kinship and friendship? Such close students of the subject as legal scholar Vicki Schultz claim to see a substantial increase in workplace regulation of intimate relations, going well beyond sexual harassment. Schultz contends that managers are engaged in a "campaign of sexual sanitization".

"A new generation of managers and employees," asserts Schultz, "has internalized the age-old message that sex is out of place in the workplace and encoded it into new sexual harassment policies and programs". Increased regulations range from "no-fraternization policies" prohibiting romantic involvement between supervisors and employees, even when consensual, to "date-and-tell" policies, where employees involved in such relationships must disclose their romance to management, and be subject to monitoring, reprimand, or transfer. The 2005 SHRM survey of human resource professionals and employees found that among employers and employees it has not only "become generally accepted that romances between a supervisor and subordinate are off limits," but "organizations are also beginning to feel the need for employees to inform their supervisors of any relationships".

Managers' fear of intimate ties goes further. In 2005, The National Law Journal reported an increase in so-called "cupid" or "love" contracts for employees about to embark on a romantic relationship. To protect firms against sexual harassment suits, employment lawyers now recommend a signed written agreement between prospective lovers which certifies that both partners understand that the relationship is consensual. Similarly, an article in the magazine of the prestigious Conference Board recommends a "personal relations policy" which includes a wide range of relatively intimate relations and: goes beyond sexual relationships and mandates disclosure of close personal relationships as defined in the policy. Even though sexual involvement is perceived as posing the greatest threat to objectivity, close after-hours friendships are important to note as well: Research supports our suspicion that "old boy" buddies-and now "old girls," too-get more job perks than "lovers."

That's why a policy should address potential conflicts with marital, extended-family, and close-friendship relationships as well as romantic ones. In a parallel move, since the 1980s employers (especially in the public sector) have been increasingly imposing no-spouse and anti-nepotism rules. What is more, legal attempts to challenge nepotism rules which prohibit couples from sharing a workplace have generally failed. Employers commonly justify bans on married couples by means of three claims, first, "the advancement of mutual interest" argument that marital solidarity might supersede employers' interests; second, a reverse "feuding" argument that couples' quarrels can seriously interfere both with their relationship and work environment; and third, a "breach of confidentiality" argument that married couples may improperly disclose secret information to each other.

These three arguments incorporate the distraction, human capital, and disorder theses I distinguished earlier. Let me not give the impression, however, that American firms generally adopt explicit anti-intimacy policies. In fact, the SHRM 2005 survey found that most companies do not have a policy designed to regulate office romances: over 70% of organizations reported they had no formal written or verbal policies. Those that did, had policies discouraging, but not prohibiting, workplace dating. The main thing we do know, then, is that both managers and management experts continue to flag the presence of different sorts of workplace intimacy and excessive familiarity as a significant management problem. As in the Wolfowitz case, these concerns often translate into organizational anti- intimacy rules, sets of defenses against contamination by intimacy.

Along those lines, Tom Rath, author of a best-selling survey of on-the-job friendships, reports that managers he talked to usually responded to the presence of workplace intimacy with caution, even fear. Some counter-trends deserve closer empirical attention. Such organizational innovations as self-managed work teams or quality circles, for example, presumably depend for their effectiveness on the fact that they promote friendship and thereby facilitate coordination of work efforts. Similarly, the shift to horizontal organizational forms seems to provide efficiency gains partly because it draws on friendships that ease communication and cooperation across divisional lines. Still, not surprisingly, managers are less concerned with friendships than with sexual liaisons within organizations.

Sexual liaisons are of course more likely to generate unfavorable publicity, lawsuits, and organizational crises than are the presence of kinship or friendship. Sexual liaisons between supervisors and employees that go sour, furthermore, most likely generate a significant share of sexual harassment complaints. In fact, experts are increasingly concerned about adequate managerial response to dissolved workplace romances which sometimes turn into sexual harassment.

The 2005 SHRM study found that concerns among human resource professionals about retaliation — meaning conflicts between co-workers after a break-up — grew from 12% in 2001 to 67% in 2005. With more women in the workforce, concern with exploitation and sexual predation (and fear of lawsuits stemming from them) grows more salient. For instance, a national survey of senior managers in 544 U.S. cities found overall favorable views on workplace friendships, but managers remained wary of office romances. Note the irony: Human relations specialists and lawyers worry increasingly about the threat of on-the-job romance, every survey reports high levels of on-the-job romance, but only 30 percent of firms surveyed have policies banning or regulating on-the-job romance.

The most likely conclusion is that experienced managers understand both that love will have its way at work and that writing regulations will not eliminate it. Nevertheless, it is not obvious either that these rules do drive intimacy from the workplace or that they actually serve organizational performance. Intimacy's Impact on Organizational Performance Surprisingly, more information is available on the overall impact of intimacy's presence in an organization than on our fourth question: its effects on intimate pairs' job performance and its third party effects. Since the 1930s, industrial sociologists have stressed the positive impact of workplace solidarity on productivity. But that older literature generally neglected practices creating solidary pairs in favor of practices fostering group identification.

More recently, a number of studies report the prevalence and even management's promotion of job recruitment by current employees of friends and kin. Mutual recruitment often benefits the hiring organization by enhancing employee productivity. So far as we can tell, mutual hiring tends to integrate new hires more firmly into workplace networks, and to give them greater access to personal attention. In a fine example of a fast-paced call center, Roberto Fernández and Emilio Castilla (2000) show that personal ties between current employees and potential employees often benefit the hiring organization by enhancing employee productivity. Castilla shows further that after mutually selective hiring newcomers tend to produce more and display greater attachment to the firm than casual hires.

He distinguishes between a "better match" account (in which referrals simply bring in new employees with more suitable qualifications for the job) and a "social enrichment" account (in which superior relations emerge between old and new employees), providing substantial evidence for social enrichment effects in the call center. Castilla reports, for instance, that the staff was considering a "buddy" system of pairing old-timers with newcomers to reduce turnover and raise job satisfaction-very much a social enrichment strategy.

"One trainer," says Castilla: highlighted the importance of having a friend on the job: "It really helps in making the job more comfortable." This trainer did not specifically say that the referrer might play an important role in this process. But when probed about the possibility that the referrer might be acting as an informal "buddy," she said this was "probably right". The work of Fernández and Castilla identifies crucial circumstances in which the presence of intimacy enhances organizational performance. Nevertheless, economic sociologists have not yet confronted intimate relations with sufficient directness or examined the supposed threat to organizational performance posed by such intimacy.

More generally, a surprising variety of studies document the positive effects of workplace intimate relationships on economic productivity. Consider these vignettes: Economist K. K. Fung provides a strong theoretical rationale for concluding that horizontal favor exchanges enhance organizational efficiency. Business School professor Francis Flynn finds evidence that employees who exchanged favors were significantly more productive than their fellows. A large 2001 Gallup poll identifies a strong connection across firms, between the proportion of workers who had best friends in the workplace, on one side, and firm profitability, productivity, safety, and customer loyalty, on the other.

In 2007, a survey of senior executives and workers in the country's thousand largest firms finds widespread agreement that workers with co- workers who were "buddies" both on and off the job were more productive and committed contributors to firm performance. Legal scholar Sally Avelenda argues that spouses who share a workplace are more likely to stay on the job, to be recruitable together, to gain more satisfaction from working together, and to adopt more favorable attitudes toward the firm that hires them. A substantial literature on family firms indicates not only that on the average they create more worker-friendly environments than their non- family competitors, but also enjoy greater organizational effectiveness.

Family businesses offer an even more decisive empirical challenge to any notion of incompatibility between intimacy and economic effectiveness. Estimates of the share of all American businesses owned by families run in the vicinity of 90% and the share of all business income from such firms appears to run around 60%. What is more, such firms perform very well, perhaps even better than non- family firms. They have lower turnover and often provide benefits such as child care, scholarships for employees' children, and profit-sharing, and are less likely to resort to layoffs.

As expert John L. Ward comments: "Family firms see employees as a long-term resource. They just believe it's the right way to go". Not those family business relations operate just like non-family relations. A compensation handbook for family business points out a series of challenges that such businesses must face, for example equity between family and non- family forms of compensation. The manual includes three striking examples of resolutions to this dilemma:

1. A family employed a diligent but handicapped son at full pay. The son made a meaningful contribution but less than the minimum expected of his peers. No one argued with or felt abused by this deviation from the company's compensation policy, probably because of the son's handicap, agreeable personality and hard-work ethic.
2. A family bent experience requirements, giving a daughter who was a single mother a chance to learn a new position to which she brought aptitude but no experience or training. The family paid the daughter the full position wage during the learning period of nearly a year. The company was rewarded with a loyal and capable

performer who had permanent ties to the organization. The family was able to help a responsible member sustain a reasonable standard of living.

3. Two brothers, both of whom worked hard, agreed to earn the same amounts. Their abilities and contributions, however, were different. From the company's standpoint, the overpayment of one brother would not have been necessary except for the sibling relationship. However, the harmony and teamwork fostered by this accommodating relationship was a major benefit to the organization.

Arguably, the organization would have been sold and dismantled if the brothers had not recognized the value of a situational overpayment in return for calm waters, productive efforts and a focus on the company's important issues. In all these cases, according to the manual, the integration of family relations into the organization enhanced organizational performance. These problems, moreover, are no more acute than those of compensation and incentives in non-family organizations. Studies of new business ventures further support the crucial role of family ties.

In a valuable survey article Howard Aldrich and Jennifer Cliff make three observations about startups of American business: First, a significant proportion of new organizations are founded by two or more related individuals, including married couples or cohabiting partners. Second, the creation of new organizations is more likely to respond to alterations in family ties rather than simply the opening of economic options. Third, families play key roles in providing start-ups with financial resources, human resources, and physical resources such as space in the family household.

Available evidence on family firms makes three points of increasing importance for the place of intimacy in economic organizations. Most obviously and uncontroversially, the sheer prevalence and relative visibility of family firms establishes the compatibility of intimate ties with a wide range of economic activity. More speculatively, descriptions of family firms suggest that they tend to substitute durable relations of solidarity for arm's length relations of short-term efficiency, and thus to gain their successes by somewhat different organizational means from firms that bar intimate relations.

Third, we have at least a hint that family firms gain some of their durability from a simple fact: Intimate ties generally operate on a longer time scale than impersonal ones, and hence provide participants with extra capacity to ride out short-term failures and downturns in favor of long-term performance. In Albert Hirschman's terms, close kin faced with organizational decline tend to substitute voice and loyalty for exit.

Intimacy's Effects on Internal Organizational Dynamics. Unfortunately, existing studies yield much less evidence on the organizational dynamics and interpersonal effects of intimate relations than on intimacy's overall impact. Those effects have two components: effects of intimacy on the pairs' work performance and the effects of intimacy on relations of the pair, singly or collectively, to third parties. In principle, we should be able to gauge intimacy's effect on organizational performance-negative or positive-simply by observing the job performance of intimate pairs as compared to the performance of non-intimate pairs in similar jobs. In practice, it is not so easy. Because of separate spheres thinking, we only have scattered evidence of workplace intimate labors.

We know little, for instance, of exactly how co-workers cover for each other's defects or absences, what sort of mentoring old timers provide newcomers, how workers console each other for managers' injustices, what sorts of favors they exchange on the job, and how they support each other by such practices as taking up collections, trading work assignments, and pooling leaves. Scattered anecdotes and complaints, to be sure, deplore the withdrawal of intimate couples from creative work and effective interaction with their fellow workers. Robert Quinn's 1977 study of the dynamics of organizational romance, for instance, identified many points in which romantic partners' work performance suffered, among them making costly mistakes as a result of distraction, covering mistakes of the partner, working less and worse, arriving late, leaving early, missing appointments, becoming inaccessible, showing favoritism, promoting the other.

Nevertheless, Quinn (1977) also documents many ways in which on the job intimacy enhanced the performance of the pairs involved. In that positive vein, other more recent studies suggest that certain forms of intimacy frequently increase the general well-being of the workers involved in these ties. Marks' 1994 GSS-based study of workplace intimacy, for example, found an association between co-workers' friendship ties and greater job satisfaction. Similarly, in her account of "intimate work" McGuire (2007) notes that for some of her interviewees, "sharing facilitated good professional relationships because it created trust and a general sense of good will between workers."

McGuire reports Larry's case: [he] described how sharing with one of his network members facilitated trust between them, which made Larry feel comfortable having "off-line conversations" with him, or confidential discussions about work-related issues. More dramatically, relying on self-reports, Rath's Vital Friends trumpets his finding that having a best friend on the job makes the worker seven times as likely to be engaged in their job. Rath and others furthermore find that having close friends on the job makes it less likely that workers will leave. In a parallel way, Groysberg et al. report that the quality of star performance among security analysts depends heavily on collaborative relations with colleagues, so much so that stars often undergo significant losses of productivity when they make solo moves from one firm to the other.

Despite the concern about romantic entanglements, office romances also often enhance worker satisfaction and performance. Lisa Mainiero's 2005 review of the literature on workplace romance identifies a number of studies which "provide support for positive impacts on performance, job involvement and enthusiasm of partners that engage in an office romance with a love motive". Along the same lines, a British survey of 221 individuals in a wide variety of organizations found that most of them reported having had intimate relations at the workplace. Most described the experience as positive: When closer and more positive relationships are formed, people report that they work better together, work harder to achieve their objectives and through such mutual respect and care, the organisation is also viewed in a more positive light.

Equally, a substantial proportion of the survey respondents view physical intimacy in a positive light, either as parties directly involved or as third party onlookers. Overall, it is reported that work effectiveness increases as a result of the relationship. For instance, a male IT Director of Financial Services made the following report: It just happened that we started working together here 10 years ago and the relationship just evolved. After two mergers we became the only two senior people from the old company. One of the key things that has been important for the development of our intimacy is the extreme nature of the work-changing technology and the business. That required quite close relations and working together . . . Consequently, the relationship gained high value for both of us, from information exchange to alliance to mutual support.

Now, we have a very intimate relationship that perhaps some would not approve of, considering that she has a partner. Thus, couples who engage in intimate relations at work frequently report both personal satisfaction and enhanced work performance. Intimacy affects not only the job performance of intimate pairs, but also individual and joint interactions of the pair with other workers within the organization. The threat to organizational performance comes from the possibility that members of intimate pairs will withhold needed communication and cooperation from third parties, and will give each other unfair access to organizational resources and rewards.

The promise, in contrast, stems from the possibility that intimate pairs will collaborate more effectively with third parties, for example by substituting for each other in cases of absence or illness. In truth, however, existing studies provide no more than glimmers of information on third party effects.

In his study of romantic entanglements among machine crew members, Roy contended that while in its early stages, "salutary effects on group morale and machine output may accompany the euphoria of a loving pair," soon the benefits soured, as "Eros and Vulcan draw apart." Eventually, Roy claimed, "the work group disintegrates, production collapses and blessings from the bossmen shrivel".

With less flourish, others have noted that a couples' close ties sometimes disrupt the flow of communications, as fellow employees may fear a breach of confidentiality. Observing work relationships within the engineering division of a large US high tech corporation, Gideon Kunda (1992) noted the impact of overlapping relationships. One supervisor married to an engineer working in the same facility shared her concerns: My husband works here too. We work on separate sides of the building and try not to see each other. I don't want to hear his voice. And I don't want any finger pointing. People might not trust you if they know you have a special relation. Some things you might not hear.

But some things I just wouldn't tell him. In a classic study, Rosabeth Moss Kanter (1977) showed how the relationship between a powerful boss and secretary affected relations-especially the boss' relationship - with the rest of the firm. Secretaries, Kanter found: Could make it easy or difficult to see a top executive. They could affect what managers read first, setting priorities for them without their knowing it. They could help or hurt someone's career by the ease with which they allowed that person access. Much of the published information on third party effects, however, rests on anecdote and conjecture.

James Dillard and Katherine Miller, speculate for instance, that romantic couples "may be attempting to impress their partners by increasing their output" or to assuage management's fears about the impact of their relationship with increased performance. However, there are wisps of evidence. In her interviews, McGuire found that co-workers' close ties: made it more likely that a work-related request would get done quickly, which was very important in this time-crunched organization. Lori described how she could call one of her network members, an administrative assistant who worked in a different area of the company, to help her with a Power Point presentation when she was "in a pinch".

Implications of the Evidence Available evidence on intimacy in organizations leaves many questions unanswered. It certainly establishes the widespread presence of intimate relations — sexual, friendship, or kinship-in economic organizations. That fact alone challenges any notion of intrinsic incompatibility between intimacy and organizational effectiveness. Separate spheres and hostile world's interpretations of intimacy hinder our understanding of organizational processes. When it comes to how intimate relations affect organizational processes, however, the evidence becomes more incomplete and complex.

On the whole, existing studies suffer from several defects. They typically: consider only one type of intimacy at a time concentrate not on everyday organizational intimacy but on extreme cases of nepotism, harassment, collusion, favoritism, and exploitation assume that the sheer presence or absence of intimate relations, rather than the intersection of those relations with non-intimate relations, is the crucial phenomenon to analyze The common view of intimacy as a general threat to organizational performance rests on two sorts of errors, analytical and empirical. The analytical errors fall into three parts:

1. Fixation on the presence or absence of certain kinds of intimate relationships instead of considering how such intimate relationships impact on third parties within the organization, and thus on overall organizational performance;
2. Failure to notice that some kinds of relationships within economic organizations actually contribute more to overall effectiveness if they involve a measure of intimacy; and
3. Uncritical acceptance of separate spheres and hostile worlds principles. How can we avoid these errors?

We must begin by recognizing a point that is obvious to organizational analysts: the overall performance of an organization is not the simple sum of individual performances, but the outcome of interactions among it members. How the performance of worker A impinges on the performance of worker B, and how their joint performance impinges on the behavior of other workers determines the effect of the relationship between A and B on adjacent relationships, and thence on the organization as a whole. To be sure, the impact of intimate work relations, including sexual interaction, varies from one kind of organization to another.

As Christine Williams, Patti A. Giuffre, and Kirsten Dellinger say in their review of sexuality in the workplace: The same behavior in different organizational contexts can have different meanings and different consequences. Thus, while many service workers are paid to be sexy and to engage in sexual innuendo with customers, in other jobs, mere rumors of sexual behavior or desire can destroy a career. What configurations should we take into account? To maintain intellectual discipline, we should begin with three-party relationships-triads-before moving on to more complex configurations.

In the simplest case, we are asking how the presence of an intimate connection between A and B affects the connection between either or both of them and C. For example, we can ask how a close connection between a secretary and a boss affects the interaction between the boss and a) his or her superiors, b) his or her peers or c) his or her other subordinates. Or we can ask how close friendship between two workers on an assembly line affects the relations of each to a) their common supervisor, b) their helpers, and c) other workers on the line. In general, then, we need to distinguish: the character and intensity of the intimate relation: breadth, duration, and intensity the relative equality or inequality of the organizational relationships involved: horizontal vs. vertical the forms of collaboration built into those organizational relationships, for example pooling of skills in complex tasks vs. sharing of confidential information.

So which configurations typically suffer or benefit from the presence of intimate relations? A whole research program awaits the question. Surprisingly and disappointingly, the concentration of organizational analysts on the sheer presence or absence of different varieties of intimate ties rather than their articulation with adjacent relationships has left us with few well documented observations on third party impacts: how fellow workers respond to a co-worker's sexual predation, the extent to which the coincidence of intimacy with informational pooling affects a pair's interactions with superiors, co-workers, or subordinates, the conditions under which intimacy-based mutual learning enhances joint contributions to collective efforts, and so on.

If my arguments hold up, investigators will identify a wide range of circumstances and relations in which kinship, friendship, or even sexual intimacy augment a pair's contribution to the effectiveness of larger collective efforts. In the absence of solid evidence, let me risk seven conjectures that follow from the argument I have just made:

1. Sexual predation of subordinates by superiors almost always damages organizational performance because it introduces coercion and injustice directly into work relationships and excites fear, indignation, or both among adjacent workers.
2. Intimate relations often threaten organizations when they involve pairs of persons one of whom has access to a third party's valuable organizational secrets, as when an affair between an executive's confidential assistant and another employee tempts the pair to share and profit by those secrets.
3. Where pooling of confidential information facilitates coordinated effort, however, intimate relations perform better than strictly impersonal relations.
4. As generations of organizational sociologists have argued, friendships within work teams, on the average, reinforce commitment to performance by the work team and the organization as a whole.
5. Where the availability of personal information within a pair of co-workers prevents errors and/or promotes superior performance (e.g. an assistant who can

compensate for a supervisor's bad day), a measure of intimacy enhances the pair's contribution to organizational effectiveness.

6. Where time-consuming mutual learning enhances collaboration because it establishes effective interpersonal routines and/or predictability, intimate relations improve organizational performance.
7. When pairs compensate for each other's failures, including sharing of tasks and compensation for absences, their joint contribution enhances organizational performance.

This does not mean, to be sure, that intimacy-even non-sexual intimacy-always enhances organizational performance. On the contrary, it means that the match between intimate relations and organizational configurations matters far more to organizational effectiveness than does the sheer presence or absence of one kind of intimacy or another. But it also means that flat bans of intimate relations are likely, on average, to damage organizational performance. Hostile worlds doctrines arise precisely because managers and organizational analysts are trying to work out good matches, but they are too blunt an instrument to do the job.

It will not do to assume that all relationships within economic organization will work better if they operate at arms-length. Nor, however, would organizations work well if any kind of intimacy occurred in any configuration. The analytic problem, then, is the identification of matches that enhance organizational performance without introducing unfairness and exploitation. Separate spheres and hostile worlds doctrines will not do the job. Policies based on such assumptions regularly: distract from the main causes of unfairness and exploitation, which are sex segregation and inequality provide a pretext for discriminating against unwanted workers curtail opportunities for productive uses of interpersonal intimacy discriminate against women who are subject to anti-nepotism rules.

The challenge consists of distinguishing configurations of relations including intimacy that a) clearly damage individual welfare through discrimination, exploitation, or injustice, b) clearly damage organizational performance in the aggregate, c) coexist without damage, d) actually contribute to organizational performance. The goal is thus to rewrite rules so that they eliminate a) and b), but not c) or d). Organizational analysts can make a major contribution to clarifying the policy issues by documenting, locating, and explaining the operation of intimate ties within economic organizations.

The challenge is to trace configurations of relations including intimate ties and their ramifications though the rest of the organization rather than settling for the observation of intimate pairs alone. We need analyses that accomplish three things: recognize and even account for the frequently positive effects of intimate solidarity within organizations on those organizations' overall performance; clarify how paired intimate solidarities affect third parties and larger networks; sort out which kinds of configurations including intimate ties commonly produce suboptimal performance, which actually contribute to organizational performance, and which have little impact one way or the other.

No one who sticks to separate spheres and hostile worlds reasoning will get very far with them. Once we understand the questions and recognize current theoretical obstacles to answering them, the investigation of intimacy within economic organizations poses a rich, challenging array of analytical problems whose proper resolution will help scholars and policy makers well outside the world of corporations.

5

Gender and Macroeconomics

The conventional conceptual frameworks and statistics used to design macro-economic policy are gender-blind. They fail to recognise that:

- Women's contribution to the economy is systematically underestimated;
- There is an unpaid care economy in which women do most of the work of maintaining the labour force and keeping the social fabric in good order, maintaining social cohesion, civic responsibility and good neighbourliness;

Looking at macroeconomics through a gender lens alerts us to the importance of non-market processes in the healthy functioning of an economy; and to the ways in which financial liberalisation places new burdens on those providing unpaid care while at the same time undermining public provision in support of this work.

More of women's work than of men's work is not counted by national economic statistics because a great deal of women's work is not market oriented. We can distinguish three kinds of non-market work that women do:

- Subsistence production
- Unpaid care work for family and friends
- Voluntary community work

Subsistence production is production for home use of goods which in principle could be marketed - such as food, clothing, soft furnishings, pottery, housing. In principle it should be included in the measurement of the gross national product (GNP). But in practice it is frequently omitted because statistical surveys do not properly count it. This is only a small component of work in Western Europe, but in poor rural countries it is very important. There is typically a social norm about which types of this work are done by men and which by women. In the UK, for instance, tasks that involve the use of power tools tend to be seen as men's tasks, whereas tasks that involve the use of sewing machines tend to be seen as women's tasks.

Unpaid care work is the work of looking after a household: cooking, cleaning, and providing personal care for family members and friends and neighbours. In principle, it is excluded from the gross national product: it is defined in the UN System of National Accounts as lying outside the production boundary. But it is vital for keeping the social fabric in good repair, and for maintaining and reproducing the labour force. Voluntary community work includes unpaid activity in all kinds of civic associations, both secular and church based. It includes everything from self-help groups of mothers getting together to run a children's play group or secure improvements in neighbourhood safety, to support work for large international charities.

Again these activities are in principle excluded from the GNP - and often are regarded as leisure activities. Voluntary work makes a vital contribution to sustaining the fabric of society, particularly the sense of civic responsibility. Unpaid care work and voluntary community work can in principle be done by men or women - but these kinds of work have been socially constituted as more the responsibility of women than men in most countries. As reported in the Special Issue of Feminist Economics, a great deal of progress is being made in many countries in measuring women's subsistence and informal sector activity, so as to include it in the GNP; and in measuring women's domestic or reproductive work and voluntary work so as to construct a Satellite Account measuring unpaid output.

UNDP (1995) estimates that in developed countries women's unpaid work produces an output equivalent to at least half of GDP. In the world as a whole women's unpaid work is estimated to produce an output of $11 trillion, compared to a global GDP of about $23 trillion. Neither national accounts, nor satellite accounts, in themselves can indicate what policies are appropriate. A conceptual framework is required in which to use them. But statistics are important for making inputs and outputs visible - without this visibility it is difficult to get them included in policy frameworks and seen as significant by policy makers.

CONVENTIONAL MACROECONOMIC POLICY FRAMEWORKS

Currently, fiscal and monetary policy is based on a concept of an economy in which private production and investment is carried out by market-oriented firms. This generates cash income for the households which own, or work in, firms. Households then either save their income, or consume it by spending it on goods produced by firms. Households are assured to act as if they were completely unified, pooling their incomes and making savings and consumption decisions so as to maximise the total benefit to the household as a whole. The role of the public sector is to levy taxes, make transfer payments, and provide public services. The economy operates so as to equate savings and investment, but not necessarily at full employment of those who want paid work, and full utilisation of the capital stock produced by previous investment.

The extent which economies automatically tend to full employment is a matter of considerable debate among economists. But all are agreed that episodes of unemployment can last a long time. In this vision, households do not produce. They are only consumers, whose function is to save or spend. The stocks of natural resources (or 'natural capital'), of labour (or 'human capital'), and the social framework (or 'social capital') are taken for granted and no work is required to maintain these resources. Non-market work is regarded for all practical purposes as outside the production boundary.

BRINGING A GENDER PERSPECTIVE INTO MACROECONOMICS

The conventional policy framework ignores non-market work, especially unpaid care work and voluntary community work. These activities tend to be taken for granted and not brought into the discussion of fiscal and monetary policy. They are often thought of as 'social roles' rather than economic activities. But they are economic in the sense that they require the use of scarce resources; and in the sense that they provide vital inputs to the public and private sectors of the economy. Palmer (1995) describes unpaid care work as a tax in kind that is levied on the domestic sector into order to reproduce the economy, a tax that is mainly paid by women. We can incorporate unpaid work into macroeconomic thinking by seeing national output as a product of the interaction of four sectors, the private sector; the public sector; and the domestic sector and the voluntary sector.

The creation of wealth in a country depends on the output of all four sectors. Sometimes there is a tendency to assume that the wealth-creating sector is the private sector; while the other sectors spend what the private sector has produced. The four sectors of the economy are interdependent. The private sector would be unable to create wealth for use by the government and by families and communities, if the government and families and communities did not in turn create wealth for use by the private sector. In particular, women's unpaid care work and voluntary work is vital for the creation of human and social capital. Of course, there are important differences between being paid to look after old people or children as an employee of the public or private sector, and looking after one's own parents and children.

This is not only a personal difference. The costs of care of old people and children in the private and the public sector show up in the national accounts, and are taken into consideration in policy decisions. But the costs of unpaid care for old people and children in the domestic sector do not show up in the national accounts are therefore not taken into account in policy decisions. But this care imposes costs of time and energy on those who do it, and when those costs are high, the careers may be unable to absorb these costs without strain.

There will always be and should always be an important role for unpaid care. But if unpaid care is treated as a free good in limitless supply, there will be negative feedbacks to the private and public sectors, reducing their productivity and increasing their costs. The tangible signs of this will be work days lost and lower productivity through absenteeism, high labour turnover, ill health and stress. There will be underinvestment in human and social capital. However, conventional macroeconomic models do not capture such links. Research is under way to develop gender-sensitive conceptual frameworks and national economic statistics which can reveal linkages and feedbacks between gender relations and macroeconomic outcomes.

In Western Europe, the public sector has nevertheless provided support for unpaid work in the domestic and voluntary sectors through public services and income transfers. Historically, the improvement of women's lives has gone hand in hand with provision of such support. However, this support is distorted and weakened by three kinds of bias: male breadwinner bias, deflationary bias, and privatisation bias.

MALE BREADWINNER BIAS

This kind of bias occurs when public sector support for unpaid care work is constructed on the assumption that unpaid care is performed by women who are dependents of a male breadwinner. When there is male breadwinner bias, women's access to social insurance, pensions, welfare benefits and public services tends to be through husbands. Married women's income may even be aggregated with that of their husbands for taxation purposes. The counterpart to this is the assumption, by private and public sector employers, that typical workers will have little or no responsibility for providing unpaid care.

This kind of bias is conducive to low labour market participation by married women, and the segregation of many women who do participate in a 'secondary earners' labour market of jobs with low incomes and few prospects. This kind of bias was common in the 1950s, when many European welfare states were built around 'the worker and his wife and children'. By the end of the 20th century, it had been considerably eroded, with rising female labour market participation and a decline in the ability of households to enjoy the living standard they expect on the basis of just one wage. But it still persists in many European countries and is reinforced by the two other biases that were not present in the 1950s, but which gathered strength in the 1980s and 1990s.

Male breadwinner bias penalises women for their unpaid investment in creation of human and social capital by denying them social entitlements on an equal basis with men. Deflationary bias Deflationary bias is a bias that gives high priority to low inflation, low public debt, low public expenditure, low taxation and low budget deficits; and low priority to full employment, high public investment and realising the full potential for improvements in the availability of goods and services. It is now deeply entrenched in the institutional framework that governs macroeconomic policy in many countries.

It is constituted in a variety of ways:

- Central banks that have asymmetrical targets, so that they aim to keep inflation below a target level, but not above a target level;
- Balanced budget legislation that constrains a government to cut public expenditure when the economic cycle takes a downturn;
- So-called 'stability' frameworks that incorporate rigid rules about ratios of budget deficits to GNP and ratios of public debt to GNP, regardless of the stage of the economic cycle, constraining governments to cut public expenditure when the economic cycle takes a downturn;
- Rules about governments borrowing only to invest that allow only for investment in physical capital and disallow investment in human and social capital.

These rules deepen the global recession rather than aiding recovery. They undermine the livelihoods of men and women and throw people back into the non-market economy. Male breadwinner bias is often exacerbated through the perception that men's jobs are more important, and women should be first to be dismissed. Women's unemployment is thus often higher than that of men, while at the same time they have less access to social benefits. Women face particular demands to provide the safety net of last resort for their families, managing a dwindling family budget to feed and clothe their children; coping with the depression, ill-health and often destructive behaviour of men whose whole sense of self-worth was bound up in the paid job they have lost.

At the same time, there are cutbacks in the public services and income transfers that would have provided some assistance to women in these tasks. The most visible cost of deflationary bias is the rise in unemployment. Less visible, but important for the longer run, is the depletion of human and social capital. Women do their best, but are not superhuman. They cannot fully compensate for the failures of the market economy and the effects of inappropriate rules for fiscal and monetary policy. Privatisation bias Privatisation bias is the bias that stems from the assumption that the private sector is inherently more efficient than the other sectors.

It can operate through three forms of privatisation:

- Complete privatisation, such as the selling of public agencies to private investors;
- Partial privatisation, such as the contracting out of services from public agencies;
- Simulated privatisation, when public services are compelled to operate as if they were privately operated.

The bias arises when faulty measures of 'efficiency' and 'value for money' are used; measures which do not take into account non-market costs and benefits; and which focus primarily on physical and financial capital. So, for example, measures are introduced to improve the 'efficiency' of public hospitals (measured in terms of monetary costs per patient) which have the effect of transferring real costs to households, increasing the amount of unpaid care work they have to provide.

One example is changing procedures to shorten the time that patient spend in hospital, and lengthening the period of convalescence at home. This cuts back on the financial costs of employing hospital staff, but increases the costs of households (and primarily women within households) in time and energy spent on caring for convalescing patients. Privatisation bias tends to intensify male breadwinner bias. One way is through worsening the pay and conditions of low paid women workers, making them more dependent on the income of a male partner. (The increasing 'value for money' that privatisation is supposed to bring is often the result of increasing the workload and reducing the pay and conditions of service of female occupations such as cleaners).

Another way in which male breadwinner bias is intensified is through the privatisation of social insurance and pension provision. This reduces the scope for pooling risks and resources and vastly reduces the possibility of social cross-subsidy. It frequently makes women more dependent on a male partner to access benefits and penalises women who do not have a male partner with whom to share household costs. Private pension provision penalises those with breaks in their employment record and longer life expectancy. It is quite legal in most countries for private insurers to discriminate against women in the annuities market. The factors which lead to the disproportionate poverty of women in old age are exacerbated.

Biased policies and false economies Deflationary bias and privatisation bias may appear to be sound economics if we ignore non- market costs and benefits. But the reduction in public provision that they imply is a false economy. Of course it is important to avoid excessive rates of inflation, excessive public debt and waste of public money. But in judging what is excessive and what is waste, we have to look at the non-market processes that create and sustain human beings and communities. A strong public sector is vital to mediate between the market pressure to treat people as mere inputs into a production process and the aspiration to live life in a fully human way.

A diminishing public sector throws more of the burden of managing the difficult balance between paid work and quality of life on to women. It results in false economies, reducing financial costs, but increasing costs in terms of health, well-being, social harmony. We need to develop innovative ways of bringing non-financial costs into the frameworks that are used to set the rules for fiscal and monetary policy. But analytical innovation is not enough. The problem we now face is that fiscal and monetary policy are primarily shaped not by elected representatives who can respond to the aspiration for a human quality of life, but by those who work in financial markets, operating with purely financial criteria and very short time horizons.

GENDER AND FINANCIAL LIBERALISATION

THE LIBERALISATION OF THE INTERNATIONAL FINANCIAL SYSTEM

The international financial system that was constructed in 1944 at Bretton Woods was built around international flows of public finance from the World Bank and IMF, both of which had social goals specified in their Articles of Agreement. In the case of the Bank, reference was made to investment in infrastructure 'thereby assisting in raising productivity, the standard of living, and the conditions of labour'. In the case of the IMF, reference was made to the promotion and maintenance of high levels of employment and real income. It was a system with a degree of public ownership, although the voting rights were not democratically distributed.

However, there was from the beginning a tension between these goals and the interests of owners of private capital, who were interested in maximizing the returns to their assets, irrespective of social goals. One expression of that tension was the shifting balance between automatic access to the pooled resources of the IMF; and conditional access, with the conditions reflecting ideas about 'sound finance' that required countries with balance of payments deficits to cut public expenditure to reduce these deficits, irrespective of the implications for social goals. From the mid 1970s, conditionality dominated and was increasingly linked to neo-liberal economic polices.

At the heart of these policies was liberalization of international financial markets, first for 'developed' countries and then for 'developing' countries. It was argued that this would lead to the most efficient distribution of finance, but efficiency was judged only in terms of the use of marketed resources. The IMF and World Bank as sources of finance became dwarfed by international banks borrowing and lending Eurodollars and petrodollars in offshore financial centers.

For instance, Singh and Zammit point out that between 1984-89 and 1990-96, net official capital inflows to developing countries fell by nearly 50 per cent, from US$27.2 billions to US$16.8 billions. In the same period, net private capital flows increased by 700 percent, from US$17.8 billions to US$129.4 billions. The most rapid increase in private capital flows to developing countries was in portfolio investment (bonds and equities), which was negligible in the 1970s and 1980s but which was US$51.1 in the period 1990-1996.

The Gender Implications of Financial Crises International markets for money are inherently uncertain and liberalized international financial transactions are fraught with risks for which no objective probability distribution exists –such as currency risk, capital flight risk, fragility risk, contagion risk and sovereignty risk. Information is necessarily imperfect and available information is unequally distributed. Such markets are argued by heterodox economists to be intrinsically unstable. Periods of economic growth lead to exuberant risk taking and the value of financial assets becomes inflated.

But eventually the growing gap between financial values and real returns leads to a subjective reevaluation of risks and holders of financial assets begin to sell them. Herd behaviour magnifies the propensity to sell and further stimulates the perception that risks have increased. The way is paved for crises in which the sudden drop in assets prices sparks panic selling; and the price of assets bought with loans drops below the value of loans outstanding, leading to collapse of credit markets and impending bankruptcy of banks and other private sector financial intermediaries.

The crisis may be mitigated by intervention by governments or international public financial institutions to co-ordinate markets, restore confidence and bail out banks and other intermediaries. But such intervention can make things worse if the wrong advice is given and the wrong policies imposed; and bailing out failing firms shifts costs from individual actors in financial markets to other members of society. Moreover the expectation of being bailed out can lead to even greater excess financial risk-taking when the economy recovers. It has been estimated that the average costs of government bailouts in banking crashes over the past 20 years amounts to about 9 per cent of GDP in developing countries and 4 per cent of GDP in developed countries.

The most immediately visible costs are to the taxpayers who fund the bailouts, and to the people who lose their jobs. But, as pointed out by Irene van Staveren (2000), the burden of excessive financial risk-taking is also shifted to the people, mainly women, who provide the unpaid care that keeps families and communities going. Particularly in poor and middle income families, women are called upon to spend more time and effort in providing non-market substitutes for marketed goods that their families can no longer afford to buy, and providing substitutes for public services that are no longer available.

In addition, women have to seek more paid work in informal employment, where new entrants making 'distress sales' tend to drive down returns. The burdens are thus not fully reflected in the GDP statistics but show up also in the additional stress and tiredness and ill-health. Though the costs of the risks inherent in liberalized financial markets are shifted to women, as provisioners of last resort, women play little role in the governance of financial markets. Of course most men play little role either. Decisions about fiscal and monetary policy, about the rules governing financial markets, about corporate accountability, are taken by a small group of officials, politicians, and financiers with little participation of citizens or their elected representatives.

The IMF (with guidance from the US Treasury) plays the key role in determining how the burdens of a crisis should be shared. Gender and the Asian Financial Crisis Attempts by the IFIs to manage the Asian financial crisis have been widely regarded as unsuccessful, not only by those outside the IFIs but also by some who were inside them at the time, most notably Joe Stiglitz, then the Chief Economic Adviser at the World Bank. The IMF in particular has been widely criticized for giving the wrong advice and imposing the wrong policies during the Asian financial crisis.

It imposed cuts in public expenditure though the underlying problem was not a budget deficit; and instead of drawing attention to the strong real economies of most of the afflicted countries, it emphasized the need for much more thorough liberalisation of markets and major changes in corporate governance, doing nothing to restore confidence among panicking investors. In the view of Singh and Zammit, 'a relatively tractable liquidity problem was thus turned into a massive solvency crisis, with enormous losses in employment and output.' There was also a substantial increase in poverty, reduced public services and increased social stress.

As yet a comprehensive study of the gender impact of the crisis is lacking. But detailed studies of survey data in both Indonesia and the Philippines show that as men became unemployed, the amount of work done by women increased, as women took up the role of provider of last resort. For Indonesia, relevant data is available from the Indonesia Family Life Surveys, which covered more than 30,000 people in 1997/ early 1998 and a follow up survey of a 25 per cent sample in late 1998. Using this source, Frankenberg, Thomas and Beegle (1999) calculate the percentage of the labour force employed in paid work in 1997 and 1998 and show that for men it decreased by 1.3 per cent, while for women it increased by 1 per cent.

When unpaid work is also included, there is an increase for both men and women, but for men the increase is only 1.3

per cent, while for women it is 7 per cent. A nationally representative survey conducted by the Indonesian statistical office sixteen months after the onset of the crisis reveals the household coping strategies underlying these figures - especially increasing the labour market participation of older married women with children and producing more goods for home consumption.

In the case of the Philippines, Lim (2000) using data from the Labor Force Survey shows that both male and female unemployment rates rose between 1997 and 1998:for men from 7.5 per cent to 9.5 per cent and for women from 8.5 per cent to 9.9 per cent. However mean weekly work hours for those employed moved in opposite directions for men and women, with those of men falling while those of women rose. Among the factors that may explain the increase for women is an increase in the hours of work undertaken by home based women working on subcontract. This increase in the average hours that women spend in paid work has occurred in a context in which women typically spend almost 8 hours a day on housekeeping and child care compared about 2 and a half hours for men.

In S. Korea, it was women who lost jobs more than men. Between 1997 and 1998, data from the National Statistical Office show that employment declined by 3.8 per cent for men and 7.1 per cent for women. In response, the Korean government promoted a national campaign under the slogan 'Get Your Husband Energized', calling on women to provide support for husbands who were depressed due to unemployment or bankruptcy - husbands were not called upon to provide reciprocal support for wives.

GENDER EQUALITY AND REFORM OF THE INTERNATIONAL FINANCIAL SYSTEM

The financial crises have lead to calls from orthodox economists for a continuation of financial liberalisation but with more international surveillance of the fiscal and monetary policies of governments. An alternative approach is the creation of new international institutions to regulate global finance. For instance, Eatwell and Taylor (1998) call for the setting up of a World Financial Authority (WFA) to manage systemic risk and pursue both financial targets and social goals such as high rates of growth and employment. It would develop and impose regulations and co-ordinate national monetary polices.

The IMF and World Bank would both have roles to play, under the supervision of the WFA which would have the responsibility of ensuring their transparency and accountability. Eatwell and Taylor are among those economists who are concerned that financial liberalization has imposed macroeconomic policies that keep employment and output below their potential and the WFA is supposed to prevent this from happening. Eatwell and Taylor seek to eliminate deflationary bias. So to do Singh and Zammit (2000), who are particularly concerned with developing countries. Full employment is the best safety net, they say. In their view developing countries must be allowed the option of maintaining capital controls.

'The right to control capital flows must be the linchpin of any reform of the international financial system from the perspective of developing countries.' In addition mechanisms are needed for more equitable sharing of the burden of bad debt between international creditors and debtors in developing countries. They argue that reforming the international economic system so as to promote growth of production and employment on a sustainable basis would benefit both men and women, but that women derive even greater benefits since they bear so many of the costs of instability. Avoidance of deflationary bias is, however, necessary but not sufficient. As Aslanbeigui and Summerfield (2000) point out, growth of GNP and increased paid employment can have different implications for men and women. Full employment can be subject to 'male breadwinner biases. Controls on international movements of capital are quite compatible with patriarchal control of women.

The so-called 'golden age' of full employment and rapid growth in the OECD countries in the 1950s and 60s was characterized by both kinds of control. Women were supposed to be fulltime housewives. Any new financial architecture must guard against male breadwinner bias as well as deflationary bias. This means that there must be other targets besides that of full employment. Employment targets must be complemented by targets for an equitable balance between work and family life; and state-based entitlements for the providers of unpaid care work as citizens in their own right (e.g. pension credits for time out of the labour market for care responsibilities).

This suggests that a target of full employment needs to be supplemented by a target of family-friendly decent jobs on comparable terms for both men and women. Just as research was done in the 1940s to define and measure employment and unemployment, research now needs to be done on identifying components of decent, family-friendly work, and constructing an index which measure how far men and women have this kind of employment. Targets for this kind of employment will be easier to reach, and a good balance between paid work and the rest of life will be easier to achieve if privatisation bias is also eliminated. This requires introduction of a target of zero transfer of non-financial costs to employees and users of privatised facilities, to set along side targets for value for money.

CITIZENS' DIALOGUE ON MACROECONOMIC POLICY

A new policy framework needs more than capital controls and additional targets and indicators. In particular, it needs to facilitate a citizens' dialogue about alternative macroeconomic policies. The ability of different interests to exercise 'voice' on macroeconomic policy are foreclosed not by the technical requirements but by fear of pre-emptive exercise of the 'exit' option by financial institutions. Their ability to exit rather than join in a dialogue is, of course, a result of the openness of capital markets. Ironically the openness of capital markets is conducive to an absence of openness in policy discussion, for fear that the wrong signals will be sent and the volatile 'sentiment' of capital markets will be disturbed.

It is difficult to conduct a participatory consultation on when some of the key players have no stake in the outcome beyond the next few hours. A neglected argument for some form of capital controls is to ensure that financial institutions have more incentive to engage in discussions with other social interests in the country whose financial instruments they have purchased, and to prevent them from foreclosing discussion by a pre-emptive exit. An example of what might be aspired to at national level is provided by the Canadian Alternative Federal Budget exercise, in which a large number of Canadian civil society groups have joined together to produce an alternative budget. It incorporates an alternative financial policy, including different types of linkage between global, national and local levels of finance and budgeting.

The AFB was first drawn up in 1995 and since then it has become an annual exercise. The initial purpose of the exercise was to challenge the budgets of the federal government which were based on public sector downsizing in order to reduce the Canadian budget deficit from five percent of GDP to a target of three percent. Federal government debt and the high cost of servicing this debt were the factors underlying the federal budget deficit, which the government argued to be unsustainable. The macroeconomic framework of the AFB reversed the government's macroeconomic framework by arguing that the high cost of debt service was due to the financial policy pursued by the government through the Bank of Canada.

The AFB accepted the importance of reducing the deficit but proposed a different route, arguing that reducing interest rates would be vital both for closing the deficit and a reduction in the rate of unemployment. The AFB recommended measures that would allow for an easier monetary policy in order to reduce interest rates, including a reintroduction of reserve requirements for banks and a requirement for the Bank of Canada to hold more federal government debt. The AFB also recommended some forms of capital control in order to reduce Canada's vulnerability to volatility in capital flows.

These forms of capital control included a surtax on Canadian interest earnings on overseas bonds, promotion of the 'Tobin tax' on international financial transactions, and a requirement by financial institutions to invest a minimum amount of their assets in community and small business development. On the expenditure side, the AFB stressed strengthening and restructuring of social programs via social investment funds in the areas of health, unemployment insurance, income security, child care, retirement income, post-secondary education and housing. The AFB aimed to reduce male breadwinner bias by improving women's entitlements in areas such as child -care, unemployment insurance and pensions.

Most of the funding (about 70 percent) for the AFB was projected to result from increased growth of the economy, while the remaining balance would come from a revamping of the Canadian tax system by raising taxes on corporations and wealthy individuals, while at the same time reducing them on low income earners. An example of such increased taxation on wealthy individuals was the introduction of a wealth transfer tax on transfers in excess of one million Canadian dollars. The AFB also promoted green taxation for protection of the environment. All the measures and proposals contained in the AFB combat the three biases elaborated above: deflationary bias, male breadwinner bias and commodification bias.

Though the AFB remains a civil society exercise and has not been implemented, it provides a valuable benchmark against which the Canadian Federal Budget can be measured. It would be good to see a similar exercise in Europe. The explicit aim of the Beijing Platform for Action was to "promote women's economic independence, including employment, and eradicate the persistent and increasing burden of poverty on women by addressing the structural causes of poverty through changes in economic structures, ensuring equal access for all women, including those in rural areas, as vital development agents, to productive resources, opportunities and public services".

As a result of this platform for action, over the past decade numerous governments have attempted to incorporate concerns for gender equality through directed programmes, targeting certain measures specifically for women, and trying to design more gender-sensitive overall policies through various forms of gender auditing. There is no question that there is greater concern on the part of governments to address the issues of gender inequality and try to achieve the greater empowerment of women. However, the current picture reflects at best a mixed outcome in terms of achieving the stated goals.

The experience of the past decade has suggested that targeted programmes for women can be less than effective in achieving desired goals, if the broader macroeconomic policies and processes are working in the opposite direction. Consider the experience of developing Asia, for example. The past two decades have been momentous for the Asian region. This is now the most "globally integrated" region in the world, with the highest average ratios of trade to GDP, the largest absolute inflows of foreign direct investment, substantial financial capital flows and even significant movements of labour.

These processes have in turn been associated with very rapid changes in forms of work and life, especially for women. Indeed, the changes have been seismic in their speed, intensity and effects upon economies and societies in the region, and particularly upon gender relations. The processes of rapid growth (and equally rapid and sudden declines in some economies) have been accompanied by major shifts in employment patterns and living standards, as familiar trends are replaced by social changes that are now extremely accelerated and intensified. We have thus observed, in the space of less than one generation, massive shifts of women's labour into the paid workforce, especially in export-oriented employment, and then the subsequent ejection of older women and even younger counterparts, into more fragile and insecure forms of employment, or even back to unpaid housework.

Women have moved-voluntarily or forcibly-in search of work across countries and regions, more than ever before, and the short-term economic migration of women in particular has had very substantial macroeconomic effects. Women's livelihoods in rural areas, dominantly in agriculture, have been affected by the agrarian crisis that is now widespread in most developing countries. Meanwhile, across societies in the region, massive increases in the availability of different consumer goods, due to trade liberalisation, have accompanied declines in access to basic public goods and services. At the same time, technological changes have made communication and the transmission of cultural forms more extensive and rapid than could even have been imagined in the past.

All these have had very substantial and complex effects upon the position of women and their ability to control their own lives, many of which we do not still adequately understand. There have been some clear gains from the relatively short-lived process of using much more women's labour in the greater export-oriented production of the region. One important gain is the social recognition of women's work, and the acceptance of the need for greater social protection of women workers. The fact of greater entry into the paid work sphere may also provided greater recognition of women's unpaid household work.

At the same time, however, unpaid work has tended to increase because of the reduction of government expenditure and support for many basic public services, especially in sanitation, health and care-giving sectors. Recent reversals in the feminisation of employment also point to the possibility of regression in terms of social effects as well. Already, we have seen the rise of revivalist and fundamentalist movements across various parts of the world, which seek to put constraints upon the freedom of women to participate actively in public life. These can have destabilising effects on gender relations and on the possibilities for the empowerment of women generally.

At the same time, advances in communication technology and the creation of the "global village" provide both threats and opportunities. They encourage adverse tendencies such as the commoditisation of women along the lines of the hegemonic culture portrayed in international mass media controlled by giant US-based corporations, and the reaction to that in the form of restrictive traditionalist tendencies. In what follows, I consider six of the more significant emerging issues, which require urgent policy intervention at both national and international levels. These include the volatility of export-oriented employment, the changing nature of work, unpaid work; the significance of informal employment, the crisis of livelihoods in agriculture, and migration. Finally, some necessary macro policy measures are briefly discussed.

THE VOLATILITY OF EXPORT-ORIENTED EMPLOYMENT

From the early 1980s onwards, the increasing importance of export-oriented manufacturing activities in many developed countries had been associated with a much greater reliance on women's paid labour. This process was most marked over the period 1980 to 1995 in the high-exporting economies of East and Southeast Asia, where the share of female employment in total employment in the Export Processing Zones (EPZs) and export-oriented manufacturing industries typically exceeded 70 per cent. It was also observed in a number of other developing countries, for example in Latin America in certain types of export manufacturing. But the relative increase in the share of women in total export employment, which was so marked for a period especially in the more dynamic economies of Asia, has turned out to be a rather short-lived phenomenon.

Already by the mid 1990s, women's share of manufacturing employment had peaked in most economies of the region, and in some countries it even declined in absolute numbers. Some of this reflected that fact that such export-oriented employment through relocative foreign investment simply moved to cheaper locations: from Malaysia to Indonesia and Vietnam; from Thailand to Cambodia and Myanmar, and so on. But even in the newer locations, the recent problems of the garments industry worldwide have meant that jobs (especially for women workers) were created and then lost within a space of a few years. This trend towards feminisation of employment resulted from employers' needs for cheaper and more "flexible" sources of labour, and was also strongly associated with the moves towards casualisation of labour, shift to part-time work or piece-rate contracts, and insistence on greater freedom for hiring and firing over the economic cycle.

All these aspects of what is now described as "labour market flexibility" became necessary once external competitiveness became the significant goal of domestic policy makers ands defined the contours within which domestic and foreign employers in these economies operated. Feminization was also encouraged by the widespread conviction among employers that female employees are more tractable and subservient to managerial authority, less prone to organise into unions, more willing to accept lower wages because of their own lower reservation and aspiration wages, and easier to dismiss using life-cycle criteria such as marriage and childbirth. This was made more relevant because of technological changes which encouraged the use of labour which could be replaced at periodic intervals.

The feminisation of such activities had both positive and negative effects for the women concerned. On the one hand, it definitely meant greater recognition and remuneration of women's work, and typically improved the relative status and bargaining power of women within households, as well as their own self-worth, thereby leading to empowerment. On the other hand, it is also true that most women are rarely if ever "unemployed" in their lives, in that they are almost continuously involved in various forms of productive or reproductive activities, even if they are not recognised as "working" or paid for such activities.

This means that the increase in paid employment may lead to an onerous double burden of work unless other social policies and institutions emerge to deal with the work traditionally assigned to (unpaid) women. However, the process of feminisation of export employment in most of the Asian region peaked somewhere in the early 1990s (and even earlier in some countries). Thereafter the process was not only less marked, and even began to peter out. This is significant because it refers very clearly to the period before the effects of the financial crisis began to make themselves felt on real economic activity, and even before the slowdown in the growth rate of export production.

So, while the crisis may have hastened the process whereby women workers are disproportionately prone to job loss because of the very nature of their employment contracts, in fact the marginal reliance on women workers in export manufacturing activity (or rather in the manufacturing sector in general) had already begun to reduce before the crisis. The reversal of the process of feminisation of work has already been observed in other parts of the developing world, notably in Latin America. Quite often, such declines in female share of employment were associated with either one of two conditions: an overall decline in employment opportunities because of recession or structural adjustment measures, or a shift in the nature of the new employment generation towards more skilled or lucrative activities.

There could be another factor. As women became an established part of the paid work force, and even the dominant part in certain sectors (as indeed they did become in the textiles, ready made garments and consumer electronics sectors of East Asia) it became more difficult to exercise the traditional type of gender discrimination at work. Not only was there an upward pressure on their wages, but there were other pressures for legislation which would improve their overall conditions of work. Social action and legislation designed to improve the conditions of women workers, tended to reduce the relative attractiveness of women workers for those employers who had earlier been relying on the inferior conditions of women's work to enhance their export profitability.

The rise in wages also tended to have the same effect. Thus, as the relative effective remuneration of women improved (in terms of the total package of wage and work and contract conditions), their attractiveness to employers decreased. In any case, the nature of such work has also changed in recent years. Most such work was already based on short-term contracts rather than permanent employment for women; now there is much greater reliance on women workers in very small units or even in home-based production, at the bottom of a complex subcontracting chain. Very recent evidence indicates that even such home-based work may be experiencing some sort of crisis, as the textile and garments exports from developing countries face increasing difficulties in world markets and the pressure of competition forces exporters to seek further avenues of cost-cutting. The extreme volatility of employment that characterises factory-based export-oriented production has also become a feature of home-based work for export production.

CHANGES IN THE NATURE OF WOMEN'S WORK

There is growing evidence that much of the paid work performed by women is increasingly under casual contracts and in the non-formal sector. It is frequently argued that women are found to be over-represented in the informal sector because the flexibilities of work involved in such activities, especially in home-based work, are advantageous to women workers given their other needs and the other demands upon their time in the form of unpaid labour. This is certainly the case to a significant extent, because much employment in the formal sector is based on the "male breadwinner" model that does not give adequate space or freedom to women who are also faced with substantial domestic responsibilities given the gender construction of societies and the division of labour within households.

However, these constraints upon women's time and freedom to choose-which are imposed by society rather than self-created-are exploited by employers to ensure much more work for less pay being performed by women. Thus, home-based work or work in very small enterprises can be for long hours and very demanding in other ways, and with conditions of remuneration (such as piece-rate wages) that effectively ensure the maximum tendency for self-exploitation. In addition, other basic responsibilities of employers, such as minimum safety conditions at work, basic health care and pension provision, are all entirely missing, which is a massive reduction of the effective wage for employers and a substantial loss for workers.

The recent tendencies towards greater informalisation of women's work must be viewed in this context. In general, these represent retrograde moves from the perspective of women's empowerment in both economic and social terms, and reflect the worsened bargaining power of labour in general in recent years. Women have always been major sources of service sector work, but they have not always been classified as engaged in service sector employment, because much of the work they typically perform comes into the category of unpaid labour, performed within the household or local community.

The care economy dominates in such work: thus, all activities such as cooking and cleaning for household members, care of the young, the old and the sick, provisioning of necessary goods (such as fetching water and fuel wood in rural areas) are typically seen as the responsibility of women members of the household. It is only recently that women's involvement in paid services has increased. While there has been some increase in women's share of paid employment in the formal sector (especially in public employment) in general, women workers tend to be concentrated into the lower paid and more informal types of service activity.

One new area of service activity that is currently widely discussed relates to the new IT-enabled services, which have become quite important especially for educated workers in a number of countries such as India, China and the Philippines. Aside from software industries (in which the share of women remains quite small) the emergence of business process outsourcing has been seen as one of the most important future tendencies, which will affect not only domestic labour markets and the status of women workers, but also the possibilities of increased foreign exchange inflows through export of this type of resident labour.

It is possible that some of the optimism surrounding this new source of employment generation may be exaggerated, especially as far as women workers are concerned. Consider recent trends in India, where the buoyancy of IT-enabled services has already received much international attention. The micro evidence suggests that women workers are reasonably involved in this sector, and in particular activities their share of employment is much higher than that for the formal sector as a whole. In the software industry as a whole the share of women workers is estimated to be 27 per cent. However, this sector shows clear signs of labour market segmentation by gender, caste and class.

Since almost all of those involved are from the urban upper caste English- speaking elite of Indian society, it has been argued that the pattern of development of the software and IT-enabled services sector brings into sharp relief the tendency of the market to reinforce or aggravate existing socio-economic inequities. While it will certainly draw more educated women into paid jobs and reduce the problem of educated unemployment to some extent, it would not bring about any major transformation in aggregate employment patterns in the near future. Further, the nature of the work involved in BPO activities can be compared to export-oriented employment, with the difference that a greater degree of education and skill is required of the workers.

Recent studies of call centers in cities in India point to the lack of opportunities for development and promotion in such activities, as well as the high degree of burnout, suggesting that absence of what could be called a "career track" in such work. Even in a few years, there is evidence of a downward trend in wages in such activities, even though the wages in these call centers remain higher than the average wages of private sector clerks, teacher and nurses. On average, female call centre workers are young and do not last in this activity beyond a few years because of the sheer pressure of the work.

So even in this emerging sector, women's work tends to be concentrated in the low end, repetitive activities with little chance of upward mobility, recreating the pattern already observed in export-oriented manufacturing production. And there are also possibilities of the future reversal of the process of feminisation of such work, in this case because changes in technology may require less of such work to be outsourced to developing countries in the first place. Such technological changes are likely to be accentuated by the protectionist pressures that are already being felt in the developed countries.

Unpaid work

One of the most important issues facing women in developing countries in particular is the change in relationship between paid and unpaid work, and the growing burden of unpaid work. The relationship between unpaid work and macroeconomic policies, especially fiscal policies which involve cutting down expenditure on social sectors such as health, childcare, nutrition, sanitation and so on is now well-known. What reduction in expenditure, and therefore deteriorating quality and quantity of public services and their effective privatisation effectively entail is a shift in the distribution of costs of such activities, from the public sphere to the household.

And within households, the social construction of gender in most countries ensures that such now unpaid activities are therefore undertaken by women and girl children. There is a dual process at work in most developing countries at the moment. At one level, as governments reduce their provision of various public goods and services, they become more expensive and therefore difficult to access for poor women, who are therefore driven to the labour market in order to increase household incomes. At another level, the same process also requires more and more women to be employed in care- giving and service sectors as other women need to farm out some of their previously unpaid domestic activities.

This can be seen as part of the overall development process-certainly it is a trajectory that has been followed by other countries in the past, whether in Western Europe or in northern America. What is different in the current context is that previously, government took up a substantial part of the costs for provision of such services, whereas now it is left to private markets. The functioning of such markets necessarily entails working conditions which are much inferior to public employment. At the lower end of the spectrum, it involves not only a double burden of paid and unpaid work for women, but also substantial increases in the sheer volume of unpaid work. The problem is accentuated as rapid social change undermines traditional ties of family, kin and neighbourhood which allowed for greater sharing of such unpaid activities.

THE CRISIS OF LIVELIHOODS IN AGRICULTURE

There is a crisis in developing country agriculture, spread across not only countries but even continents, which has continued for the past few years. This crisis reflects the combination of effects of trade liberalization which has exposed developing country farmers to unequal competition from highly subsidized northern exporters; reduced subsidies on inputs such as power and irrigation and increase role of private p[layers in other input markets; the removal of state protection in a variety of ways; the decline in institutional credit to agriculture which has typically resulted from financial liberalisation measures.

This crisis has definitely affected adversely the economic conditions of women, since agriculture remains the largest employer of women in many developing countries, and very large proportions of women are indirectly dependent upon the incomes from agriculture because of their family incomes and rural residence. In a number of countries it has been found that present distress has been associated not only with worsening health and demographic indicators, such as slowing down in rates of reduction of maternal and infant mortality, but also social regression such as the removal of girls from schooling. Therefore government policies designed to regenerate agriculture and the rural economy generally are absolutely crucial to improving the conditions of the bulk of women in the developing world.

WOMEN'S MIGRATION FOR WORK

In many parts of the developing world, there has been an explosion in short-term migration for work, not only across countries but also within countries, and often taking seasonal form. Cross-border migration results in remittance flows which have become the single most important (and most stable) source of foreign exchange for many smaller countries (Philippines, Sri Lanka, Central American countries) and are also extremely important even for relatively large economies (India, Mexico). The substantial movement of women as part of this process is relatively new, especially as women are increasingly moving on their own.

Cross-border migration tends is highly gendered, with women migrants largely found in the service sector, especially in the domestic and care sectors, as well as in entertainment work. Male migration by contrast tends to be more in response to the requirements of industrialisation, in construction and manufacturing, as well as in semi-skilled services. Obviously, migration is a multidimensional phenomenon, which can have many positive effects because it expands the opportunities for productive work and leads to a wider perspective on many social issues, among migrants and among the population of host countries. But it also has negative aspects, dominantly in the nature of work and work conditions and possibilities for abuse of migrant workers by employers and others.

In addition to the economic and social advantages of migration (remittance inflows, training of workers, spread of knowledge and skills) for sending countries, there are social costs, which are often borne more directly by families or specific home bases of migrants. The absence of the migrant may have important negative effects upon the family, the separation and disruption of relationships and possible adverse effects on the education and socialisation of children, especially when women migrants have to leave young children behind.

Conversely, remittance incomes provide crucial benefits, and typically enable families back home to lead better material lives than would otherwise have been possible, and may even contribute to expenses towards children's education, better health care for the sick and elderly in the household, and so on. Women migrant workers tend to be concentrated in the low paid sectors of the service industry, in semi-skilled or low-skilled activities ranging from nursing to domestic service, or in the entertainment, tourism and sex industries where they are highly vulnerable and subject to exploitation. They rarely have access to education and other social services, have poor and inadequate housing and living conditions.

When they are illegal or quasi-legal and dependent upon contractors, they also find it difficult to avail of existing facilities such as proper medical care and are almost never found to organise to struggle for better conditions. In general, host governments tend to less than sympathetic to the concerns of migrant workers, including women, despite the crucial role they may play in the host economy. Host country governments tend to view migrants as threats to political and social stability, additional burdens on constrained public budgets for social services and infrastructure, and potential eroders of local culture.

There is little recognition by officialdom, in terms of ensuring decent working conditions and remuneration for migrants, or safekeeping the health conditions. This is an important issue for women migrants in particular, since they are specially vulnerable to various forms of economic and sexual exploitation, not only when they are workers in the entertainment and sex industries, but also when they are employed in other service activities or in factories as cheap labour.

POLICY MEASURES

In this context, there are important measures which governments in the region can-and must-take in order to ensure that work processes do not add to the complex pattern of oppression of women that continues in Asian societies today. More stable and less exploitative conditions for work by women cannot be ensured without a revival of the role played by governments in terms of macroeconomic management for employment generation and provision of adequate labour protection for all workers. Changes in labour market regulation alone do little to change the broad context of employment generation and conditions of work, if the aggregate market conditions themselves are not conducive to such change.

More direct employment generation through increased public investment and provision of public services is useful; in addition, indirect employment generation through encouraging the expansion of activities which use female labour in stable and remunerative ways should be encouraged through fiscal incentives and other means. Given that external competitive pressures are creating tendencies for more exploitative and volatile use of all labour including women's labour, this has to be counteracted with pro-active countercyclical government spending policies.

The basic elements of a gender-sensitive macroeconomic strategy would include: the focus on employment-led growth rather than growth-led employment; and to ensure the public provision of essential goods and social services of reasonable quality with universal access. In addition, it is evident that the strategies enumerated below require not only national level action but also regional and international co-operation and assistance.

1. *Fiscal policies*: Fiscal policies have to be non-deflationary, have to allow for countercyclical expansion in particular, and have to be designed to ensure that important areas of public spending (such as on nutrition, health, sanitation and education) are never cut but rather are increased in per capita terms. This is more important for the overall conditions of women than simply increasing expenditure on women-targeted programmes as is common through gender budgeting exercises.
2. *Financial and monetary policies*: It is important to note that it is extremely difficult for a country to embark on any gender-sensitive macroeconomic strategy as long as rapidly moving capital flows can create destabilising effects and even seek to indirectly put pressure on the policies themselves. There, some degree of control on capital flows is absolutely necessary even to contemplate the other elements of the policy. Monetary policies should focus not only on inflation targeting but more crucially on employment targeting. Banking policies have to ensure greater provision of credit to small producers in all sectors, including agriculture, through some measures for directed credit.
3. *Trade policies*: Trade policies that encourage export-oriented employment must also be conscious of the problems of volatility of such employment and competitive pressures leading to reduced wages and working conditions in such sectors. This may call for specific forms of protection for producers and workers in trade-related sectors.
4. *Public provision of services*: There must be substantial increases in the public provision of basic goods and services in most countries, especially in the developing world. Such provision must ensure universal access at reasonable quality.
5. *Employment programmes and labour market regulation*: There is a case for public employment programmes (which must

be designed to ensure the maximum participation of women workers) which would also contribute to the public provision of goods and services described above.

6. *Food and nutrition*: There is some evidence of stagnation and/or deterioration in nutrition indicators of women and girls in several parts of the world, and increasing gender gap in such indicators. Reversing this and reducing the gap requires a proactive strategy of public intervention and ensuring basic food security among the population.
7. *Policies towards agriculture*: The crisis in agriculture needs to be addressed on a priority basis, with government strategies for redirecting public investment to rural areas, providing some degree of protection from input and output price volatility to farmers, ensuring access to institutional credit, and so on.
8. *Policies towards migration*: Both host and home countries need to be more sensitive to the specific concerns and needs of women migrants, and to formulate policies to ensure basic workers rights and protection from exploitation of such migrant workers. Such policies may also have to be developed at regional level or through bilateral agreements between sending and receiving countries.

6

Gender Mainstreaming and Regional Trade Governance in APEC

Despite the distance, trade policy is increasingly being confronted with social and gender issues. This is mainly due to the politicisation of trade policy, the connections being made between trade1 and development and the expansion of trade to services. All these factors are involving trade policy more directly in the lives of citizens and communities. The gender aspects and implications are thus becoming clearer. At the same time, an emphasis on 'gender mainstreaming', the idea that gender awareness should be incorporated in all aspects of policy, has been accepted by many governments.

While this has only sketchily been implemented, and hardly at all in macroeconomic policy, it does represent an attempt to move policies on gender equality away from small targeted interventions, towards a more cross cutting general remit. Trade policy, with its link to development and north/south relations, and its increasingly high profile, has become a prime site for testing out these commitments. As a result, there has been a build up of activism and research directed by civil society organisations such as the International Gender and Trade Network (IGTN) and Women in Development Europe (WIDE).

Academic research has produced substantial studies on the effects of trade on women's employment and livelihoods in various parts of the world, and on the position of women in global production chains. The Bridge Cutting Edge Pack on Gender and Trade (2006) usefully summarises some of these activities. International institutions and government departments have also become involved. Both UNCTAD and the Commonwealth Secretariat have produced substantial studies on trade and gender in the last two years and the OECD has issued a cautious working paper.

In 2003 the UK Department of Trade and Industry (DTI) set up the Gender Expert Group on Trade (GEGT) to advise it on the gender dimensions of trade policy. The question remains: are there inbuilt inequalities within the system, and what should be done about those who do not benefit? The need to answer these questions coincides with greater public attention to and concern about international development and poverty. How the evidence and arguments are interpreted, and the significance given, depends very much on the perspective from which they are surveyed.

Much of this work, along with other development literature, suggests that what is needed in internationally negotiated trade policy is a period of reflection and monitoring, in order to reconsider the present system and the assumptions upon which it is based. However, a slowing down suits neither the dynamics of trade competition, nor the impetus of trade policy, as was made very clear at the recent World Trade Organization (WTO) ministerial held in Hong Kong in December 2005. The message there was that a broad agreement was needed at all costs. Without it the Doha Development Round would be a failure and the WTO in danger.

Hong Kong also made clear how difficult it is for the current negotiating process to take on board development issues let alone those involving a consideration of gender relations. How to explain this disconnect? In order to do this, we need to examine the make up and content of these two concepts, gender and trade, both of which embody different theoretical and political approaches to the globalised world. Each represents an attempt to prioritise a certain perspective and use this to suggest forms of organisation and shifts in structure at the global level which embed the concerns more fully. In this situation, gender is the challenger, the demandeur. At the moment, power lies with the trade process, although negotiating agreements, even among those with 'standing' on the issues, is becoming increasingly difficult.

GENDER ANALYSIS AND ACTIVISM

Gender is a social construct, and gender analysis foregrounds relations between women and men and the ways in which aspects of these are embedded in culture, tradition, institutions, forms of regulation, and political and economic processes. The impetus for gender analysis comes from women since overall the way gender relations have been embedded has tended to favour men over women in terms of access to power and resources. At the same time, the activities in which women predominate, which can be summed up in the term 'social reproduction', have been undervalued and in particular not 'counted' in classical economic analysis. Social reproduction is the term normally used to encompass the roles which women have traditionally played.

These include: biological reproduction, maintenance of the household, transmission of education and values, and protection of the community. Women are a diverse and diffuse constituency who approach and are affected by these issues in a myriad of ways. Some accept the world as it is, some like the traditional division of gendered labour as long as they are given sufficient status, some want to participate more fully in public life and work on a more level playing field, others want a more profound transformation.

Some campaign for themselves; some for other women who they feel are voiceless. In general, however, gender analysis and activism starts from social relations and concerns about the distribution of power, and works up from the micro and personal experience toward the macro and general regulation. It has been difficult for women's organisations, starting from these concerns, to find an appropriate voice and level through which to address trade negotiations.

As far as the application of gender analysis to the trade environment is concerned, a number of points are made:

- Women overall are more likely than men to suffer through the disruption that opening an economy may bring; they have fewer resources and less capacity to benefit from the changes.
- Food sovereignty' and 'food security' are of particular importance to women. Subsistence agriculture and local production can be threatened by trade liberalisation and cheap imports. This may offset the advantages of lower prices.
- Work in global production chains may give extra employment opportunities to women but research suggests that their vulnerability is being used to depress wages and reduce costs.
- Women are under-represented in trade negotiations and women's organisations (and citizens groups in general) are inadequately involved and consulted in the formulation of trade policy.
- Women have overall an intricate involvement with public services. Many rely on them for support while others contribute to them or are employed by them. The changing functions of the state and in particular the designation of services as traded goods may be damaging in this respect.
- While trade liberalisation in itself may overall be beneficial, and may create new employment and commercial opportunities for women, more needs to be done to anticipate and monitor its effects and manage and embed the consequences.
- Finally, economic analysis generally, and with it trade theory, sees the household and the domestic as mainly outside the market, and yet the market itself crucially depends on the maintenance of families, the labour force and the community.

This in turn depends to a large extent on the unpaid work of women. These points rest on sustained work by feminist economists, carried out over many years, addressing particularly what they see as the gendered assumptions upon which economics rests, and the problems which both the theory and practice of caring present for economic analysis. Against this background, we need now to examine trade theory and trade policy and the very different worlds which they inhabit.

TRADE THEORY

Trade theory maintains that trading is generally good, a natural activity, from which both parties to the exchange will gain. Open markets are flexible, create opportunities and generate export led growth. They lead to efficiency and better use of resources, which in turn produce cheaper goods for the consumer. Protection and government intervention generally are seen as trade distorting and therefore to be discouraged except in cases of market failure. For developing countries increased trade is seen as a kick-start for growth, for developed countries as a way of expanding or maintaining growth.

The basic assumption of neo-classical economics as a body of theory is that the main participant in economic activity is the utility maximising individual engaged in exchange and acting out of self interest. What economists and theorists are concerned with is not whether this or other assumptions are realistic but whether the models they build on this basis yield good predictions. This equally applies to trade theory. Trade theory is based on the theory of comparative advantage, that is that a country will have a trade advantage if it has lower opportunity costs than other countries producing similar goods, and hence will benefit by specialising and from economies of scale.

This prioritises difference-trade is not about equality or sameness. Comparative advantage can, however, be undercut or modified by competitive advantage where countries (or companies) are able to gain an advantage by offering greater value to consumers through increasing performance and appeal, creative advertising or superior distribution and support. This is increasingly the case in a globalised economy. Trade theorists are not generally concerned with the consequences or social effects of trade liberalisation.

As they see it, trade is an overall good for the economy, even if it involves changes in the composition of economic activity which advantage some and disadvantage others. In a way this is the intention: those disadvantaged will provide resources for new enterprises or will be forced to be innovative and do something different which is more competitive. The effects of international trade, therefore, will almost certainly be uneven both within and between states. These effects will be specific to each country, and trade policy is likely to be only one causal factor among many. The effects, according to trade theory, should normally therefore be managed by other policies.

The process of management is 'not observed'-that is it is not taken account of, or factored in - by the trade community. It is somebody else's problem. An example of this is the WTO's Trade Policy Review Mechanism which looks primarily at how the WTO's rules have been implemented by governments, and their effects on the multilateral trading system, and not at what the effect has been in terms of wellbeing. It is clear from this that trade theory in fact relies heavily upon the state to manage and mediate the consequences of trade policy. This, however, is becoming more difficult given the current change in state functions, encapsulated by the reduction in the welfare role of states and their increasing role in ensuring competitiveness.

At the same time, trade liberalisation reduces the types of instruments that states can use to mediate social effects and their ability to experiment with new social arrangements. It is this that has fuelled the demand from some developing countries for more 'policy space' in the trade environment. The current political situation is, however, forcing trade theorists to argue rather more concretely about the effects of trade on poverty. Krugman and Obstfeld deal quite extensively with the arguments (or wrong perceptions as they would see them) underlying popular protest about low wages and bad work conditions in, for example, export processing zones in poor countries.

Given no other alternative, they argue, a low wage and bad conditions may still be preferable to rural poverty and stagnation, and may in the long run provide an important trigger for development. They also make clear that although trade affects the distribution of income between different resource holders this is not necessarily in the direction of the poor.5 Other polices will be needed to compensate for disadvantage and force some redistribution from gainers to losers.

Another work by development economists, Trade Liberalisation and Poverty, makes similar points about the specificity of poverty, and gives rather precise advice to developing country governments about how to deal with particular aspects of trade policy which may increase poverty in the short run. One must conclude from this, that just as gender has difficulty finding a terrain upon which to engage with macroeconomics, so the trade community finds it hard to deal with arguments rooted in poverty and disadvantage.

TRADE POLICY

Trade economists and negotiators admit that while trade theory underpins policy, the negotiation of actual trade arrangements involves a different process altogether. This is because politics intrudes. Negotiations are driven by 'predominant pressure groups', those that are best organised and have coherent interests. As Pascal Lamy put it recently, each trade negotiator has 'his authorising environment'. So Peter Mandelson, the EU's trade commissioner, at a meeting with civil society before the Hong Kong ministerial, faced forceful and targeted interventions from agricultural and business organisations, leaving little space for arguments around development.6 Diffuse constituencies, like consumers or women, have much less influence.

Development has come up the trade agenda because it has had some powerful advocates (southern governments, some influential NGOs and some disquieted northern consumers) and because the evidence of continuing and increasing inequality has become an embarrassment, and a danger to stability. Despite this, the negotiations in Hong Kong showed the interests of northern pressure groups and lobbies predominating, so that the prevailing question was not 'what needs to be done for development' but 'what do we need to give on development issues in order to keep the momentum of trade liberalisation going?'

The emphasis is on reciprocity. At the same time, the development groups were far from united, demonstrating both conflicting interests, and for some, a lack of capacity to intervene effectively. The emphasis on and pressure for services liberalisation in Hong Kong was striking, given that this is the most problematic area of liberalisation for many developing countries. The attitude of southern governments on gender is also mixed.

Despite the presence of a number of activist women in delegations, gender issues were hardly raised in Hong Kong-the shape of negotiations leaves little space for social issues to be debated except on the fringe. Southern governments have in general opposed linking trade negotiations with issues about labour standards or decent work in the belief that cheap labour is their main comparative advantage and those provisions of this kind would be used against them.

THE SAME ARGUMENTS APPLY TO PROVISIONS ON GENDER EQUALITY

The above accounts make clear that starting points and perspectives are key components in the disconnect between trade and gender. Gender analysis is informed and inflected by the degree of poverty and disadvantage at the base and gender activists cannot understand how officials and policy makers can apparently ignore these facts. Trade theorists and policy makers on the other hand take the broad and long view and argue that trade is overall beneficial and that open economies are superior to any likely alternative.

They point to the women who do benefit, and to the counterfactual:-would people be better off without trade liberalisation? However, trade theory remains relatively closed to the problems of social consequences and to the distortions in trade policy that a bargaining model creates. Although at this point the disconnect between gender and trade may seem fairly absolute, in fact around the edges changes are taking place.

First the various small but maybe significant policy initiatives which have been undertaken in response to pressure on gender issues and for gender mainstreaming, and second the alternatives which are emerging under the general title of 'fair' rather than 'free' trade. Though the latter are not particularly gender aware they do (or could) provide spaces where gender issues can be taken seriously.

POLICY RESPONSES

There are at the moment some small but potentially significant initiatives taking place which attempt either to address the real needs of women within the trade process, or sensitize the broader trade community to gender issues. The first concerns support for women entrepreneurs. This is an area where a broad level of agreement is possible. Women entrepreneurs in northern as well as southern countries who wish to take advantage of new trade opportunities can find themselves disadvantaged by lack of skills, knowledge and credit and can find traditional ways of achieving these either inaccessible or discriminatory.

Greater awareness of these limitations and assistance in combating them can have a considerable effect. The history of the Uganda Women Entrepreneurs Association (UWEAL), described in detail in the Bridge Cutting Edge Pack (2006), is a good example of this. This group was formed in 1987 to assist women members trying to develop enterprises, mainly in handicrafts, textiles, education and tourism, in overcoming the barriers they faced as women. They needed very specific gender sensitive training and advice.

They have subsequently received help from the Commonwealth Secretariat and the gender section of the World Bank in exploring export markets. Another example of help to women entrepreneurs concerns the Northern Homebased Worker's Network, part of Homenet Thailand, which was set up to support women in handicrafts production who needed advice and expertise in extending export markets. They had experienced extreme difficulty (and still do) in managing the global market place but were assisted by the Asian Pacific Economic Cooperation Forum (APEC) and Canadian International Development Assistance (CIDA).

In addition to marketing issues, Homenet also advises and tries to encourage collective action on issues such as social protection and childcare. It is a unique trade and economic forum which aims to share experience and concerns and develop a 'concerted unilateral approach'. From 1998 onwards a strong monitoring organisation and structure was developed within APEC to assess how women were affected by its agenda for trade and investment, and to enforce a three pronged action based on gender analysis, collection and use of gender disaggregated data, and increased participation of women.

Leadership from Canada and the Philippines, and support from a high level group of women, seems to have been crucial in initiating this. But because of the Asian financial crisis in 1997, there was also a stronger appreciation among some of the Asian members of APEC of the links between the economic and the social, and also of the costs for women in coping with the consequences of economic crisis. The effects of this effort seem to have been more procedural than substantive, largely because, despite all the activity, the core assumptions of the institution were hardly challenged and because 'gender equity and liberal trade are not directly resonant norms'.

Nevertheless, APEC did initiate an important study on the ending of the Multi-Fibre Agreement, looking particularly at the effect on women workers. APEC also funded the report on the Thai Women Exporters, mentioned above and tabled in Session 4. The third example concerns the introduction of gender criteria into the impact assessment and general monitoring of trade measures and outcomes which are beginning to be introduced.

One of the most important of these are the Sustainability Impact Assessments (SIAs) which the EU has been developing over the last seven years.8 Through the SIAs, the European Commission undertakes to monitor all the trade negotiations which it carries out (multilateral, regional and bilateral) in terms of the sustainability development criteria adopted at the Rio World Summit in 1992.

These cover economic development, social development and the environment. The SIA process takes place during and after particular negotiations. Significantly, however, it does not form part of the process which sets up the Commission's negotiating mandate for such negotiations, and which represents the power bargaining stage in determining the EU's trade strategy. Nor is it entirely clear how the findings will feed into the policy process and if money will be available to back up proposals.

There are two gender criteria included in the equity subsection of the social dimension of the monitoring, one concerns discrimination at work and the other follows the aim of the Millennium Development Goals to end gender disparity in education by 2015. The process by which these two came to be selected is by no means clear; nor do they seem to correspond to the references to the situation of women which are made in the examples given of monitoring procedures already completed.

WIDE, the main women's NGO active at EU level, was involved in the early days of the SIAs, and made a critique of the Mercosur agreement from the point of view of women. However, they seem now to have backed off, partly at least it seems because they do not feel they have the level of resources and expertise required to participate in an exercise of this kind. The SIAs represent a change in the conceptualisation of trade at the level of the EU and a willingness to concede that trade liberalisation alone may not produce development and that there are consequences that need monitoring. How far that will influence the hard bargaining remains to be seen.

Whether the SIA process will apply to the Economic Partnership Agreements (EPAs) is by no means clear. Peter Mandelson has said that there will be some monitoring, but not what or when. Again, the determining of the EU's negotiating mandate and a considerable part of the actual negotiations have passed, without any obvious monitoring process in place.

Women's organisations are often happier working outside the formal process. So, for example, the Women's Edge Coalition in the US has developed a trade impact review (TIR) which it applies to trade and investment agreements to highlight the effects on poor women. It has so far applied this to Mexico under the NAFTA agreement and Jamaica under the proposed Free Trade Area of the Americas.

The increasing interest in the monitoring of trade agreements opens some possibilities for bringing gender issues and analysis closer to the trade process. Women's organisations have a strong role to play in this and in creating the mobilisation without which such measures will be hard to implement. The difficulties in dealing with big bureaucracies and the resources this requires remain real obstacles.

These then are three examples. We need to consider what the effects are of these sorts of initiatives and if they can act as entry points for the gender sensitising of trade policy. They clearly meet the needs of some women and begin to make small inroads at the margins of policy. Do they have an incremental effect? Can they be sustained? With this in mind I want to go on to consider two initiatives which explore more centrally the trade process and put the emphasis on fair rather than free trade.

FAIR TRADE ALTERNATIVES

What would a 'true' development round look like? In the aftermath of the failed Cancun summit, the Commonwealth countries, representing a cross section of both developed and developing countries, requested Joseph Stiglitz, formerly chief economist at The World Bank, to undertake a study and make proposals on the WTO's Doha Development Round. They wanted to know what a true development round 'one reflecting the interests and concerns of the developing world, one which would promote their development' would look like.

Stiglitz, together with Andrew Charlton, produced the report and has subsequently developed it as a book. The book attempts to review both trade theory and trade policy from the point of view of developing countries. While recognising that trade can be good for development, the authors point out that conventional theory is flawed in the sense that it assumes full employment and no restraints on resources, whereas most developing countries suffer from high unemployment and limited resources.

This limits the gains that can be expected from trade. They also make clear that more successful developing economies like the East Asian countries and India have not pursued trade liberalisation relentlessly but have slowed it down when necessary and have introduced important complementary policies. They also criticise the failure of trade economists to do good empirical monitoring of the impacts and consequences of different trade regimes. However, their main criticism is directed at the self-interested bargaining procedure through which trade policy is made.

The WTO has been unable to meet development objectives, they maintain, because to do so would have required some discussion of collective principles and an idea of what a 'fair' agreement would be. This in turn would require impact assessments of different proposals and detailed monitoring of effects. The debate on this is interesting and comes near to the argument developed by Matthias Risse who also reached the conclusion that some broader principles are needed at the level of the WTO in order to achieve 'fairness in trade'.

Such arguments open the way to a view of development nearer to that of Amartya Sen's capabilities approach, which sees development and individual well being as being based on a broader range of factors than economic growth and increased income. With this broader view of well-being, Sen has no problems in including gender in the equation. Stiglitz and Charlton are not in fact saying much that is new. They are drawing together work by development economists and attempting to give it more coherence and political punch. They make no suggestion as to how their ideas could be implemented.

They seem to intend the book as a contribution to the debate about international trade and have the merit of recognising the positive aspects of trade while showing very concretely how inequities come about. No mention is made of gender or women (except for one reference to discrimination) and the authors show no sign of having read any of the gender and trade literature mentioned earlier. Nevertheless it would not be difficult to include gender considerations in the analysis. The space is there and the link between the social and the economic already made.

THE FAIR-TRADE MOVEMENT

The Fair-trade movement has not waited to convince officials or theorists of the rightness of what it is doing. It has acted instinctively and from conviction to bring the micro and the macro together in the trade field and link producers directly with consumers. The development and growing importance of this movement is a fairly recent phenomenon though it is miniscule in global trade terms and total sales in 2003 represented only £500m. Fair-trade sales in the UK, however, have increased by over 40% in the last two years, though admittedly from a low base.

The Fair trade system provides a basic minimum price for producers of certain commodities in southern countries calculated on costs of production and embodying a reasonable return to the producers. There is also a small social premium in the price which must be used for development projects in the community. Producers sell to buyers who guarantee at least this price, and meet certain other standards, and who can then use the Fair-trade logo on their products. Unlike the agricultural price support in the EU, the producers have to sell in order to get the subsidy. This acts to discourage overproduction.

The emphasis is on high quality production which at the moment sells mainly in niche markets. Examples of coops selling to Fair-trade markets suggest that the stability of the return, together with the development premium, creates a situation where projects which are geared to improving gender relations are more likely to be implemented. The Fair-trade system is based on a recognition of development needs and entails a subsidy from consumers in the north to producers in the south.

Its strength lies the fact that it is a market based mechanism which aims to restructure markets. It assumes a subject other than the utility maximising individual acting on self interest. Nor should it fall foul of WTO market liberalisation principles since it is a market based arrangement between consumers and producers not involving government measures. Some economists, however, have been sceptical about the effect of Fair-trade on the choices of individuals and overall on the economy.

By subsidizing uncompetitive production, they argue, Fair-trade is enticing people into something they would be better off not doing. However, this seems a somewhat abstract argument. In fact, Fair-trade support should encourage diversification, as well as a shift to non-traded goods and food production, just because there is more money in the community. However, it is true that diversification does not at the moment form part of the criteria.

In addition, having some additional resources and a more stable community should also open a wider range of options for the individual. The questions for the future for Fair-trade would seem to be how far this form of exchange can be expanded, both in terms of products covered and market share, and how the expansion of this sector affects more conventional trade flows and economic activity.

In the long run its future depends entirely upon the willingness of a segment of northern consumers to continue to buy Fair-trade products at Fair-trade prices. Neither of these two examples of how to make trade fairer, is particularly gender sensitive. However, both of them by seeking to alter the norms upon which trade policy operates open the way for gender initiatives. This chapter has demonstrated the extent of the disconnect between gender and trade policy and has attempted to examine both how this operates and some of the reasons for it.

It poses the question of what kinds of policies and actions can help to bridge the gap rather than reinforce divisions, while encouraging real and, necessary changes in the way in which trade policy is made. Are gender initiatives as described above, and research into the situations of women, primarily ameliorative, in the sense that they help to cope with the undesirable side effects of trade policy, or can they, together with other similar initiatives, provide a starting point for bringing social and gender issues more centrally into trade bargaining?

GENDER MAINSTREAMING IN NATIONAL BUDGETS

There are still unacceptably wide gaps between policy commitments to women's empowerment and gender equality and the resource allocations to meet the goals set. Budgets at different levels are one of the most powerful instruments for bridging this gap, as well as for promoting women's equitable access to public resources and mainstreaming gender perspectives into national development frameworks.

Presentations and discussions stressed the importance of clear objectives in efforts to mainstream gender perspectives in budget processes, i.e. to develop awareness of gender perspectives in different sector areas which need to be addressed; to establish accountability for commitments to gender equality; and to make necessary changes in resource allocations through budget processes. Experiences of incorporating gender perspectives into budgeting processes in different countries of the region demonstrate the importance of clarity on the responsibilities and accountabilities of organizations and individuals involved.

The involvement of economic and planning bodies, finance and budget departments and the legislature, as well as oversight by an informed and committed group of gender advocates, are important to the process of making budgeting processes gender responsive. The role of the national machinery is critical for ensuring the necessary political and technical support. To be effective and sustainable, gender mainstreaming in budgets has to be supported by an active constituency for gender equality, both within government and in the civil society.

The presentations highlighted the importance of adequate research on the gender perspectives in different sector areas which need to be taken into account in resource allocations. While gender research groups and institutions play an important role in carrying out research and making information available, experience has shown that it is also critical to develop the capacity of staff in Ministries of Finance and line ministries, to be able to identify areas where gender is relevant and know where to go to get necessary information.

The importance of availability of sex-disaggregated statistics was emphasized. Some of the strategies utilized to achieve gender-responsive budgets were discussed. To raise awareness of the gender implications of budget processes, sex-disaggregation of statistic is one important strategy. Improvement of data at household and individual level is critical, as is increased research on unpaid work. Initiatives are also needed to raise public awareness. The importance of challenging the notion of "neutrality" of particular sectors to gender equality in the budget process was highlighted.

To increase accountability of budget processes to policy goals on gender equality-assessing where resources went, through which process, and with what results - a number of strategies have been developed. These include making information on budget processes more accessible to the general public; including information on budgets in reporting to CEDAW; making gender-responsive budgets an election issue; and using media effectively. One strategy which was mentioned but has not yet been utilized involves using general audit processes to monitor the gender-responsiveness of budgets at different levels.

Assessing changes in the budget allocations requires consistent monitoring. Assessing impacts of budget changes on the situation of women and gender equality, i.e. the extent to which women as well as men benefit from resource allocations - requires systematic data collection and research, involving the full commitment of relevant line ministries. Positive experiences reported included the fact that efforts to bring greater attention to gender perspectives in local budget processes had resulted in the empowerment of women to engage in discussions with local politicians and administrators on resource allocations.

In these contexts, politicians and administrators were increasingly forced to motivate decisions taken and to increase consultation with women as well as men. At national level, efforts to bring gender perspectives to the centre of resource allocation decisions were more formalized. Requirements for the development of Gender Action Plans and regular reporting on progress by line ministries has led to the development of greater awareness, commitment and capacity to take gender perspectives into account. The fragility of the gains made, and the constant need for the national machinery and civil society groups and networks to advocate and monitor, was, however, highlighted. Issues of good governance - participation, transparency and accountability - were raised in the discussions on budget processes.

It was pointed out that there is little transparency in relation to the process of developing budgets. In most countries the final products are presented, with little information on the processes behind critical decisions on resource allocations. Empowerment of women in relation to budgets includes skill development in relation to understanding the budget processes at national and local levels, in order to be able to initiate an informed dialogue with budget and finance departments and hold them accountable to policy commitments.

The need to work to bring gender perspectives to the whole of the budgets at national and local levels, rather than working to secure a portion of the budgets for specific support to women, was emphasized in the discussions. Gender mainstreaming in national budgets should aim to ensure that resource allocations are based on gender analysis of needs and priorities in all sector areas and that policy commitments to gender equality in different sector areas - health, education, agriculture, and infrastructure - are backed up with resource allocations.

In the context of globalisation, the importance of incorporating gender perspectives into all the issues of financing for development was highlighted, not just in relation to domestic resource allocation through national budgets. Issues of foreign direct investment, external debt management, trade and development assistance are also critical.

In relation to debt, questions of what the loans are used for and who repays and in what manner must be raised. Issues of revenue-raising, for example through taxation, are also important. Is the burden of taxation on households or individuals: is it detrimental to the poor: are there differential impacts on women and men? Social policy and social security measures are also identified as critical.

RESPONSIBILITIES AND ACCOUNTABILITIES FOR GENDER MAINSTREAMING

Ms. Patricia Licuanan (Miriam College, Philippines) moderated the discussion on the responsibilities and accountabilities for gender mainstreaming. Experience from within Government was provided from New Zealand (Ms. Wendy Moore), the Republic of Korea (Mr. Ji Kyu-Taek) and the Philippines (Ms Ermilita Valdeavilla). Experience on the role of NGOs in ensuring government accountablity for policy commitments was presented from Sri Lanka (Ms. Swarna Jayeera, CENWOR). The discussion is summarized below.

Copies of the full presentations will be made available in the separate report prepared by ESCAP. The participants discussed mechanisms to clarify the responsibilities for gender mainstreaming of different actors and ensure accountability. This included different actors within country contexts, such as Government (line ministries and national machineries, National Statistical Offices, Census Offices, etc.), Parliament, NGOs and civil society groups and researchers. Within organizations, responsibilities need to be clearly spelt out - including for top management, middle-level management, programme staff, budget officers, gender focal points, etc. - and linked to overall policy commitments.

Accountability at the highest levels, while sometimes difficult to build, is critical for stimulating accountability at lower levels. The central role of national machineries in promoting gender mainstreaming was raised in the discussions. The critical role of national machineries is, however, a very difficult one. There was agreement among participants that national machineries should play a catalytic role in promoting gender mainstreaming - advocating, advising, supporting in different ways, without taking over responsibility, and monitoring and reporting on progress.

This requires the development of collaborative working styles, sound knowledge of gender analysis methodologies and special skills to promote and facilitate gender mainstreaming. A key constraint facing national machineries in their catalytic role in gender mainstreaming is the pervasive resistance of organisational cultures in many government bodies to gender equality values. The constraints to gender mainstreaming in different line ministries need to be identified and strategies developed to overcome them.

It was recognized that national machineries should also move beyond promoting gender mainstreaming within individual sectors to identifying and promoting gender perspectives in overall development frameworks. Greater engagement with macro- economic issues is required. New challenges such as globalisation and HIV/AIDs need to be given particular attention. Within the region the national machineries in some countries are well established and catalytic frameworks in support of gender mainstreaming are already in place; while in others, such as in countries in economic transition or post-conflict reconstruction, the national machineries are still under development.

The importance of ensuring that the development of the national machineries in these latter countries builds on the lessons learned in other countries in the region was stressed. The importance of finding ways and means of ensuring that line ministries take responsibility for gender mainstreaming in their respective sector areas was highlighted. The need for specific accountability mechanisms was raised. The importance of high-level commitment within line ministries was also identified as critical. Participants shared examples, in this session and in following sessions, on ways and means of developing awareness, commitment and capacity within line ministries.

These included training and capacity-building inputs, development of concrete approaches, methods and tools, and provision of technical support. Apart from developing adequate policies and strategies, the need for establishing effective oversight functions in relation to gender mainstreaming in line ministries was also noted. An innovative approach to developing accountability for gender mainstreaming, involving the requirement of Gender Implementation Statements on all policies going to Cabinet, was discussed. The Gender Implementation Statements outline the gender implications of the policies being presented to Cabinet.

These include clarification of the gender perspectives on desired outcomes and the nature and extent of potential impacts on women and men, both directly and indirectly, as well as policy options for addressing any gender implications identified. The process should involve consultation in the development of the statements and monitoring of results by collecting sex-disaggregated data. The objective is to legitimize the framework for gender analysis in areas other than social sectors. Political commitment at highest level is critical for successful implementation of the strategy.

The national machinery plays an important catalytic role in the process, by providing training and information materials and tools to the departments. Constraints identified included the lack of capacity for gender analysis in departments; the lack of data disaggregated by sex and ethnicity; the failure to understand the gender approach (that it is not only about women); and the reliance on the national machinery to provide all back-up.

The importance of building new constituencies for gender mainstreaming among the general public and NGOs and civil society groups was highlighted. This involves broad dissemination of information on what the government has committed to in global intergovernmental processes, in treaties such as The Convention on the Elimination of All Discrimination Against Women (CEDAW) and in policies and strategies at national level, as well as regular reporting on efforts made and concrete results on the ground.

Training in advocacy and monitoring for civil society partners actors is essential. Research organizations have particular responsibilities, as well as specific potentials, for securing accountability for commitments to gender equality. Examples of the innovative work of such organizations were shared. These included development and dissemination of regular reviews of the situation of women; in-depth research in critical policy areas and monitoring of state policies in these areas; carrying out of gender audits of organizations, including line ministries; policy dialogue and specific contributions to policy formulation; preparation of information materials, guidelines and tools; and provision of training and sensitisation programmes.

Statistical bodies play a key role as access to adequate sex-disaggregated and gender-sensitive statistics was identified as essential for successful gender mainstreaming. Gender perspectives need to be mainstreaming into all statistical areas. This is involves, over and above sex-disaggregation, changes in approaches and methods for data collection, production, analysis and dissemination as well as identification of areas where gender-sensitive data is still not collected and utilized in policy and programme development.

The importance of donors for the effective implementation of gender mainstreaming was raised. It was pointed out, however, that there are serious gaps between policy commitments to gender mainstreaming of international organizations, including the United Nations, and their practice on the ground. The fact that many international organizations have ghettoised gender equality concerns, including the promotion of gender mainstreaming, within their own organizations is a constraint to gender mainstreaming within their partner countries. The need for Governments and NGOs and civil society groups to demand greater accountability of international organizations and donors for gender mainstreaming in their policies and programmes was emphasized in the discussions. Donors should be required to make attention to gender perspectives mandatory in all support in the region.

STRATEGIES FOR GENDER MAINSTREAMING - CASE STUDIES

In discussing the different case studies-gender mainstreaming in specific sectors (education and forestry), through census exercises, development cooperation activities, efforts of national machineries and other government bodies, as well as in relation to human rights, political participation and in post-conflict situations - a number of generic approaches were identified, as will be outlined below. Participants pointed out the importance of access to gender specialists to advocate, advise, support and monitor progress on gender mainstreaming. Specialist expertise is particularly essential for the development of strategies and action plans for gender mainstreaming and providing competence development for staff.

At project level gender specialists were considered important to assist in the identification of relevant gender issues, support consultation with women as well as men, and recommend strategies for overcoming barriers and obstacles to the equitable participation of women. Use of gender focal points within organizations has increased, although there are constraints to their effective utilization. Their roles and responsibilities need to be made very clear - particularly the fact that they are resources rather than those with full responsibility for gender mainstreaming. In many cases gender focal points are not experts and are not provided with adequate training to allow them to play an effective role.

In community level projects, grassroots motivators, organizers or promoters can be effective catalytic agents - ensuring increased consultation with women as well as men, increasing equitable participation and highlighting discriminatory attitudes and practices at the local level. These groups need, however, considerable support. Gender training was also identified as an essential element in strategies to promote gender mainstreaming. Training is required at all levels to increase awareness and knowledge on gender issues, ensure commitment and develop capacity.

Training programmes need to focus on developing necessary leadership, communication and problem solving skills for working with gender equality issues. Experience has shown that capacity development for gender mainstreaming involves a long process. A one-off training programme of one or two days produces few changes. More innovative process-oriented methods need to be developed, including different types of follow-up training. Capacity development can also be achieved through the development of methodologies, guidelines and toolkits, particularly if done in a participatory manner. Training should also be offered to top and middle-level management levels.

Development of gender analysis methodology was highlighted as critical for effective gender mainstreaming. Some capacity for gender analysis is required for all professional staff, not only gender specialists or gender focal points. Gender analysis should be applied to all sector areas. In some areas particular skills are required. Professional staff also need to know where they can go to get support if they are not able to carry out the analysis themselves. Gender analysis can be carried out as a separate analysis or included as an integral part of other analyses being undertaken. Gender analysis findings should be fed into the design and formulation stage of project development. Access to sex-disaggregated data is critical.

Gender mainstreaming guidelines - general overall guidelines, handbooks or manuals or such tools for specific sectors - have proven useful for promoting greater implementation of the strategy. Participatory development of such tools increases the "ownership" of the tools and potential for their utilization. Strategies for gender mainstreaming need to include efforts to increase consultation with and participation of women as well as men. Networking to provide ongoing support to women and gain access to their perceptions, priorities and needs, was also an important strategy at grassroots level. Sharing of experiences between different groups of women was also an important strategy. Establishing effective monitoring mechanisms was also identified as vital for successful gender mainstreaming in different sector areas.

At project level participatory monitoring procedures are important. Ensuring access to information is essential for participatory monitoring processes. Accountability was reported as a constraint, and even with built in monitoring mechanisms, ensuring compliancy was often a problem. The importance of a rights-based approach and effective use of CEDAW was highlighted. The effective utilization of different treaty bodies and human rights rapporteurs should be increased. CEDAW provides an excellent framework for assessing gender mainstreaming, emphasizing equality of opportunity, access and results.

The low participation of women in political decision-making was identified as a constraint to gender mainstreaming. Innovative strategies for incorporating gender perspectives into governance and public administration need to be developed. The mainstreaming of gender perspectives in local governance in the context of decentralization remains a huge challenge. Experience in the region has shown that even where increased participation of women is made mandatory, considerable supportive inputs are required to ensure that women can participate in an equitable and effective manner.

Systematic monitoring is necessary to identify constraints. In complex emergencies, including conflict and post-conflict situations as well as natural disasters, incorporation of gender perspectives can meet resistance because of the attitude that gender mainstreaming is only relevant when all major problems are solved, as well as the perception of women as primarily victims. Greater emphasis needs to be put on the gender perspectives in both the emergency assistance inputs as well as more long-term development activities. The perception of women as key actors and agents of change should be promoted.

The opportunities for changing the situation of women and gender relations in these post-conflict and post-disaster situations need to be identified and capitalized on, particularly through providing access to information and training as well as job opportunities. The equitable participation of women should be promoted in all areas. The need for a strong focus on human rights was highlighted. Support to the development of an active role for women's groups and networks is also important. The example of gender mainstreaming in census exercises was discussed. Ways and means of eliminating male biases in the processes, caused by inadequacies in methodology and instructions for and training of enumerators, were discussed.

Effective strategies to make the census more gender-sensitive included ensuring that the Master Trainers are gender sensitive; training of all enumerators on gender issues; hiring of more female enumerators; modifying the forms for collection of information at household level; including a specific chapter on women in the instructions; and raising awareness among the general public through posters, banners, advertisements and radio and television programmes.

GENDER MAINSTREAMING IN INTER-GOVERNMENTAL PROCESSES

In the discussion it was noted that in the context of globalisation there is increased interdependence within regions and sub-regions. Many emerging issues require intergovernmental collaboration, for example trafficking, migration, HIV/AIDs and trade. Intergovernmental processes at regional and sub-regional levels have become increasingly critical. Participants pointed out that intergovernmental mandates - both global and regional-provide important political support for gender mainstreaming and are essential instruments for securing necessary financial resources.

The importance of expanding the use of intergovernmental processes, and the intergovernmental mandates emanating from them, to ensure increased and sustained attention to gender mainstreaming was raised. The intervention frameworks of intergovernmental organizations are determined by their respective governing bodies, and these were often focussed on a few strategic issues. Work programmes are determined by global mandates and international instruments. Efforts must be made to more broadly disseminate the Platform for Action, the outcome of the Twenty-third special session of the General Assembly and CEDAW as critical mandates for all intergovernmental bodies.

It was noted that many Governments and donors still perceive gender equality as a marginal issue and therefore a campaign to keep gender mainstreaming on the agenda, at the highest political level, especially through intergovernmental mechanisms, must be continued and reinforced. Participants pointed out that strategic allies had to be identified on various intergovernmental bodies, including in subcommittees or working groups; stronger collaborative initiatives need to be developed by different actors to influence intergovernmental bodies; and constant contact and communication needs to be maintained with constituents and support groups in civil society.

The need for specific gender expertise within intergovernmental bodies to support gender mainstreaming through catalytic roles was stressed. Those servicing intergovernmental bodies need gender training in order to be sensitized and equipped with the necessary professional skills and expertise to mainstream gender perspectives into their substantive work. The role of donors in facilitating gender mainstreaming in intergovernmental processes was discussed. This role should be primarily catalytic, supporting the efforts of individual Member States as well as their collaborative efforts in intergovernmental contexts.

Donors can also play an important role by facilitating the creation of space for inputs from NGOs and civil society groups, as well as for bringing critical stakeholder together for dialogue on the implementation of the Platform for Action and the outcome of the twenty-third special session of the General Assembly. The importance of taking a broad focus on gender mainstreaming was emphasized throughout the discussions. Stakeholders include not only Governments but also NGOs and civil society groups, the private sector, academia, religious institutions, media and other actors in society. Within government the focus should not only cover the executive branch but all other branches, including the judicial branch.

The need to incorporate gender perspectives in the overall macroeconomic framework for development was highlighted time and again as critical for effective gender mainstreaming - moving beyond individual sectors to the larger development framework. Gender mainstreaming was seen to be very much about identifying and challenging existing gender biases, for example, in relation to values and norms within organizations and in macroeconomic frameworks. Gender mainstreaming cannot be seen simply as a technical issue-involving the development of strategies, methodologies and skills.

There are important political dimensions to be taken into account. Specific capabilities need to be developed to address both the political and technical dimensions. Issues of good governance - in particular participation, transparency and accountability - were identified as critical for gender mainstreaming. The importance of a rights-based approach was highlighted in many discussions and the value of CEDAW, as a framework for promoting gender mainstreaming, was emphasized by many presenters. While there is increased understanding that incorporating gender perspectives into different areas of development supports other development goals as well as promoting gender equality, there is need to provide new examples of how and why incorporating gender perspectives into policies and programmes supports the achievement of sectoral goals.

Good practice examples are needed in this respect-with clear evidence that the incorporation of gender perspectives provides a "valued-added" impact. Organizational change in support of gender equality within Governments, donor organizations, NGOs and other bodies can only be successful if grounded in the broader goals of development, peace and equality, as expressed through women's mobilization on the ground. Organizations cannot promote gender mainstreaming effectively in isolation from the women's movement at national level. The voices of women have to be heard and their expressed priorities and needs taken into consideration. Consultation with women as well as men is essential for successful gender mainstreaming.

The need to always link the strategy of gender mainstreaming to the overall goal of promoting gender equality was highlighted throughout the discussions. The importance of placing the goal of gender equality in a broad socio-economic context was also raised. Gender equality cannot be seen in isolation from other socio-economic criteria such as race, class, poverty levels, and age. Institutional change for gender mainstreaming Progress could be reported in a number of areas of institutional development to support gender mainstreaming.

Efforts have been made to move the responsibility for gender mainstreaming out of gender units within national machineries or other organizations and into line ministries and other mainstream bodies. National machineries and gender units within organizations are increasingly working in a catalytic manner promoting and facilitating rather than doing the work themselves. A broad range of mechanisms have been adopted in support of gender mainstreaming. These include use of gender focal points, taskforces and high-level advisory groups; training - including for top management; development of analysis methodologies and strategies for making use of analysis mandatory; development of action plans; carrying out audits; establishing strategic reporting mechanisms - such as to Parliaments; and positive collaboration with NGOs and civil society groups.

Challenges in institutionalizing gender mainstreaming approaches within organizations were discussed. Experiences shared highlighted several common issues. These included the need for an informed and vocal constituency that could demand change and hold public agencies and authorities accountable for addressing the interests of women as well as men, and the importance of developing accountability mechanisms within organizations, including sanctions for behaviours which perpetuate discrimination against women. An important constraint identified is the fact that in many organizations gender equality policies and gender mainstreaming strategies have been implemented from the top down, without adequate internalization of the values embedded in these policies by staff at lower levels.

As a result, there is little progress in implementation of these policies. In some contexts, organizations have established strong policies on gender equality and made explicit commitments to gender mainstreaming but then assumed that implementation would be automatic. Monitoring and evaluation mechanisms are not put in place and this reduces the potential for constructive self-criticism and further development. There are many ways in which good policies and strategies can be subverted within organizations, especially in contexts where there is little explicit management support, over and above the existence of these policies and strategies.

Active support and demands for accountability from all management levels is essential for successful gender mainstreaming. Commitment of top leadership and management would take various forms such as developing clear directives and articulation of support for gender mainstreaming in the work of the organization, and demanding and supporting the development and implementation of gender action plans with clear time-frames and targets. Although it is recognized that accountability mechanisms will be critical to successful implementation of gender mainstreaming, there are few examples of good practice in this area to share. Development of accountability mechanisms must be a priority for the future. Indicators of progress in gender mainstreaming, with emphasis on outcomes, need to be developed to facilitate effective monitoring.

Without incentives and sanctions for non-compliance, informal processes within organizations can jeopardize the implementation of very positive policies. The specific constraints, particularly related to oversight and accountability, of institutionalizing commitment to gender mainstreaming in large countries with decentralized systems were raised in the discussions. Institutional development is related to establishing a core set of values within organizations that should inform a body of policies and strategies, in which gender perspectives are incorporated as an integral dimension.

Gender-biased institutional norms are not always immediately visible or explicit but are embedded in the hierarchies, work practices and beliefs of organizations. Unchallenged gender biases and gender stereotypes within organizations can seriously constrain efforts to implement gender mainstreaming. While there has been progress in setting up the infrastructure to support gender mainstreaming in many organizations, little has been done to combat deeply embedded organizational values that discriminate against women in subtle and insidious ways. There is a clear need for strategic action to develop more conducive institutional environments for gender mainstreaming.

One concrete example of efforts to produce a more conducive institutional environment for promoting and securing accountability for gender mainstreaming was discussed. This involved the mandatory institutionalization of a methodology for gender analysis. The process involves establishing the basic gender equality principles on which work programmes should be based; clarifying the responsibilities of all actors; and stipulating the gender analysis provisions to be implemented. The methodology requires that in the planning and implementation of programmes the specific roles and situation of women and men should be taken into account, so that the potential differential impacts are understood.

Although emphasis is placed on the value of gender mainstreaming for programme efficiency and effectiveness and the gains in terms of transparency and accountability are outlined, one of the most difficult constraints to overcome remains the attitude that incorporation of gender analysis makes processes burdensome and that there is a risk of sacrificing project efficiency in the process. The need to emphasize the value added of incorporating gender perspectives for the achievement of overall development goals as well as sector-specific goals in this context was highlighted.

Constraints identified included weak gender analysis capabilities within line ministries and inadequate accountability mechanisms, both in terms of incentives and sanctions. The importance of the national machinery retaining a catalytic and supportive role and developing effective partnerships with line ministries and other actors, to ensure effective institutionalisation, was emphasized.

It was also noted that there are important links between gender equality policies of the organization itself (including on equal opportunities, a gender-sensitive work environment and harassment issues within the organization) and commitment to gender mainstreaming in work programmes.

Organizations which are poor performers on gender equality within their own organizations can be assumed to perform poorly on gender mainstreaming. In particular organizations with poor records on open and flexible management styles, and/or with extremely hierarchical structures, do not have potential to do well on gender mainstreaming.

7

Governing Globalisation

Feminist Engagements with International Trade Policy

In 1944, an international UN conference in Bretton Woods, New Hampshire (USA) established-in large part at the political urging of the United States of America-a system of international monetary management, which was to set the rules of commercial and financial interactions and relations among independent nation-states. Central to this system, which was to prevent global economic downturns such as during the Great Depression of the late 1920s and help in post-war reconstruction with an initial focus on war-torn Europe, was the establishment of the International Bank for Reconstruction and Development (IBRD), now one of five institutions in the World Bank Group, and the International Monetary Fund (IMF).

These organizations, the so called Bretton Woods Institutions, became operational in 1946 after a sufficient number of countries had ratified the agreement. Founded originally as part of the United Nations system and which their focus on financial and monetary stability (IMF) and poverty alleviation (World Bank) respectively, these institutions over the course of the past 60 years have grown to be the most powerful public creditors in the world, taking on a gatekeeper and signaling function for all development-related aid and support, be it bilateral, private sector or multilateral. Especially the poorest countries of the world depend on the IMF and World Bank for financial liquidity (to offset balance-of-payment problems and to repay or renegotiate debts).

Low-income borrowing countries since the early 1980s have been required to follow a formulistic set of Neo-liberal economic reform policies, initially known as structural adjustment programs (SAPs). These policies, which came to be known as "The Washington Consensus" mandated tight macroeconomic and fiscal policy reforms including decreased government spending, tightening of money supply to curb inflation, a reduced public sector, privatization of state-owned enterprises and liberated trade, thus greatly restricting and limiting the policy space of developing countries in formulating their individual path to development.

While somewhat reformulated and adjusted over the past several years, the basic premises of these policy mandates are still at the core of the policy advise and capacity building in trade, public sector management (including health care and education), institutional governance, tax and fiscal policy that the IMF and World Bank staff provide on a daily basis. Critics maintain that contrary to the stated aim of reducing poverty and increasing stability through economic growth, the economic policy mandates of IMF and World Bank policies have largely harmed and further impoverished hundreds of million of people around the world, most of them women-while failing to deliver the economic growth (especially in Sub-Sahara Africa and Latin America) needed to alleviate poverty and growing inequalities worldwide.

Although the Asian continent is usually cast as a success story of IMF and World Bank reform policies, many observers are convinced that strong economic growth there over the past two decades resulted from a willful ignorance rather than faithful acceptance of IMF and World Bank mandates by strong governments following their own path to development and carefully sequencing needed reforms at their own speed. Despite being usually cast in gender-neutral and beneficial terms, standard World Bank and IMF policy mandates for the poor developing countries impact the poorest people the most, although men and women differently.

Since the Neo-liberal economic model on which the IFIs growth projections and policy mandates are based does not recognize women's unpaid, yet substantial labor in the home, the agricultural and the informal sector, many IMF and World Bank policies have actually increased and worsened gender inequality-and the feminization of poverty - in developing countries. The burden of public health expenditure cutbacks in developing countries is overwhelmingly borne by women who have to care at home for sick family members and thus reduce their time available for paid work; this is especially a burden in many developing countries ravaged by HIV/Aids. At the same time, the introduction of "user fees" prices health services out of the reach of many poor people.

Public sector and enterprise restructuring, as for example mandated by the IMF and the World Bank after the fall of the Iron Curtain in the former Soviet Union and in Eastern Europe, eliminates many jobs and benefits with women being often the first to be fired and the last to be rehired because they are assumed to be only secondary breadwinners. Unreciprocated developing country import tariff reductions, so-called "autonomous liberalization", threaten the livelihood of manufacturing sector workers in the poorest countries –many of whom are women, especially in sectors such as electronics or garments.

In the agriculture sector, where the majority of women in developing countries still work as subsistence farmers, export-oriented agricultural production, as mandated through structural adjustment programs, and subsidized agricultural dumping by the industrialized countries threaten food security and local markets. Likewise, the introduction of value-added-tax or consumption taxes in many developing countries as mandated by the IFIs affects poor consumers, a majority of them women, disproportionately. These are just some of the examples that indicate how macroeconomic structures and policies, perpetuated and promoted by the IFIs, have an effect on microeconomic conditions and gendered rights, access to resources, labor and livelihoods.

While most critical observers of the IFIs from civil society organizations worldwide have long concluded that the IFI-approach to development is not delivering the hoped-for benefits, those critics-and the international movement of IFI-watchers-are split on the remedies. Some, including many groups in the Global South, have given up hope that the IMF and the World Bank can be satisfactorily reformed and are calling for an abolition of the Bretton Woods Institutions. Others are still optimistic that reform of the IFIs is possible and see incremental change happening through continued and consistent civil society engagement with the institutions.

Finally, after many critical observers have addressed their demand for change directly with the institutions in the past decades, more recently campaigns all over the world are focusing on national governments, particularly in the North, as the real decision-makers behind misguided IFI policies. The main focus of all this criticism-whether directed at the institutions, the national member governments, the broader world opinion or affected communities on the ground-is ultimately what these advocates see as a misdirected development-approach of the IFIs that focuses on narrowly defined economic growth to the detriment of a wider concept of sustainable human development.

They demand a human development approach that puts human rights –to livelihood, access to resources and also gender equity– at the core of the IFI loans, projects and policy recommendations and would force the institutions to be more accountable and transparent. Since the 1970s, pioneering feminist economists have highlighted the contributions of women's unpaid labor to the economy. They highlighted how unequal power relations and the gender division of labor translate into different impacts of development and reforms on women and men.

More recent work by feminist economists has focused on macroeconomic policies and the effects of globalisation on income distribution and gender inequality, including IMF and World Bank mandated structural adjustment policies. They are among the critics of the so-called gender neutral neo-classical economic models of the IFIs and have conceptualized gender-sensitive macroeconomic models. The Summer School will take a closer look at these approaches and models and will analyze and discuss what IFI policies and projects that follow these gender-aware theoretical foundations will have to look like.

It will also discuss and analyze how effective the concept of gender mainstreaming can be at the IFIs in the current economic thinking. Ultimately, the hope is that a broader knowledge and understanding of new economic gender-sensitive macroeconomic concepts can help in influencing not only institutional operations but also member countries' policies and policy contributions on the Bretton Woods Institutions-especially by the industrialized countries which hold the largest influence and voting power in the IMF and the World Bank.

Objectives of the Summer School 2007 on International Financial Institutions:

1. Capacity building on the policies and projects of the International Financial Institutions, their importance in the current global governance system, and the effects of their macroeconomic policy advice and mandates from a gender perspective.
2. Understanding of linkages between macroeconomic and microeconomic systems, between international monetary, financial and trade policies as set and overseen by the International Financial Institutions, and national policies and the livelihoods, labor and resource rights of women, using feminist economic concepts.
3. Envisioning a feminist concept of macroeconomic policy which links sustainable economic growth, a country's right to its own path of development, social equity and gender justice toward an alternative to the Neo-liberal model of fiscal austerity and export- and foreign investment-led growth and which breaks the dominance

of the IFIs in determining the "right" development path for emerging market and developing countries.

4. Enhancing global and regional alliances and networking between HBF-partners, feminist economists, experts, like-minded policy makers, and grassroot activists in their struggle to reform the IFIs toward greater democratic accountability, greater social justice and gender awareness.
5. Enhancing the capacity of these alliances and networks, as well as of the individual participants to intervene with and lobby the governments of individual member countries of the IFIs on behalf of more gender-inclusive and pro-poor alternative macroeconomic policies at the national level so as to inform these countries' contribution in IFI decision making.
6. Bridging the gap between economic theory and political practice with regard to macroeconomics and financial, monetary and trade policies, as well as with respect to incorporating and considering gender justice and gender democracy through an effort at coordinating strategies directed at the global, regional, national and local level.

PROGRAM

The program consists mainly of lectures and panel presentations and workshops, organized on a regional or sector basis. Some off-site visits (to the World Bank and the IMF, possibly to the US Department of Treasury with sets American policy-priorities for the IFIs) are planned. Participants will be connected to civil society representatives from the Washington area currently critically engaging the IFIs.

The lectures and panel discussions will provide a general introduction to the IFIs and their global role, a short introduction to the basic vision of a gender-aware macroeconomic theory, contrast the vision with the actual outcomes of the macroeconomic Neo-liberal model the IFIs employ (which negatively and disproportionately affect women in developing countries), and will look for ways how to make the IFIs and their policies more gender-aware and publicly (and legally) gender- accountable through advocacy and campaigning by civil society.

Where useful, and in order to strengthen, supplement and practically apply information learned in the plenary, workshops will be offered. They will serve to exchange information on the effects of IFI policies and projects in respective regions and sectors, will provide space for participants to assess and connect their prior knowledge on IFIs and their impact on their country to other regional experiences and will give them room to network and strategize for possible joint and/or follow-up activities.

THE ECONOMY THROUGH WOMEN'S EYES

There has been much analysis in recent times of increasing inter-relatedness and interdependence at a local and global level. The term 'globalisation' describes this understanding that we are now 'living in a global village'. Globalisation has come to be associated with the spread of capitalism and neo-liberalism, western cultural dominance and the influence of the international media and information technology. Globalisation also has political, economic and socio-cultural effects at local, national, regional and global levels.

Some are positive, such as transnational social movements and opportunities for dialogue and action at local and global levels. Others, such as increasing global inequality and lack of access to decision-making at international levels, very negative. Internationally, women's organisations-such as Women in Development Europe (WIDE), the International Gender and Trade Network (IGTN), the Caribbean Association for Feminist Research and Action (CAFRA) and Development Alternatives for Women in a New Era (DAWN)-have made key contributions to developing critiques of the negative impacts of globalisation.

These organisations develop alternative ideas and lobby policy makers for a gender and human rights perspective in international economic and trade policy. As a feminist organisation that is part of the international women's movement, Banúlacht works to link locally based women's groups with the experiences of women in the South and with national and international decision-making processes that address the political, economic and sociocultural effects of globalisation. Banúlacht is particularly concerned with the effects of globalisation on women and on gender inequality.

In April 2004 we launched a new publication, 'Looking at the Economy through Women's Eyes'. Based on five years of work promoting critical debate on aspects of globalisation within women's organisations in Ireland through our 'economic literacy' programme, the book aims to provide a resource for trainers and facilitators.

ECONOMIC LITERACY

A real barrier to women's engagement with economic policy making is the elitism of economics, which can make it seem inaccessible and overwhelming. Therefore, those most adversely affected by the negative impacts of globalisation are those who are likely to have least access to the concepts and skills for challenging it and creating alternatives on the basis of their knowledge and experiences. It is critical therefore those women develop the skills and confidence to engage with economic policy.

One response to this need is the development of economic literacy programmes for women by women's organisations such as CAFRA, WIDE and the IGTN. The use of the term 'literacy' is not intended to imply that participants are 'illiterate' about the economy. Rather, it is used to refer to a Freirean adult education process that is grounded in the values of community development, and aims to facilitate critical engagement with ideas. In 1998, Women in Development Europe (WIDE), a network of women's organisations working on gender and development issues, produced a pilot training manual for economic literacy.

Through this manual, WIDE aimed to bring together its work on alternative, feminist economics and popular education methodology. Banúlacht found the idea immediately attractive as a new way to bring a global focus into its work with women's organisations. In developing a curriculum, we were fortunate to have the opportunity of working with Emily Kawano, an economist from the Centre for Popular Economics in the US. Drawing together WIDE's economic analysis, Emily's popular economics methodology and Banúlacht's experience in gender analysis and development education, we devised a programme for economic literacy in an Irish context.

Since 2001, we have organised over 35 workshops on economic literacy with 21 different women's organisations. Through this process, the training methodology and content have been developed and expanded, and the feminist approach strengthened. Banúlacht's economic literacy training aims to contribute to women's empowerment through a process of demystifying the economy. The training is based on a feminist approach to the economy. This does not mean that we attempt to provide a definitive feminist analysis of the economy, or to provide all the answers to all the questions on the economy.

For Banúlacht, feminism is a mode of analysis, a method of approaching life and politics, a way of asking questions and searching for answers. Starting with their personal experiences and opinions, women explore how the economy works and its impact on their everyday lives. The training facilitates women to critique the prevailing values that underlie economic policy and to develop their own visions of alternative value systems and alternative economic policies. They discuss strategies for women's organisations to use international agreements on gender equality to strengthen their analysis of and advocacy on issues affecting women in Ireland and women in the South. For Banúlacht and the groups we have worked with the experience of engaging in economic literacy training has been powerful.

Participants have come to recognise and value their own knowledge of the economy. They have recognised their right to critique government policy based on their lived experience of the economy. Crucially, they have explored frameworks with which to analyze and critique economic policy, not as abstract notions, but in the context of personal and local experience. Looking at the Economy through Women's Eyes

Aimed at tutors, facilitators and trainers, the book is a compilation of analyses, resources and activities that have been tried and developed through interaction with women's groups in community development settings.

The name 'Looking at the Economy through Women's Eyes' aims to reflect that economic literacy training is about looking at the world differently, seeing what mainstream economists do not see and about re-visioning alternative economic systems. Vast areas of human activity, including much of the work carried out by women in the home and community, becomes invisible in economic calculations and unregarded in economic policy, simply because it is unpaid. This publication aims to make this sphere visible, and to explore the implications of visibility.

They have a key role to play in shaping the social and political contexts of their lives. Women are entitled to alternatives. They have a right to make choices about policies that impact upon them. Our aim in publishing this facilitator's guide is to contribute to the empowerment of women, to give women space to critique economic policy and to imagine alternatives to prevailing economic models. As the competence and confidence of individual women and women's organisations and networks to engage with economic policy grows, we hope that policy makers and decision makers will be able to see the economy through women's eyes.

It is well known to readers of the f word that feminism is frequently portrayed as anachronistic and irrelevant. I shall not discuss this particular issue here. What I will discuss is a related, though different, perception of feminism. This is the view that feminism, as well as having declined, has become less radical to the point that, where it does exist, it is seen as watered-down; lacking the critical force it once had. Crucially, this view can be found both within the popular media, but it is also a view frequently expressed by both academic feminists and veterans (for want of a better word) of second-wave feminist activism. The term 'deradicalisation' could, I argue, be used to describe this view of contemporary feminism.

Whilst it is accurate up to a point, it overlooks important processes going on within contemporary British feminism, as I shall explain.

The 'deradicalisation' idea is based on a particular set of assumptions about the recent history of British feminism, centered around the view that contemporary feminism has completely lost its more radical and critical dimensions. Often, but not always, the view is expressed with a distinct tone of melancholy, a longing for a return to the 'good old days' of militant activism. Basically, this view contends that there was once a time (typically around the mid 1970s) when feminism attracted large-scale grass roots support and was militant, hard-line, radical and uncompromising. Whilst there were differences between the various strands of feminist thought, it is widely assumed that they all shared a commitment to radical, grass-roots activism.

What is also crucial is that they also tended to regard looking to the state, or British political institutions more generally, as illegitimate from a feminist perspective. Put simply, these feminists took the view that if political institutions are run according to patriarchal / anti-feminist principles, then feminists would have to make severe compromises if they were to look to these institutions for support.

There is a perception that some time around the mid 1980s, feminists moved into British state institutions (the Labour Party, the Greater London Council (GLC), other local councils, the Equal Opportunities' Commission (EOC)) and that in doing so, they lost their links with grass-roots support, and consequently became less radical. Feminists are therefore now seen as simply trying to make small-scale reforms *within* these institutions, rather than expressing grander visions of more fundamental change.

Often, there is seen to be a trade-off between remaining autonomous (i.e. not becoming involved in political institutions) but being faithful to your principles on one hand, and having influence within decision-making bodies whilst compromising your principles, on the other. In the BBC4 documentary, Linda Bellos epitomised this viewpoint, arguing that she preferred to do her politics on a shoestring but remain true to her principles. She was deeply critical of feminist involvement with the GLC which she saw as leading to feminist principles being compromised.

It is no coincidence that the two terms used to describe the movement of feminists into institutions have slightly derogatory connotations. The word 'femocrat' originated in Australia but has become used as a general term referring to feminists, or women with feminist sympathies, working within state bureaucracies. It is derogatory to the extent that it emphasises feminist involvement within institutions which are seen as being anti-feminist: it implies that these women have compromised their principles, or 'sold out.' In the BBC4 documentary, the feminist journalist Julie Bindel highlighted this view when she talked rather disparagingly of the increasing feminist involvement with the GLC in the mid-1980s: 'I couldn't bear all that town hall feminism… femocrats we called them,' she says.

So, the term 'femocrat' conjures up images of women working in state institutions without significantly *changing* those institutions. Similarly, the term 'liberal feminism' has roughly similar connotations, with its emphasis on the involvement of women in public life without having a theory of 'systemic' oppression. But is this view of 'femocrats' and 'liberal feminism' justified? Well, for the most part, no. The stereotyped view of liberal feminism is basically just an artificial construct created by more radical feminists. This might all sound rather abstract, but this is a hugely important issue for contemporary feminists in the UK. I would argue that the whole debate is based on an artificial opposition between two kinds of feminism: radical, autonomous, grass-roots feminism on the one hand, and reformist liberal feminism operating *inside* British political institutions on the other.

This is especially the case in some strands of academic feminism, in which one finds a strong tendency to debate the pros and cons of feminist engagement with 'the state.' This is interesting up to a point, but it is all rather abstract and, as such, tends to reinforce certain negative stereotypes of liberal feminism. What it overlooks is the way in which, while it is true that feminists have recently become more willing to work with, rather than against, British political institutions, this does not mean that British feminism has necessarily lost its radical or critical edge.

A quick look at the Fawcett Society, arguably the most important pro-feminist organisation in the UK at present, confirms this view. In many ways, Fawcett adheres to the stereotype of liberal feminism outlined above: they emphasise campaigning within British political institutions (e.g. by asking politicians to address women's issues, and trying to get more women into the House of Commons), and a lot of their proposals seem relatively modest. For this reason, when more radical feminist authors mention the Fawcett Society, they are often rather dismissive of the organisation. However, this view overlooks the ways in which Fawcett's policy agenda is in fact informed by a much more radical vision of social transformation.

Whilst their proposals in terms of issues of women's political representation (e.g. use of all-women shortlists) might seem fairly moderate, their proposals on issues such as maternity and paternity leave, domestic violence, the criminal justice system, and reform of the EOC would all require quite profound changes in the structure of gender relations in the UK. When one reads their literature, which outlines the need for a new 'equalities' body to replace the EOC, one sees that they are profoundly critical of the popular assumption that feminism is no longer necessary and that all remaining inequalities are simply a matter of choice. In that sense, there is a belief in the need for large-scale structural change to combat existing gender inequalities, as well as an emphasis on the need to profoundly alter public perceptions.

These moves are arguably more in keeping with radical feminism than the stereotype of moderate liberal feminism outlined above. Furthermore, their proposals regarding maternity and paternity leave would require a profound shift in popular understandings of the work/life balance, as it would lead to a less aggressively competitive understanding of the job market. In addition, their biting criticisms of the criminal justice system emphasize that nothing less than a profound shift in understandings of gender within the system will be sufficient. In this sense, it is profoundly misguided to regard an organisation like the Fawcett Society as a moderate liberal feminist organisation which only seeks to advance small-scale change within existing institutions.

Whilst the Fawcett Society may not be radical feminist in the traditional sense, its vision is nonetheless fairly radical (given that its goals would require a profound transformation of gender relations), even though that vision may be informed by liberal rather than radical feminist insights. One must also bear in mind the fact that contemporary feminist/gender equality organisations are typically not especially resource-rich. Kate Bellamy of the Fawcett Society pointed out that she would like to see Fawcett engage with more activist forms of campaigning but that, at present, this not really feasible given the organisation's limited resources.

In terms of the issue of liberal versus radical feminism, Women's Aid is an interesting case. Women's Aid's roots are in the more radical grass roots feminism of the 1970s, but have since become a more professional campaigning organisation. Women's Aid publishes smart, glossy documents, often plays an advisory role in the formation of relevant policy, and also uses celebrity endorsement to further its aims (Will Young is a Women's Aid Ambassador at present!). Thus, a case could be made that Women's Aid has lost its critical edge in moving form a more radical to an arguably more liberal position.

However, this is categorically not the case. A cursory glance at Women's Aid's policy proposals reveals an emphasis on the need for profound changes in how domestic violence is treated by politicians, the legal system and the public at large. Crucially, Women's Aid emphasize how nothing less than a profound change in gender relations will be sufficient to end domestic violence, given that they see the latter as being rooted in historically entrenched structures of male supremacy. Thus, although Women's Aid has moved from a defensive to a more engaged position in terms of state institutions, the idea that this necessarily compromises their ability to push for broader, more radical change is fundamentally unsound.

Women's Aid has maintained its critical, uncompromisingly feminist message despite having become more willing to engage with British political institutions. This points towards a number of conclusions. Whilst radical feminism as an activist movement is arguably less influential than it used to be, a number of radical feminist concerns can still be found both in academic and activist feminist circles. Of particular interest here is the issue of feminist involvement with the state and political institutions more generally. In much feminist literature, one often finds a reluctance to endorse feminist involvement with state institutions: in fact, there is often something of a romanticisation of autonomous feminist activity.

This view argues that engagement with British political institutions forces feminists to compromise, reducing the effectiveness of the feminist critique. However, when one looks at the Fawcett Society and Women's Aid, one can see that this view is not helpful: whilst these organisations do engage with the state, they are still willing and able to articulate visions of a profound shift in gender relations. Therefore, the view that feminists used to be radical militants and are now all moderate liberal reformists simply does not hold. It is true that since the 1980s feminists have looked increasingly to existing political institutions to further their aims, but this has clearly not resulted in an automatic compromising of feminist principles.

This means that feminist engagement with British political institutions is not necessarily a bad thing. After all, some of the major feminist advances of the twentieth century could only have been achieved through particular policy changes. It is therefore important to resist having a romantic view of militant and autonomous politics, and to accept that engaging with existing British political institutions is necessary for feminism to be effective. Similarly, what this also shows is that the distinction between radical feminism and liberal feminism might actually be quite problematic.

This is somewhat remarkable given that these two positions are often seen as polar opposites. Liberal feminism might be characterised as a feminism which is not in any way prescriptive in terms of the sort of sexual, cultural and economic choices woman make, and this is certainly the basic view underpinning both the Fawcett Society and Women's Aid's campaigning activities. However, this does not mean that their views are not radical, as both organisations are seeking broad structural change. What this points towards is that it would be worth our while trying to move beyond the distinction between radical and liberal feminism.

Perhaps what we are dealing with might be called 'radical liberal feminism.' It might be a bit far-fetched to try to persuade everyone to join together in a big radical liberal feminist coalition, but it might be a helpful term to use. It could have the potential to help devise a feminism which could gain popular support by moving away from the more alienating aspects of traditional radical feminism, but without losing the feminist vision of a radical transformation of gender relations. Given that radical liberal feminist sentiments are fundamental to the Fawcett Society, Women's Aid, and indeed many of the views expressed on this website, perhaps the seeds of a large radical liberal feminist coalition are already in existence!

Maybe this is wishful thinking, but I think it is important to try to think beyond rather false oppositions (such as liberal vs radical feminism) which can have a rather paralysing effect on feminist activity. Given that the seeds of a 'radical liberal feminist' movement are perhaps already in existence, it might be worth our while thinking about trying to establish connections between 'grass roots' activity (such as this website) and more formal organisations such as the Fawcett Society and Women's Aid.

These groups are arguably the most significant feminist groups in the country, and have similar agendas, and might allow for a greater flow of ideas between grass-roots groups /

sites and more formal organisations which have closer links with established political institutions. These ideas are all rather cursory at the moment, and I am not really sure how they might be put into practice, but I think it would help the feminist cause if these groups were able to join together a little more rather than exist in isolation from one another.

GLOBALISATION AND TRADE

Early in the nuclear age, Albert Einstein lamented that the atomic bomb had changed everything but the way humanity thinks. Today, the same can be said of the impact on American politics of economic globalisation - the increasing integration of international markets being brought about by rapidly expanding worldwide flows of goods, services, capital, information, and sometimes people.

Prominent Americans in and out of government proclaim the new global economy to be the defining reality of our age, powerful enough (along with technological change) to transform such age-old institutions as the job, the nation-state, and the family itself. Yet aside from discrete trade policy controversies, globalisation has not been meaningfully incorporated into American politics or policy-making. In fact, most social and even economic policy issues are debated in America today as if globalisation did not exist or were happening somewhere else.

Take the ongoing controversy this year about domestic monetary policy and the relationship between economic growth, employment levels, and wage pressures. Eyeing a steadily falling national unemployment rate and understandably determined to stop inflation before it starts, Federal Reserve Board chairman Alan Greenspan has been holding real interest rates high enough to keep economic growth modest and therefore labor markets loose enough to inhibit workers from seeking significant raises. Most Wall Street observers and economists have praised Greenspan, expressed amazement that inflationary pressures have not reappeared at today's unemployment levels, and continued to warn that rising labor costs must be just around the corner.

If these observers recognized the United States economy's steady internationalization, they would understand that the employment rate of American workers is no longer the only significant determinant of American wage levels. With more and more American companies hiring foreign workers for their overseas facilities, it is equally important to look at global unemployment rates. According to the International Labor Organization, roughly one-third of the world's workforce is jobless or underemployed.

Moreover, given the explosive growth in the number of workers entering the world economy in huge, low-wage countries like China, India, and Indonesia, it is easy to see how American workers could continue to be afraid to press for higher pay even if United States unemployment rates sank even lower. Welfare reform is another issue with a critical but neglected international dimension. Both supporters and most opponents of today's welfare reform schemes apparently believe that the United States economy is full of opportunities for minimally educated and generally unskilled workers to earn a living wage - either through the magic of the marketplace or with a little help from retraining and reeducation programs.

What both overlook is that most of the industries that paid decent wages to American workers without world-class skills and education - such as apparel, textiles, and steel - have been decimated by foreign competition and the inadequate response of United States trade policy. Moreover, wages in those jobs that remain have fallen precipitously in the past quarter century. The failure to fully incorporate globalisation into American foreign and domestic policies has had serious consequences. As suggested earlier, it has obscured the global dimensions of - and therefore, key elements of the solutions to - many major national economic and social problems. It has also crippled American trade policy, saddling the country with narrowly conceived globalisation approaches that have benefited relatively small numbers of Americans.

Not coincidentally, the poll ratings for America's globalisation policies keep sinking lower and lower. American politics and policy are not taking globalisation seriously enough for several reasons. One is perceptual. To most Americans in and out of government, globalisation means "trade." This is especially true in discussions of globalisation's impact on American living standards, which are usually brought to a premature halt with the observation that, despite 20 years of steady growth, two-way trade in goods and services still represents less than 30 percent of the United States economy. Thus it is said to be mathematically impossible for such flows to be responsible for most wage stagnation.

Leave aside for the moment the conveniently forgotten fact that mainstream economic theory emphasizes the decisive influence that even marginal changes in supply, demand, and prices (including labor prices) tend to have on each other. What about the impact of immigration on wage levels'? What about investment'? Technology flows? For some reason they are invariably left out of the debate - an especially ironic tendency, given that immigration is now widely blamed for about one-third of the wage decline experienced since the early 1970s by low-income Americans (a point made by Harvard professor George Borjas in the November 1996 Atlantic).

Other reasons for the globalisation non-debate combine the emotional, the intellectual, and the ideological. Today, at the end of the twentieth century, many Americans are inhibited from thinking critically and rigorously about globalisation for the kinds of reasons that inhibited their forebears at the end of the nineteenth century from thinking critically and rigorously about laissez-faire capitalism in the domestic sphere. Unfettered economic activity and the absolute sanctity of private property were that era's unassailable orthodoxy.

Their moral and practical superiority were firmly established by Adam Smith's The Wealth of Nations and subsequent works of neoclassical economics. As Eric F. Goldman explained in his brilliant 1952 history of American reform, Rendezvous with Destiny, these certitudes formed the main links of a "steel chain of ideas" that created an overwhelming bias against government intervention in domestic economic and social affairs. Today, although welfare capitalism has sunk deep roots in the industrialized world, free trade, unrestricted capital mobility, and economic integration are the watchwords of international economic policy. Their moral and practical superiority has been firmly established by two epochal events - the Great Depression and the fall of communism.

Today's noninterventionist trade ethos has become so strong that even many liberals who have pushed hard to expand the welfare and regulatory state at home recoil at the thought of any regulation of international trade or investment. Indeed, no modern American political cliché has been more predictably invoked than when Vice President Al Gore confronted former presidential contender Ross Perot at their 1993 televised NAFTA debate with a photo of Senators Smoot and Hawley. Their 1929 tariff bill, after all, is almost universally - but inaccurately - blamed for deepening and even starting the Depression.

The power and persuasiveness of laissez-faire orthodoxy have another, equally important dampening effect on debating globalisation - portraying globalisation issues as a series of black-and-white, either-or choices. Free trade versus protectionism is how the debate is typically framed - as if anyone were advocating either removing all controls over international commerce or permitting no such commerce whatsoever. The situation is analogous to the debate over American foreign policy, with most commentators endlessly and fruitlessly debating "engagement versus isolationism," and neglecting what form engagement should take.

This dichotomous portrayal of globalisation choices is convincing in large part because of the way globalisation itself is depicted. Critics of current globalisation policy are right to complain that its champions simply assume that the global economy will unfold along Anglo-American-style free trade lines, even though most of the world practices forms of capitalism significantly different from this approach. But the problem runs even deeper. It entails the view of globalisation as a monolithic, undifferentiated phenomenon, with a structure as interesting as a lump of coal.

In fact, like any sweeping trend with widespread, profound effects, globalisation is highly complex. The term describes a bewildering number of relationships and arrangements that are inevitably subject to strategic, political, social, and cultural - as well as "purely economic" - influences. Elsewhere around the world, where mixed economic systems and the difficult trade-offs they require are more openly acknowledged, the complexity of globalisation seems more apparent. Policymakers and analysts alike seem to recognize that their challenge entails not simply promoting or stopping globalisation, but ensuring that its terms serve specific local, national, and regional interests.

Efforts are under way to strike the right balance between benefiting from globalisation's efficiency-enhancing effects and promoting the equally valid noneconomic goals set by all human communities. Eisuke Sakakibara, a vice minister in Japan's powerful Ministry of Finance, provided an unusually comprehensive statement of this position in his 1993 study, Beyond Capitalism: The Japanese Model of Market Economics: "Taking the pluralistic position that capitalism can differ across national borders and according to various historical and cultural backgrounds, our views on the world economy and world trade should be transformed as well. Indeed, in this increasingly interdependent world, many aspects of different national economies need to be harmonized. Yet to the extent that different regimes continue to be different, they will have to accommodate each other in certain ways. In some instances, these accommodations may take the form of modification of the principle of laissez-faire."

In the United States, the failure to perceive the real, highly nuanced choices presented by globalisation, plus the ideological bias against intervention in the economy, severely undermines the very legitimacy of thinking critically about these matters. The clearest evidence of this is the labels that have been successfully hung on the parties in globalisation disputes: supporters and opponents of prevailing policies are simply and misleadingly labeled "pro" and "anti-trade," respectively. Proponents of current globalisation policies have also been able to portray their preferences in terms connoting objectivity and inevitability. They have explicitly described themselves as the "party of the future" or, more specifically, of the "New Economy." Their depiction of their policies as "bridges to the twenty-first century" fails to provoke much protest, even from opponents.

Critics, meanwhile, are widely dismissed as voices of the past, clinging stubbornly but naively to outmoded industries and ways of life. (At least one - columnist and erstwhile Republican presidential hopeful Pat Buchanan - actually does talk openly about returning to the "Old Republic.") Paul Gigot of The Wall Street Journal used all of the major stereotypes in a September 12, 1997, column: "Free trade has its political compensations even in a Democratic primary. It lets [Vice President Gore] seem future-oriented and presidential, instead of hostage to special interests and the old blast-furnace economy."

President Clinton, perhaps characteristically, tried to have it both ways in his September 22, 1997, speech to the United Nations General Assembly. "The forces of global integration are a great tide, inexorably wearing away the established order of things," he intoned, hastening to add, "but we must decide what will be left in its wake." Superficially, these labels and stereotypes seem at least partly justified. After all, some of the leading champions of current globalisation policies are high-tech companies like Microsoft, IBM, and AT&T while some of the leading opponents include industrial unions, like the United Steel Workers and the United Auto Workers, which provide the workforce for the so-called blast-furnace industries.

The problem is that the high-tech companies still employ surprisingly small numbers of high-wage, highly skilled workers. Many more of these workers are employed by the blast-furnace industries, which have also undertaken a large and growing incorporation of high-tech components into their products and manufacturing processes. Still, the CEOs of the blast-furnace economy are sending production abroad just as fast - and fighting just as hard to keep United States markets open to their output - as their counterparts in high-tech industries.

Although the globalisation debate often bums white hot when it erupts, the contending factions are anything but perfectly cohesive or coherent. The confusion is understandable; after all, any phenomenon with effects as powerful and wide-ranging as those of globalisation is bound to stimulate myriad responses from many different interests and individuals. Still, the blurring of disagreements even over fundamental issues make productive discussion of globalisation all the more difficult.

For most of America's history, globalisation policy has mainly meant trade policy, and its politics was mainly sectional. The manufacturing-heavy north favored high tariffs to protect and nurture its industries; the largely agrarian south, which not only imported manufactured goods but relied heavily on commodities exports, favored much more open trade. These powerful sectional influences in turn produced a clear partisan divide. Republicans were so devoted to tariffs that their presidents and especially members of Congress championed protectionist policies well into the Nixon era. Democrats generally favored more trade liberalization even after they transcended their base in the "Solid South."

At the same time, it is crucial to note that the early nineteenth century triumph of federalists and nationalists in American politics and economic policy placed the nation on a predominantly mercantilist course until the mid- 1930s. During that decade, powerful domestic and international developments began to rival sectionalism as a determinant of trade politics and policy. Domestically, nationalizing forces, such as the continuing spread of manufacturing to the south and the creation of national cultural tastes and economic markets by movies and radio, started to flatten sectional differences. Internationally, protectionism was blamed for the Great Depression (and ultimately World War II).

By the end of the war, a strong bipartisan consensus in favor of multilateral trade liberalization had been produced by the determination not to repeat the mistakes of the 1930s, the overwhelming supremacy of American industry and technology, and the emerging perceived need to win or aid cold war allies by unilaterally opening United States markets.

In the years to follow, many politicians and analysts credited these free trade policies with sparking unprecedented peace and prosperity in the noncommunist world - further reinforcing free trade's legitimacy and popularity.

Starting in the 1970s, the fading of United States global economic predominance, the slowing of worldwide and domestic growth, and the steady decline in Americans' real wages significantly weakened the free trade consensus. Additional blows were delivered in the late 1980s by the end of the cold war and by the steady transformation of many large American companies into truly global firms. The former development undermined the strategic arguments for tolerating continued protectionism by allies even as their own economic strength burgeoned. The latter development began to open an unprecedented gap between the fortunes of American workers and those of American businesses, as companies responded to competitive pressures, new market opportunities, and investment incentives by building more factories and even laboratories abroad, exporting possibly millions of high-wage jobs in the process.

At the same time, one powerful countertrend enabled free traders to prevail in most of the increasingly contentious policy disputes of the 1980s. President Ronald Reagan's ringing rhetorical support for trade liberalization convinced many conservative and moderate Americans that traditional free trade policies were integral parts of the campaign against big government - even as the president approved skillfully targeted trade barriers to help hard-hit United States industries like semiconductors and autos regain competitiveness.

In the late 1980s, globalisation's increasingly differentiated impact on Americans and the collapse of the cold war rationale for free trade, coupled with the end of the Reagan economic boom, greatly complicated the politics of globalisation. The effect on Republicans and conservatives was especially profound, as their long-standing postwar consensus on free trade was shattered. At the end of World War II, the Grand Old Party was comprised of often vigorously clashing clusters of Eastern seaboard internationalist financiers, pro-tariff New

England and Midwestern industrialists, Western and Midwestern isolationists, opportunistic McCarthyite red-baiters, and a small but influential band of paleo-conservative intellectuals battling against the modernizing, secularizing spirit of the twentieth century.

The onset of the cold war persuaded them to set aside their differences and unite on an emergency basis behind interventionism, peacetime military alliances, and free trade. Over the next three decades, these Republican factions broke up, evolved, and recombined into their contemporary forms - including laissez-faire-oriented supply-siders and libertarians, moral majoritarians, neoconservatives, nativist communitarians, deficit hawks, blue-collar ethnic "Reagan Democrats," and a dwindling band of moderates and liberals who retain influence in Congress and in Washington media circles. Yet with the cold war emergency over and the unifying presence of Reagan gone, America's conservative coalition has been pulling apart at the seams. And one of the main polarizing issues - even more at the rank and file than at the leadership level - has been globalisation.

A February 1997 survey by prominent Republican pollsters Fabrizio McLaughlin and Associates showed how deep and wide the split runs. All five factions into which they divided the party - including the normally ardently pro-free trade supply-siders - showed plurality support for the proposition that recent trade agreements had sent more jobs abroad than they had created at home. Just as surprisingly, a late-July NBC - Wall Street Journal poll reported that Republican respondents were more strongly opposed to NAFTA than Democrats. The end of the cold war had a less dramatic impact on Democrats. Instead, their internal splits over globalisation stem from the gap opened up by the Vietnam War between the party's moderate and left wings.

The fault lines have remained more or less intact, but the dispute has been transformed into a battle between contrasting visions - if not realities - of the new and old economies. Moderates - most of whom eventually turned against the Vietnam War - continued to insist that cold war internationalism was a viable framework for United States foreign (and by extension, trade) policy. The left-wingers pushed a more fundamental critique of the war and the society that spawned it. At the same time, cross-cutting issues and clashing institutional imperatives have repeatedly confused the picture. Among congressional Democrats, the hardening of organized labor's opposition to conventional free trade policies - led by unions whose leaders tended to support the Vietnam War until the bitter end - has helped shift the balance of power against current globalisation initiatives.

At the presidential level, many Democratic leaders persuasively argued that electoral success depended on candidates distancing themselves from the party's best-known constituencies (including not only big labor but civil rights groups and feminists) and from the unpopular federal bureaucracies they had allegedly captured. Instead, the moderates counseled, Democrats should embrace the technological progress and entrepreneurial spirit that was fueling the booming information-based New Economy. Greatly enhancing the New Democrats' power has been the skyrocketing costs of political campaigns.

Since business - which is traditionally pro-Republican - is the greatest potential source of funds for the media advertising that can make or break candidates, Democrats have had to "follow the money" and step up their efforts to win corporate support. Under the leadership of former Connecticut Congressman Tony Coelho, the Democratic Congressional Campaign Committee turned into a big-time money machine and full-time Wall Street presence, starting in the late 1980s. In fact, one of Bill Clinton's most effective fund-raisers in 1992 was Treasury Secretary Robert Rubin, then head of the Wall Street investment giant Goldman Sachs.

Because the large companies pursued by the Democrats have been the strongest proponents of current globalisation policies, the New Democrats who preach that America should "compete, not retreat" in the world economy (to quote Clinton) have seen their influence grow. (The Democrats have made no special efforts to target small businesses - the vast majority of which do not export or are found in domestic-oriented service industries.) The fly in the ointment has been the environmental issue.

Although many environmentally minded voters are high-income Americans who consider themselves to be globalisation's winners, many fear that uncontrolled globalisation will greatly increase industrial pollution - and enhance corporations' ability and authority to pollute. Thus, major environmental organizations like the Sierra Club have been leading opponents of NAFTA and the General Agreement on Tariffs and Trade (GATT) Uruguay Round agreement that gave birth to the World Trade Organization.

One critical result of these intraparty changes has been the emergence of nonpartisan "strange bedfellows" coalitions on globalisation issues. Numerous commentators and analysts have noted that the anti-NAFTA and anti-GATT campaigns united Pat Buchanan and Jesse Jackson, Ralph Nader and Ross Perot, paleo-conservatives and big labor. Less remarked on have been the mirror images of these pairings among globalisation enthusiasts - Bill Clinton and Newt Gingrich, Henry Kissinger and Jimmy Carter, the Brookings Institution and the Heritage Foundation. At the same time, below the surface of these coalitions lurk major globalisation-related disagreements that make coherent debates difficult to hold - and difficult for most voters to follow.

Today's globalisation enthusiasts are divided between self-styled competitiveness advocates and free-market conservatives. The former - many of whom serve in the Clinton administration-speak of current globalisation policies as integral parts of a broader "proactive" government strategy to restore America's relative economic position on the world stage. Indeed, many also favor a significant government role in developing and commercializing new technologies, as well as public sector efforts to restructure labor-management relations along more cooperative lines and improve America's primary and secondary schools.

Although often insisting that trade in particular is not a zero-sum game, they repeatedly emphasize the importance of

American exporters not only getting their appropriate share of foreign markets, but also beating the competition in the race for business opportunities whenever possible. Early in the Clinton administration, many of these competitiveness advocates vowed to reduce America's global trade deficits and its major bilateral trade deficits, which they blamed largely on foreign protectionism. The continued growth of these deficits, however, led them to abandon these goals in favor of simply boosting exports.

Nowhere was this approach more apparent than in the campaign to pass the original NAFTA in 1993. The agreement was sold as a way to create millions of high-wage jobs and improve the relative competitiveness of United States companies by securing for them significant advantages in Mexican consumer markets as well as important investment preferences. NAFTA supporters even warned that without these preferences valuable business opportunities would be lost to European and Asian companies allegedly poised to dominate the Mexican economy. Revealingly, the same arguments are being made today in the debate over expanding NAFTA to the rest of the Western Hemisphere.

The free-market conservative allies of these competitiveness advocates are distinctly uncomfortable with most of these arguments. They tend to see any trade expansion as a good in itself that enhances global efficiency and maximizes global welfare - thus benefiting America indirectly. Convinced (somewhat inconsistently) that international markets can, do, and should operate completely independent of international power politics, they oppose as counterproductive government efforts to shape worldwide economic flows for national advantage. The only exception entails maintaining sound macroeconomic policies. Significantly, these conservatives' laissez-faire instincts are so strong that they vigorously oppose government trade policy activism even when market forces are fettered.

In other words, true to David Ricardo's teachings (although not to Adam Smith's), they regard government as inherently so incompetent that they believe in tolerating foreign protectionism rather than retaliating. To be sure, they attribute America's trade deficits primarily to its relatively low rate of savings and high rate of consumption, not to foreign barriers. More important, however, most attach no significance to these international trade balances. Consistent with their free-market beliefs, they also oppose dedicated United States government efforts to promote exports, not to mention anything smacking of "industrial policy." Indeed, they - like Ronald Reagan's rhetoric - see opposition to protectionism as central to their plans to shrink government.

Critics of current globalisation policies face significant disagreements of their own, which tend to divide along left-right, nationalist-internationalist lines. Right-wing critics generally take a strongly nationalist view of international economics. They see the main challenge of United States globalisation policy as defending and promoting purely American interests against the predations of foreign actors. Consequently, they scorn international organizations like the World Trade Organization as mechanisms largely designed by weak countries to handcuff great powers like the United States, and as unacceptable threats to America's sovereignty and the principles of representative, accountable government.

In addition, they are fully confident that the unilateral use of United States power - especially regulating access to the American market - can achieve America's essential globalisation policy goals, including removing foreign trade barriers and ensuring that exports to the United States are "fairly" traded. Yet like the competitiveness advocates, the right-wing globalisation critics leave unclear whether they simply want a perfectly level playing field in world trade and investment and equal opportunity for American producers, or whether they want guarantees of successful outcomes. These critics understand that promoting economic development and sound environmental policies in low-income countries can help buoy wages and environmental standards at home. But they fear that significantly closing the North-South gap will take too many years - if it can be done at all.

Therefore, they tend to see the interests of American workers and their foreign counterparts as being in unfortunate but unmistakable conflict. Most left-wing globalisation critics see entirely different fault lines in the world economy. Generally unconcerned with the globalisation-related tensions among countries, their main interest is the struggle they see between the world's workers and international capital. Unlike the conservative nationalists, they believe that developing world living standards can be raised relatively quickly with few sacrifices from workers in the industrialized world, and they are confident that international institutions can and should play constructive roles. The main problem they have with these institutions is not that they are anti-American, but that they are controlled by worldwide corporate interests.

If only unions and consumer groups were adequately represented, these left-wing critics suggest, they would have no objections to significant reductions in American sovereignty. At the same time, one faction on the left, convinced that multinational businesses have all the advantages in a truly global economy, seems to oppose the idea of increasing worldwide economic integration itself, and argues for greater self-reliance at the national and especially sub national levels. Unquestionably, the American globalisation debate has been hampered by the diversity of the nation and by globalisation's uncanny ability to subdivide even the factions described above, as well as by ideological blinders.

The globalisation of production does indeed create obstacles to identifying which firms are truly serving the entire nation's interests and therefore where and how to target globalisation policy initiatives. Powerful links are forming between the prosperity of American workers and foreign countries - whether the former work in exporting industries or hold stock in foreign enterprises or major United States exporting companies. And globalisation issues can pit not only different industries against each other, but different companies within industries against each other - witness the current feud among American airlines over access to Japan. At the same time, although organized labor and United States multinationals are battling tooth and nail over the trade and investment dimensions of globalisation, they are cooperating to defeat a

UN environmental initiative that both believe will damage American competitiveness.

Precisely because its effects are distributed in such a wildly uneven, frequently shifting manner, globalisation raises serious questions about America's future as a cohesive, successful society - about American nationhood itself. Globalisation's ability to set worker against manager, industry against industry, and companies within industries against each other is clear even during today's ongoing economic expansion and relative prosperity.

These developments will only become more frequent and pronounced when the economy slows. Observing the growing tendency of wealthier Americans to literally wall themselves off from the problems of their fellow countrymen with private schools, gated communities, and private security forces, writers as different as Robert Reich, the former labor secretary, and conservative military strategist Edward Luttwak warn that parts of America are starting to resemble chronically divided, class-ridden third world societies.

Should these trends continue, globalisation could represent the greatest challenge to national unity since the Civil War. It is, of course, certainly possible that Americans ultimately will be better off as members of transnational labor or corporate communities, or even as citizens of tightly contained subnational groups; no political form lasts forever, and the nation-state cannot automatically be assumed an exception. But questions so monumental should be confronted openly and decided deliberately, not backed into unwittingly, heedless of the full consequences.

WOMEN CONTRIBUTE TO WORLD TRADE

Women are important economic actors. Today, 54% of working age women are in the labour force. In 1960, women's participation in the formal labour force was only 33%. These statistics do not come close to telling the whole story though. They do not include women working in what economists call the informal and household sectors. In plain English, that means women whose work is not "recognized, recorded, protected or regulated by public authorities", or women who are caring for their children (and thus providing the next generation of economic actors). The ILO has estimated that if only the value of unpaid work that is done by women were counted, global output would be almost 50% greater.

Trade liberalization has had a particularly striking effect on the number of women working in developing countries' manufacturing sectors. According to the ILO, export-oriented industrialization is associated with a rising share of women's manufacturing employment - especially in the textiles, apparel and electronics sectors. Some 70-90% of the workers employed in export processing zones (EPZs) are women. Women also produce more than half of the world's household goods and their share of informal employment generally matches or exceeds men's.

In the more traditional agricultural sector, the FAO has estimated that women may produce over half of the world's food. As economic actors, women wield their pocketbooks as well as their diverse skills: women are significant consumers as well as important producers. As consumers, they typically make purchasing decisions for themselves as well as their families, compounding the economic impact of their decisions.

Like virtually all economic actors today, women are greatly affected by world trade. New paid employment opportunities, for example, can enhance women's autonomy. They can also offer women greater negotiating power within households and communities. Over time, this is likely to lead to improved social status, self-confidence and awareness of rights. Recent studies, however, suggest that this interface is generally more problematic. Much as the relationship between trade liberalization and poverty is now widely recognized to be complex and controversial, there is growing evidence that trade liberalization can have both positive and negative effects for women.

What kind of evidence exists? Studies to date have basically focused on three questions:

- How does trade liberalization affect women's employment opportunities, income and consumption?

- What impact does trade expansion in specific industries and geographic locations have on women?
- Does trade have non-economic implications for women's well-being, rights to human potential and freedom from poverty?

The results of these studies present a varied and inconclusive picture. It is one, nonetheless, that must be considered. The following are just a few of the reasons why:

Women have gained new jobs in the export sector, but these jobs may be socially problematic. According to UNCTAD, workers in EPZs put in hours that are 25 percent longer than in other firms. Women working in these zones, in turn, are paid 20 to 50 percent less than men. This has increased the overall wage gap between women and men and decreased the prospects for closing this gap. It may also be reinforcing gender bias in the labour market.

Imports can displace local production that was an important source of livelihood for some households. In the agricultural sector, women produce 90% of the food for home consumption in the developing countries. But they are small-scale producers. Trade liberalization, by introducing import competition, tends to advantage larger producers. The market access opportunities that it creates, in turn, can be difficult for women to take advantage of. This is because in many societies they have limited property rights and lack access to things like credit, modern technologies and marketing expertise.

Finally, tariff reductions and the elimination of import licensing requirements reduce government revenues. This could indirectly compound any existing gender inequalities by limiting governments' discretion to introduce policies to remedy them. More generally, it might also reduce the capacity of governments to provide services or safety nets for the most vulnerable.

What has the WTO done to date to factor women's needs' and concerns into trade policies. The answer is, very little. Trade policy is made on the basis of an assumption that trade policy and trade liberalization are gender neutral. This assumption needs to be reassessed and examined in the light of evidence, increased involvement of women in the global economy, and the growing importance of the WTO in regulating trade policy. Governments could begin by respecting their existing commitments to gender equality and mainstreaming.

Virtually all WTO Member states have endorsed the UN's Beijing Platform for Action. This legal instrument is the international reference point for governmental commitment to women's advancement and gender equality. It obligates governments to promote active and visible policies of integrating gender perspectives in all their policies and programs. It also requires that they take actions to correct any imbalances that a policy might create. This includes economic policies.

Subsequent UN resolutions place responsibility on international organizations-including the WTO-to support government efforts to achieve the objectives of the Beijing Platform. They also provide for the mainstreaming of a gender perspective into all policies and programs of the UN system. Early examination of the issue of gender mainstreaming could provide guidance for the on-going implementation of existing trade rules and ensure that development of future trade rules would be gender-neutral, thereby leading to a strengthened WTO.

INTERNATIONAL TRADE LIBERALISATION

Mainstream economic theory teaches that international trade is beneficial to all countries and their citizens. This belief is based on the idea of "comparative advantage" — each country should focus on what it does best and trade for other products in order to reach the most efficient allocation of resources in the global economy and the highest levels of output and growth in all countries. It is assumed that trade leads to growth which in turn promotes national development and reduces poverty. While it is recognized that trade produces both "winners" and "losers" in every economy, the theory is that the "losers" can be compensated from the net gains. The evidence, however, does not support these simplistic assumptions.

Furthermore, the "comparative advantage" of some countries is their low wages, poor environmental regulations and lax labour standards. Comparative advantage based on the exploitation of women and the environment is incompatible with a human rights and human development approach, irrespective of the perceived economic benefit or efficiency for the country. The stated objective of the WTO is "to help trade flow smoothly, freely, fairly and predictably." The original *GATT* was limited to facilitating trade in goods by eliminating so-called 'trade barriers' (e.g. quotas, tariffs) and articulating the basic principles of free trade (i.e. non-discrimination, fiscal and regulatory independence of states). The scope and power of the organization, however, has greatly increased.

Today, the WTO's reach includes issues of service provision, intellectual property, health and safety standards, and a vast array of products. It is now the primary actor in international trade, administering multilateral agreements, hosting negotiating sessions, handling disputes, monitoring national trade policies, and providing technical assistance and training for developing countries. With good reason, the WTO has been described as "the institutional face of globalisation" and has been the focus of many so-called "anti-globalisation" protests in recent years. The organization's structure has been non-transparent, unaccountable, non-participatory, undemocratic, and imperialistic, and trade liberalization has become an ever-expanding end in itself. Furthermore, the WTO's contribution to human rights protection and sustainable development is questionable.

Case studies reveal that women's time, labour, sexuality and health are at times exploited in the pursuit of gains from trade in various countries. In fact, some governments overtly appeal to sexism to increase their country's trade revenues, for example, by using low wages of women as a basis to compete internationally in export industries or through campaigns to encourage married women to do home based work. Furthermore, men and women experience poverty differently and women do not have equal access to and control over resources, do not enjoy equal protection of human rights, and have distinct roles in terms of production and reproduction. For these reasons, women and men may benefit from or be harmed by trade policies in different ways. They may also respond differently to the economic incentives set up by the governments' chosen strategies. Trade policy, however, tends to be gender-blind and silent about gender-specific repercussions.

Consider the following examples:

- *Women's unpaid work:* Trade liberalization policies have pulled many women into the formal labour force and also affect the cost and availability of food, medicines, household goods, and social services. Each of these impacts can increase the demands on women's unpaid labour — women may have less time available for reproductive work but simultaneously face greater demands to provide services. Unfortunately, studies show that men are not picking up the slack.
- *Women's conditions of employment:* Women are increasingly at risk of working in highly exploitative and dangerous conditions because trade liberalization tends to increase their employment in the industrial sector, in commercial agriculture and in export processing zones, which are characterized by low rates of pay and sub-standard conditions. Globalisation has also fueled informal employment arrangements and subcontracting in female-dominated industries (such as food and garment production), threatening the security, status and rights of workers.
- *Gender inequality constrains productivity*: Gender based inequalities (especially in education, health and training) hinder women's abilities to take advantage of new opportunities created by trade liberalization such as skilled employment and entrepreneurial opportunities. This in turn constrains the "output response" to the economic incentives created by trade promotion policies and constrains the export capacity of the whole economy.

Gender analysis reveals that the relationship between trade and gender relations is complex and ambiguous. The question we need to ask is not whether trade liberalization is good or bad for women as a group, but how trade policy can contribute to the achievement of human rights for everyone and promote sustainable development in all societies. Gender analysis demonstrates how pushing forward with more of the same "one-size fits-all", gender-blind trade liberalization policies — which do not consider local social factors and human needs — will not remedy inequalities in the economy or eradicate poverty. The challenge is to implement policies that will.

The rules of the international trading system (including the trading rules, conflict resolution mechanisms, etc.) currently reflect the power of rich countries and transnational corporations. These vested interests are apparent at two different stages: a) the making of the rules, and b) the implementation, enforcement and interpretation of the rules. The rules are contained in a set of agreements which have been elaborated in successive rounds of very political, intense and often biased negotiations between state representatives. This set of agreements includes the *GATT*, the *Agreement on Agriculture*, the *Agreement on Technical Barriers to Trade* ("TBT"), the *General Agreement on Trade in Services* ("GATS"), the *Agreement on Trade-Related Aspects of Intellectual Property Rights* ("TRIPS"), among others.

Establishing the rules is only the first stage of the game however; the implementation, enforcement and interpretation of the rules is another matter altogether. While the agreements that make up the WTO system are the product of political negotiations, they become public international law once they are adopted. As international law they are enforceable, binding on states, and subject to the rules of international legal interpretation (as opposed to U.N. conference documents for example, which are aspirational but do not have the force of law behind them). In other words, international trade rules "have teeth".

This is at least in part because through the advent of the WTO, the international trade system was transformed from a political/diplomatic regime to a highly legalistic one. When a country is not following the rules, another country can bring a case against them in a court-like setting known as a dispute settlement panel. The panel makes a judgement as to whether the country is violating the law, and if so, orders them to comply with the law or face sanctions. This is not a negotiation; it is a litigation based enforcement system. The judgements can be appealed to the Appellate Body (sort of like a "supreme court of international trade").

So for example, while the *Convention on the Elimination of All Forms of Discrimination Against Women* ("CEDAW") states that countries must grant women equal nationality rights with men (Article 9), many countries do not and there are few consequences for their defiance. In contrast, when a WTO member country does not meet the standards for the protection of patents mandated by the *TRIPS* agreement, or imposes a tax that makes locally-produced products cheaper than foreign ones (prohibited by *GATT* Article 3), the countries who are harmed can bring a case against the defiant country and punish the offender for their breach.

Untempered trade liberalization not only runs the risk of further marginalizing women from key activities in the national economy but may itself engender significant violations of women's social and economic rights- *Mariama Williams.*

The legal stature of these rules also means that if circumstances change or a government realizes that the provisions are not "a good deal" for their country, they can not simply back out of their commitments or negotiate different provisions. And unlike some other legal regimes (e.g. human rights treaties including *CEDAW*), states must accept the entire package of WTO rules or none at all. This is a major problem for developing and less powerful countries since they are less able to influence the formulation of the rules in the first place.

Finally, the legal nature of the trading system is important because some of the most complex WTO agreements have important provisions that are subject to differing interpretations. While the words on the paper may be clear, how to apply them in real-life scenarios can be more difficult.

In a dispute settlement proceeding, the "judges" interpret the rules based on the arguments put forward by the participants in the proceedings and principles of legal interpretation (much like in national constitutional litigation). Hypothetically, they may decide whether clothing produced under sweatshop conditions and sweatshop-free clothing must be treated as the same products, whether a pesticide ban is necessary for the protection of public health, or whether providing drugs necessary for the treatment of a pandemic at a low cost is "a circumstance of extreme emergency".

Legal imagination, not hard economics, determines these cases. While the answers to these questions may seem inconsequential, they can have huge impacts on the actions governments take and hence on the lives of women. On the one hand, legal enforcement removes flexibility and the possibility of adopting trade policies that coincide with national development strategies. The mere threat of legal action may be sufficient to force a government to change their policies. The dispute settlement process also limits participation and transparency because only governments can act as complainants and defendants in the proceedings. Furthermore, effective participation in a dispute proceeding is very costly and requires specialized training. Finally, the legal forum focuses very narrowly on specific rules and facts, ignoring the broader context and full range of values and factors relevant to justice and development. Gender issues, for example, are usually not "legally relevant".

On the other hand, as opposed to negotiations and 'behind closed doors' deals, the judicial setting at least formally places the parties on an equally footing and allows them to present their positions in front of formally impartial decision-makers. The judicial setting also provides an opportunity to develop the law and interpret provisions in ways that further a social justice agenda. In deciding whether a state is acting in a manner consistent with the rules, the panelists look at the relevant provisions and must decide what they mean in light of modern day values, the overarching objectives of the agreement (which often include environmental protection and human development), and the entire body of principles that constitute international law. Given the intensified advocacy around the WTO by women's groups, we should consider potential of legal interpretation and dispute settlement proceedings to steer existing WTO rules pro-poor, pro-equality direction.

THE POST-DOHA AGENDA

The Ministerial Conference is the WTO's top decision-making body; it meets at least once every two years. Country representatives come together to negotiate new agreements and market access commitments, clarify existing agreements and set the organization's agenda. The most recent Ministerial was in Doha, Qatar, in November 2001. The official outcomes were a 10-page Ministerial Declaration plus a declaration on intellectual property and public health (focusing on pharmaceutical patents, including HIV/AIDS medications) and a decision on "implementation" (i.e. the concerns of developing countries).

The mandate coming out of the meeting is several years of intense and complex negotiations with an ambitious deadline of January 2005 for a new set of agreements. Despite the official "development" focus of the conference, the outcomes fall far short of any development objective and were achieved by undemocratic, manipulative and biased processes. In light of Doha, analysts and activists from around the world are articulating an action agenda. Here are some of its components:

- *No new issues*: The WTO's mandate must be limited to trade issues. It is not the appropriate venue for issues such as labour, the environment, human rights, and competition policy. Other institutions (e.g. the International Labour Organization, the World Intellectual Property Organization and U.N. committees) should be given the resources they need to properly address these other issues.
- *New systems of governance and accountability*: The WTO has been secretive, undemocratic and unaccountable for too long. Political will and creativity must be devoted to establishing structures for consultation, dialogue, and stakeholder involvement in decision-making and monitoring. Clear

ground rules must be established concerning information sharing, reporting and stakeholder participation. Participation needs to be based on principles of transparency, collaboration, learning, equity and flexibility. Furthermore, governments need to be accountable to their own citizens for their actions at the WTO.

- *Judicial independence*: The dispute settlement system needs to have complete independence from the WTO Secretariat, member governments and transnational corporations who may try to inappropriately influence outcomes. Dispute panelists and the Appellate Body must apply the full body of principles of international law and interpret WTO rules consistently with the objectives of equality and sustainable development. In addition, clear and fair procedures for the participation of non-governmental stakeholders, including NGOs, need to be developed.
- *Human development as the central guiding principle*: We need to re-think the dominant model of international trade and challenge its underlying values and assumptions. Why not 'co-operation' instead of 'competition' as a basic assumption, for example? Trade policy must be situated within the overall development strategy of a country and each country must have the flexibility and policy autonomy necessary to achieve their development goals. Trade liberalization can no longer be seen as an end in itself. The WTO should be evaluated according to its contribution towards poverty reduction, equality and sustainable human development.
- *Putting developing countries first*: Imbalances in the WTO must be redressed and the needs of developing countries should define the WTO's agenda. The negotiating and monitoring capacity of developing countries must be increased and mechanisms must be developed to hold transnational corporations accountable for their actions. Developed countries need to open their markets to the products of developing countries and grant them appropriate exceptions to liberalization commitments. Finally, developed and developing countries need to work together to redistribute opportunities in favour of the poor and women.

- *Gender analysis*: We simply don't yet know enough about the relationship between gender and trade policies. We need comprehensive gender analyses of current trade policies, specific WTO agreements, different sectors and the full range of trade-related issues. We need to determine when women stand to win and when they stand to lose from new trading relations and also how different trade-related policies impact on women's empowerment. Researchers and women's rights advocacy groups need to work together to articulate alternative, appropriate policies that guarantee women's rights and contribute to a more just and sustainable world.

GENDER ACROSS THE FULL RANGE OF TRADE ISSUES

Trade between different countries is regulated by a large number of negotiated agreements, including bilateral agreements between two countries, multilateral agreements between groups of countries (including regional free trade agreements such as NAFTA, Mercosur, CARICOM, etc.) and also a group of agreements that fall under the umbrella of the WTO (most of which were the outcome of the 1986-94 'Uruguay Round' of negotiations). These agreements are like contracts between the countries that sign them, granting each country certain rights and confining their actions to within certain limits. While these texts are almost without exception silent on gender, consider the following examples of gender issues in WTO agreements:

- *GATS: The General Agreement on Trade in Services* applies to service providers including banks, telecommunication companies, tour operators, health care providers, energy companies and education providers. This agreement has profound impacts on women who are the majority of workers in the service sector, on access to and availability of public services, and on governments' abilities to regulate the quality of health care and education provided.
- *TRIPS*: The agreement on *Trade-Related Intellectual Property Rights* sets out the rules of how intellectual property rights

(including copyrights, trademarks, product names, industrial designs and "trade secrets") should be protected when international trade is involved. Its ramifications include public health, food security, biodiversity, agriculture and traditional knowledge, all of which have gender specific impacts.

- *Agreement on Agriculture:* This agreement seeks to promote trade liberalization in the agricultural sector and is therefore of concern with respect to food security and small farms producing food for local consumption as well as to sustainable livelihoods of many female agricultural workers.
- *SPS* and *TBT*: These two agreements (*Agreement on Sanitary and Phytosanitary Measures* and *Agreement on Technical Barriers to Trade*) aim to promote the harmonization of domestic health and safety standards. Their potential implications for women's health are immense. These agreements should also be of particular concern because they set very high standards for governments that wish to implement precautionary regulations to protect the health of their citizens or the environment and because they greatly expand the scope of governance by the WTO by condemning measures that are not discriminatory but are simply deemed to be *excessive*.

STRATEGIC APPROACH

Nowhere at the policy level is the disjuncture between the reproductive and the productive spheres more apparent than in the area of international trade. Most often, international trade is seen as a technical, class-and-gender-neutral process for transforming national input/output into internationally accepted currencies and for augmenting national endowments for the enhancement of consumption and production. Yet, none of this can occur without the involvement of women's and men's labor. None of this can occur without the active involvement of the reproductive sector in producing food for domestic consumption, in producing and nurturing labor, and in caring for the environment. Gender concerns in trade policies and trade agreements, therefore, arise out of the gender division of labor, gender differentiated access to economic and social resources, and women's socially prescribed responsibility for child-care, food production and preparation.

These cause women to have different perspectives on development and trade as they are differently impacted by policies related to economic and social development. These gender divisions underscore the need for better integration of the social reproduction and production spheres as the underlying basis for fashioning trade policy. Some key questions that must be addressed include:

1. Do trade policy and agreements promote better access to services that are essential for social reproduction (water, electrification, sanitation)?
2. Do trade policy and agreements increase, lessen, or have no bearing on women's access to education and health care?
3. Is trade policy complemented by social and other policies that promote human development?

In this case, policy interventions and strategies should begin with a situational analysis of men's and women's time in providing social care and participation in the labor market and an assessment of the nature of existing essential services and how these will be impacted by trade policies and agreements.

MICRO-MESO-MACRO LINKAGES, GENDER AND TRADE AGREEMENTS AND POLICIES

The dynamics between women's location in and identification with social reproduction, and critical gender gaps regarding access and ownership of resources are impacted by changes in trade policy and trade agreements. What does this mean for women's and men's daily survival and long-term strategic advancement? Since women in most economies generally have less access than men to tangible and intangible economic and social resources-land, credit, training, etc.- gender concerns are generally wrapped with gender inequality. Inequality in the present system of allocation means that women have greater need for specific types of goods and services.

This need is not counterbalanced by women's contribution to economic activity in their multiple roles as care givers in the household and community and workers, knowledge providers, and entrepreneurs in the formal and informal sectors of the market economy. Thus, when we look at trade agreements from the perspective of gender issues, we must necessarily focus on critical and pervasive gender gaps and how these under gird the system of trade and development. Longewe identifies these gaps as 'the observable and often measurable gap between men and women on some important socio economic indicators: ownership of property, access to land, and enrollment in school'.

Changes in agreements and, hence, trade policy may alter the absolute or relative nature of the gaps between men and women to the greater disadvantage of women. From this vantage point, a number of core questions about gender and trade must be examined. Answers to these questions will differ for every economy across different points in time but they do provide some initial guidelines towards strategic gender equality- oriented strategies.

Some key questions to be considered include:

1. Where are women and men located at the point of introduction of trade liberalization or change in trade policies? What mechanisms and measures are incorporated into the policy changes to account for these differences?
2. What were the expected results of the changes in trade policy? Were these results generated?
3. What mechanisms and measures are needed to promote a gender equality- sensitive trajectory?

In this case, policy interventions and strategies should focus on: Identifying gender based constraints and considerations in specific areas such as land, credit, and technical assistance. Identifying the specific directional shifts in trade policy and how trade liberalization is occurring. Assessing the possible impacts of trade liberalization/export promotion on women and on gender equality. These may include new or the exacerbation of traditional factors that impede women's access to productive resources. Identifying the nature of change in a competitive environment.

For example, the casualisation of work, more EPZs, and new sources of employment. Identifying the trends in terms of power and access to resources between men and women, employment, and the range of alternatives available to members of the households in response to trade liberalization. Identifying and monitoring changes in intra household power and income and distribution. Trade liberalization is an inherently political process that generates winners and losers internationally and nationally and, thus, poses particular dilemmas for women and men, even in spite of the existing gender relations.

Trade liberalization is a key facilitator of the globalisation process. Thus, the multilateral trading system is geared towards trade liberalization which promotes decreasing tariff and non-tariff barriers, the elimination of behind the border measures, competition policy, intellectual monopoly privileges in the form of intellectual property rights (IPR), and the harmonization of product standards and investment liberalization. In conventional economic analyses, trade liberalization has at least five important effects on a country.

It impacts:

1. Consumption,
2. Production,
3. Fiscal revenue,
4. Employment, and
5. Balance of payments.

However, from a gender sensitive perspective, there are at least two other effects that must be explicitly considered when analyzing trade liberalization: poverty/equity and environmental/ecological effects. These seven clearly identifiable effects of trade liberalization have particular implications for the process of economic development in developing countries as well as for gender relations. Changes in consumption obviously impact social reproduction in terms of its effect on the cost and availability of household items and the nature and scope of family and individual budgets.

Depending on the effect on the commodities that are critical to the daily food and survival needs of individuals and families in a country, this can mean more or less work for women in terms of securing the family's welfare. The reality is that the former is more likely than the latter. Changes in production, whether it improves the access of local business to national or international markets, will clearly impact the number, size, and profitability of local female-and- male-owned enterprises. Ultimately, whether female or male entrepreneurs can compete will depend on the rules, access to capital, credit, training, marketing, and distribution. Employment effects can mean increased jobs for women and men or imbalances in the distribution of jobs between the two sexes depending on which gender dominates the sector that is more favored by changes in trade rules.

Fiscal revenue impacts the government's ability to provide services to individuals, families, and communities. The balance of payments effect, which will be due to trade deficits, will tend to exacerbate consumption, production, and fiscal effects. Overall, with trade liberalization, different sectors in the economy may gain or loose access to jobs, markets, and livelihoods. Thus, trade liberalization, as reflected in the lived experiences of children, women, and men, can create new opportunities for business, growth, employment, and income. However, it can also be linked to rising poverty (in new and traditional forms), rising inequality, joblessness, gender discrimination, gender violence, and greater informalization of the economy.

The depth of the severity of the experiences of women and men varies for different sectors of the population depending on existing realities of class, ethnicity, and gender. Trade agreements and trade policies are inherently political, social and economic processes grounded in gender and other power based asymmetries Trade agreements are the set of modalities, rules, and procedures governing the setting of tariff, non-tariff barriers, and the bounds of reciprocity and non-reciprocity between and among countries with regard to the flow of goods and services across national borders. They also include concerns for a level of flexibility for contingent trade measures such as anti-dumping duties, countervailing and safeguard measures, as well as dispute settlement rules and procedures.

Traditionally, trade agreements provided some of the key elements for national trade policy design, development and implementation. They also tended to focus on border and cross border measures affecting the international trade of goods and services and, thus, were restrained within the foreign economic policy scope and apparatus of the national authority. However, under the increasingly expanding nature of WTO and subsequent trade negotiations, multilateral trade rules are expanding into more and more domestic policy areas. Trade policy refers to the rules and procedures for controlling the inflow and outflow of goods, services, and capital into and out of a country.

Its scope may also include measures directed at the promotion of exports. Thus trade policy, broadly constituted, consists of sets of instruments- tariffs and non-tariff barriers, and export promotion measures, all focused on capturing, to whatever extent possible, the best possible gains from trade for a nation; thereby providing an impetus for increasing national income and employment. Traditional trade policy objectives and priorities were conditioned by and subordinate to the imperative of national economic development and social objectives and strategies.

Today, however, national trade policy, at least in the context of developing countries, is operating under the increasingly binding constraints of multilateral trade rules. It is also dominating and superceding all other objectives and policy areas. Thus trade policy measures and instruments are unidirectional (biased towards trade liberalization) and unresponsive to national/domestic objectives.

Trade agreements and trade policies impact all spheres

of human activity, human development, economic growth, and gender relations. Yet, trade agreements at the bilateral, regional, and multilateral levels are completely gender blind. Trade agreements certainly do not incorporate policy goals related to gender equality. Trade and official economic decision-makers often argue that their policies are gender neutral because these policies make reference to so-called gender-neutral terms such as 'people, farmers, and target group beneficiaries'. However, these are 'easy formulae for gender blind treatment' which obscure gender biases and gender inequality in the economy and overlook or ignore gender-differentiated impacts, which are often disproportionately negative for women.

Ultimately, they are inimical to sustainable poverty eradicating economic development. Clearly, there are gender concerns at the trade negotiation table, there always have been and there always will be. The problem is that the perspective and formulation of trade policy has been from the point of view of one gender-the male- with the perspectives and concerns of the female gender subordinate to, ignored or left out of the policy making process. Yet women are active contributors in key spheres of the economy that are affected by trade agreements and trade policies. Likewise, underlying trade agreements are the different power relations between various groups of developing and developed countries. Thus, trade agreements reinforce and build on power asymmetries that imposed the wills, concerns, and priorities of economic actors in powerful countries on less powerful economic actors in poor countries.

This process is being strengthened by the following four characteristics of trade agreements at the multilateral level:

1. The practice of appending the term 'trade related' to those areas of economic activities that international capital would like to regulate favorably for themselves and in the interest of the developed countries while appending the term 'trade barriers' to those rules and regulations that are believed to be unfavorable to international capital and to the competitive advantage of developed countries. Examples of the former include the Trade-Related Intellectual Property Rights (TRIPs), Trade-related Investment

Measures (TRIMs), and the focus on creating a multilateral agreement on investment in the WTO. Examples of the latter usually include most social and environmental regulations-these are precisely the areas that are often most critical to women's social and economic needs and activities.

2. The concept of 'single undertaking'. In these two words, the differences and diversity of experiences and stages of development of countries are erased since all countries must implement all agreements without regard to their capacity and growth stage. Thus, the history of developed countries that became 'developed' by virtue of being able to differentiate themselves and to selectively apply the appropriate standards and instruments conducive to their level of experience and development is being precluded as suitable models for developing countries to follow. Developing countries find themselves applying standards that have evolved over the history of a developed country such as the U.S. and the UK without regard to where they are in terms of the level of education of the population and labor force, the very factors that are critical for social reproduction and production.
3. The increasing process of formalized 'coherence 'between the international financial institutions that provide development financing and ensure liquidity in the trade and monetary system and the World Trade Organization. Increasingly, the interaction between the IMF, the World Bank, and the WTO is geared towards 'harmonious implementation of common and complimentary objectives'-mainstreaming trade into development. In the case of the World Bank, its PRSP and CAS function as mechanisms and processes that lock in privatization of essential services and the elimination of behind the border measures. Ultimately, this 'coherence' presents dangers of cross conditionalities.
4. Trade liberalization is intertwined with social, labor market and fiscal policies, etc., and thus has tremendous implications for development, poverty eradication, and gender equality. Summary Gender biases in social and employment relations and gender inequalities in ownership, control, and access to

economic resources such as land, credit, and technical assistance play an important role in the multilateral trade system to the detriment of women.

Interestingly, however, the existence of these biases and constraints do not seem to play a significant role in the formulation of trade negotiation positions and trade policies. At the same time, trade expansion and trade intensification, as promoted by the structural adjustment and other programs of the World Bank and the IMF, and the trade liberalisation agenda of the World Trade Organization, rely explicitly on the incorporation of women' s labour both in the formal and informal sectors of the economy. In addition, the cost of adjusting to the consequence of trade liberalisation (such as cuts in public services due to budget shortfall from the reduction of trade tariffs) is disproportionately borne by women.

Overall, liberalisation and the economic adjustment which accompanies it often leads to the intensification of women's care activities. Thus, from a gender perspective, what is important is that trade policies, programs, and mechanisms promote sustainable human development and enhance social policies which protect the poor and promote the economic and social advancement of women and men. Furthermore, they should take into account differences in country needs, nature and scope of business size, activities, constraints and ability to compete, and recognise and develop mechanisms and processes that seek to overcome the special constraints that women face in the economy due to gender biases and gender inequality. There is a need for an integrated framework for sustainable, gender sensitive human development.

Trade policy must be examined in the context of all other macro-level policies. In this context, trade policy should be one of many instruments (along with industrial, fiscal and monetary policies, etc.) aimed at promoting gender equality, sustainable economic development, poverty eradication, and the improvement in the standard of living of all citizens. Finally, trade rules should be constrained and bound by existing international agreements that promote human rights and women's rights, ecological sustainability, and human dignity and life. Moreover, there should be fairness, transparency, democracy, and participation by civil society in the WTO system.

8

Transforming Global Governance Challenges and Opportunities

The deepest, broadest, and most persistent financial crisis in decades has the world in its grip. It has taken a significant toll on consumer and business confidence, and led to a sharp slowing in global economic activity. Much of the developed world (including Canada) is in recession and the slowdown is spreading to major emerging and developing economies. In a recent speech, OECD Secretary-General Angel Gurría stated: "The only way out from this crisis is multilateral co-operation. But the world economy has changed to such an extent in the last years that we need a new type of multilateralism, more inclusive global governance."

He added: "It is time to change. It is time to re- write the rules of a more reliable and balanced globalisation. But this will not only require better international organizations and better global governance; this will also demand a change of mind, a change of culture." This chapter focuses on the role of global steering committees and multilateral institutions in governing the global economy, and the increasing calls for their reform. It highlights some of the major challenges facing the world and the opportunity presented by the upcoming G-20 Leaders Summit to cement change.

Lastly, it concludes that Canada is in an excellent position to assume a leadership role to drive change. What is Global Governance? Global governance is a process of cooperative leadership that brings together national governments, multilateral public agencies, and civil society to achieve commonly accepted goals. It provides strategic direction and then marshals collective energies to address global challenges. To be effective, it must be inclusive, dynamic, and able to span national and sector boundaries and interests. It should operate through soft rather than hard power. It should be more democratic than authoritarian, more openly political than bureaucratic, and more integrated than specialized.

Examples of multilateral institutions that mold economic and political relations are the United Nations (UN) and its Security Council, the World Bank, the International Monetary Fund (IMF), and the World Trade Organization (WTO). Each of these organizations pursues its own objectives and priorities, according to its mandate. The lack of a comprehensive system of oversight has been filled by a succession of ad hoc groups of states that act as a steering committee for the world economy, for example, the Group of Seven/Eight (G-7/8) Heads of State, and the Group of Twenty (G-20) finance ministers and central bank governors.

As the OECD Secretary-General noted, dramatic changes have taken place in the global economic structure in recent years. Emerging market economies have grown in importance, both in terms of population and economic weight. They have integrated into the global economy through both trade and finance. China and India, for example, have emerged as economic powerhouses and formidable global competitors. China is the largest creditor nation to the United States. Russia, Brazil, Mexico, South Korea, Indonesia, South Africa, and the Gulf States are also ascending in the world order. Yet, major global economic, financial and social concerns are, for the most part, discussed by the traditional forums of industrial countries-the Group of Seven/Eight (G-7/8).

Emerging countries have been invited to G-8 meetings on an ad hoc basis largely as observers. Some repeatedly asked to be present at the "whole lunch and not only at the dessert." Emerging and developing nations also have little influence in multilateral institutions-like the IMF, and the World Bank-even though they are deeply affected by their work. Because of the global nature of the economic and financial crisis, calls for dramatic and lasting change in global governance-reformed institutions that are more inclusive, effective, and legitimate; and a more inclusive global steering committee-appear to have reached an apex.

In 1999, the G-20 4-the Group of Twenty finance ministers and central bank governors was formally created as a forum for cooperation and consultation on matters pertaining to the international financial system. It advances discussion, study and review of key economic and financial policy issues. The goal is to promote stable and sustainable economic growth, and international financial stability. The G-20 consists of 10 industrial countries (Australia, Canada, France, Germany, Italy, Japan, Russia, the United States, the United Kingdom, and the EU which is represented by the rotating president) and 10 emerging market economies (Argentina, Brazil, China, India, Indonesia, Korea, Mexico, Saudi Arabia, South Africa, and Turkey).

The G-20 arose out of the need to deal with the Asian financial crisis of 1997-98. Canadian leadership was instrumental in the creation of G-20. Paul Martin, then Canada's Minister of Finance, championed the idea within the G-7. He believed that emerging economies have a vital role to play in maintaining global economic stability and prosperity. After all, the 1997-98 financial crisis emanated from Asia and had global repercussions. Emerging economies had to be at the table and be part of the solution. He also championed the idea of transforming the G-20 into an L-20, a leaders-level (Heads of State) group.

The concept of the L-20 came to fruition some nine years after the creation of the G-20. Another financial crisis was the catalyst of the first ever G-20 Leaders Summit which took place in Washington DC on November 15, 2008. For many, this meeting was seen a historic breakthrough-a major step toward a new, more inclusive architecture in global financial and economic relations, and global governance more specifically. The communiqué of the November 15, 2008 Leaders Summit set a date of April 2nd, 2009 for the next meeting of G-20 Leaders to be held in the United Kingdom.

The Summit is the opportune time to showcase global cooperation and demonstrate strong leadership to tackle the immediate and longer-term global challenges. The ongoing financial crisis and the ensuing global recession deserve and demand the world's immediate and utmost attention. At the same time, the world does not have the luxury to postpone work on long- term issues-like climate change, energy security, nuclear proliferation, the fight against terrorism, possibility of a global pandemic, and endemic poverty.

There is growing consensus that we must deal with these issues before they become a crisis. The G-20 can play a unique and important role in addressing these issues collaboratively and informatively. There have been calls for the G-20 Leaders to explicitly commit to making the G-20 Leaders group a permanent global steering committee which would meet regularly, and have a clear and strong mandate. Heads of State have the political power to advance discussion and broker key compromises. Does this mean there is no role for the G-7/8? Indeed, there is. The G-7/8 can continue to meet as an assembly for industrial countries to discuss issues of mutual importance.

The G-7 Finance Minister and Central Bank Governors can play a critical role by laying the foundation and completing the groundwork on key global financial and economic issues to effectively prepare their Leaders to address them at G-20 summits. They can collaborate to collectively use a full range of policy tools to strengthen the global economy and stabilize financial markets. The G-7 countries also have considerable resources at their central banks and ministries of finance to devote to G-20 matters. The IMF is an organization of 185 countries. It oversees the international monetary system, and monitors the financial and economic policies of its members.

It keeps track of economic developments on a national, regional, and global basis. The IMF also provides guidance and training to low- and middle-income countries on how to upgrade institutions and design appropriate macroeconomic, financial, and structural policies. Lastly, the IMF provides loans to countries that have trouble meeting their international payments and cannot otherwise access financing on affordable terms. Most resources for IMF loans are provided by member countries.

The IMF also provides concessional loans to low-income countries to help them develop their economies and reduce poverty. These loans are financed through separate contribution-based trust funds funded by members, and the IMF itself. As a result of the global economic crisis, a number of countries have turned to the IMF for financial assistance. The IMF currently has about US$250 billion in financing capacity. IMF Managing Director Dominique Strauss-Kahn has called for a doubling of its resources. Japan has provided the IMF with a US$100 billion loan-the largest loan ever made by an IMF member country-but the institution needs an additional US$150 billion to deal with the current economic and financial crisis.

The upcoming G-20 Leaders Summit is expected to focus on ways to adequately resource the IMF. The world financial crisis has led many in the international community to question the IMF's ability to effectively deal with it, and its overall role and responsibilities in crisis prevention and management. The IMF's legitimacy has also been brought into question. The institution is run by an Executive Board composed of 24 Directors who are appointed or elected by member countries, or by groups of countries. The Managing Director has traditionally been a European. There have been calls for a more open, transparent and merit- based selection process to capture the confidence of emerging nations.

The voting structure of the IMF has also been criticized. Voice and influence is distributed largely according to economic weight and financial contribution, thus, developing countries have very little influence even though they are greatly affected by the IMF's work. Five of the 24 Directors are appointed by the members who constitute the five largest shareholders of the IMF (the United States, Japan, Germany, France and the United Kingdom). Collectively, these five Directors have 38.39 of the total votes. All other economies are grouped within 19 constituencies each represented by one Director. For example, 20 African countries are represented by a single Director and have a combined voting share of merely 3.01 percent.

Six South American countries are represented by a single Director and have a combined voting share of just 1.96 percent. The United States has 16.77 percent of the votes and veto power over special categories of important decisions. While IMF member nations approved reforms in March 2008 for developed countries to give up a fraction of their voting rights to the benefit of emerging and developing countries, it was criticized as inadequate. A strong case can be made for significantly realigning voting power to give developing nations a greater stake in the institution to enhance its legitimacy, effectiveness and relevance. U.S. Treasury Secretary Timothy Geithner said: "We need to send a strong signal that we are ready to give developing countries a voice within the IMF that is commensurate with their importance to the world economy."

There is great expectation for the upcoming G-20 Leader Summit to conclude with an inclusive package of IMF reforms that address these issues. The World Bank Membership in the World Bank is open to all 185 members of the IMF. The World Bank provides financial and technical assistance to developing countries. It consists of two development institutions-the International Bank of Reconstruction and Development (IBRD) which focuses on middle income and credit worthy poor countries, and the International Development Association (IDA) which focuses on the poorest countries. Together, they provide low-interest loans, interest-free credits and grants for investment in education, health, public administration, infrastructure, financial and private sector development, agriculture, and environmental and natural resource management.

Like the IMF, many believe the World Bank is in need of governance reform. The IBRD Board is comprised of 24 Executive Directors. The Executive Directors select a President, who traditionally has been an American. The Executive

Directors of the IBRD serve ex-officio as Directors of the IDA. Five of the 24 IBRD Executive Directors are appointed by the members who constitute the five largest shareholders of the Bank (currently the United States, Japan, Germany, France and the United Kingdom). Collectively, these five Executive Directors have 37.38 of the total votes. All other economies are grouped within 19 constituencies each represented by one Executive Director.

For example, 23 African countries are represented by a single Executive Director and have a combined voting share of only 1.92 percent. Six South American countries are represented by a single Executive Director and have a combined voting share of just 2.32 percent. Recently (February 2009), the World Bank's Board of Governors approved a proposal to create an additional seat for developing nations on its executive board-a chair for Sub-Saharan Africa. The Word Bank recognizes that "expanding the developing world's voice is central to delivering effective aid and promoting shared prosperity and development within a 21st century economic reality." The Bank will also undertake a comprehensive and intensive work program to move towards an equitable voting power between developed and developing countries.

While these are seen as steps in the right direction, there is broad support for more ambitions reforms to make the World Bank a more legitimate and inclusive institution that commands the confidence of developing nations. After all, developing nations (especially the poorest of countries) are the most affected by its work and in need of its services. As more countries become more active participants, ongoing coordination is important to enable timely decision-making and informed action.

The G-20 Leaders Summit is the opportune occasion to discuss and develop action plans to reconcile a number of global concerns. While the global financial and economic crisis is the top priority, the G-20 Leaders have reaffirmed the importance of the Millennium Development Goals and have indicated they are "committed to addressing other critical challenges such as energy security and climate change, food security, the rule of law, and the fight against terrorism, poverty and disease."

FINANCIAL AND ECONOMIC CRISIS

Since the G-20 Leaders met in Washington, DC in November, 2008, the outlook for the global economy has deteriorated significantly. Reflecting the seriousness of the situation, the global macroeconomic response has been unprecedented in both size and scope. Governments and central banks have utilized a variety of tools at their disposal aimed at stabilizing the financial system, including: reducing monetary policy rates to ensure access and affordability of credit for businesses and consumers; guaranteeing bank deposits and borrowing; purchasing bad assets; and injecting capital into financial institutions.

Most of the world's leading advanced and emerging economies have also injected significant fiscal stimulus focused largely on the expenditure side, in particular infrastructure spending. The G-7 countries combined have announced over $1.2 trillion in fiscal stimulus. Almost half of G-20 countries have announced cuts in personal income taxes and one-third have announced reductions in indirect taxes. About half of the G-20 countries have plans to cut corporate income taxes. The Bank of Canada believes the effects of the fiscal and monetary stimulus in place in Canada and globally to support the recovery will begin to be felt in the second half of 2009 and will build through 2010. However, "stabilization of the global financial system remains a precondition for the global and Canadian economic recoveries."

This means that international cooperation and coordination will continue to be critical in designing and implementing policies to strengthen credit markets and the economy. In November 2008, the Chambers of Commerce of the G-20 (including the Canadian Chamber of Commerce) issued a joint statement in advance of the G-20 Leaders Summit in Washington, DC. The statement is still relevant as we head into the April G-20 Leaders Summit in London, UK. "The G20 proposals should aim at strengthening supervisory structures at national and supranational level, and at enhancing cooperation between developed and emerging economies with the aim of reducing economic, monetary and trade global imbalances.

The quality of regulatory standards should be improved in the framework of a broad reform of the global financial system that must also include a higher degree of financial and macroeconomic surveillance and improved crisis prevention mechanisms, as well as early warning systems." Mark Carney, Governor of the Bank of Canada, expressed a similar view during his appearance before the House of Commons Standing Committee on Finance on February 10, 2009. "G-20 countries need to act in concert to improve domestic and international regulatory frameworks. In this regard, measures to improve transparency and integrity, to implement a macro-prudential approach to regulation, and to adequately resource the IMF are vital."

It is expected that the April G-20 Leaders Summit will culminate in a concrete action plan to address these issues. Bank of Canada Governor Mark Carney also made the case why emerging nations need to be at the table. "Key emerging markets not only have first-hand experience of financial crises but also are the major surplus countries who, as major capital providers, need to be part of a global solution."

INTERNATIONAL TRADING SYSTEM

The World Trade Organization (WTO) is the only global international organization dealing with the rules of trade between nations. It provides a forum for negotiating agreements aimed at reducing obstacles to international trade and ensuring a level playing field for all. The WTO also provides a legal and institutional framework for the implementation and monitoring of these agreements, as well as for settling disputes arising from their interpretation and application. It has 153 member nations. The Doha Round ('Doha Development Agenda') of the WTO negotiations was launched in late 2001 to create new market access opportunities and help developing countries gain more from trade liberalization.

Some eight years later, a deal on new trade rules has yet to be reached. The global economic recession has spurred calls to revive talks to promote trade, stave off protectionist actions, and promote an economic rebound. A successful conclusion to the Doha Round would be a boon to the global economy. The WTO estimates that a Doha deal would translate into an annual US$35 billion boost in agricultural trade. For trade in other goods, the expected global gain is as much as US$95 billion annually. For Canada, the benefits of a successful Doha Development Agenda would mean greater access for Canadian manufacturers in key markets, such as the EU.

There is also the possibility of even greater global market access through sector-specific agreements. Liberalization in the services sector could yield even greater benefits-Canada had received signals that new opportunities would be made available in areas such as environmental, energy and financial services. Pascal Lamy, Director-General of the WTO, issued a statement at the 2009 World Economic Forum in Davos, Switzerland expressing hope that the April 2nd, 2009 meeting of the G-20 Leaders will "provide further impetus" to the negotiations.

The April 2nd, 2009 Summit presents the G-20 Leaders with an excellent opportunity to reaffirm their commitment to reject protectionism, refrain from erecting new barriers to trade and investment, abstain from imposing new export restrictions, and avoid implementing WTO inconsistent measures to stimulate exports. It is important that the Leaders send a strong signal that they are committed to reaching an agreement "on modalities that leads to a successful conclusion to the WTO's Doha Development Agenda with an ambitious and balanced outcome."

Trade and foreign investment protectionist measures would further exacerbate the global economic crisis and pose risks to sustained growth. "Business is concerned that a panic-driven slide towards protectionism may prolong the economic slowdown", stated BIAC Secretary General Tadahiro Asami. He added: "Political leaders must resist the temptation to shield their industries from foreign trade and investment, as any measures to fence off domestic economies would deepen and widen the negative impact that the financial turmoil has already had on global growth and job creation." "It is essential to finalise the modalities for trade in agricultural and industrial products before the end of this year and to conclude the trade round successfully with meaningful results in 2009."

In the final analysis, international cooperation is necessary if there is to be a recovery in international trade. Respect for international trade rules will promote stability and economic growth. The fact the WTO is working with the World Bank and the IMF to improve the conditions for financing international trade is extremely encouraging.

CLIMATE CHANGE

There is general agreement in the international scientific community that reducing the buildup of greenhouse gas emissions in the atmosphere is fundamental to mitigating climate change. Canada is a member of the Kyoto Protocol, which contains emission reduction obligations for 36 industrialized countries. It requires no commitment from large emitters, like India and China. The United States did not ratify the Kyoto Protocol. As the 2012 expiration date of the Kyoto Protocol draws near, formal negotiations on a successor agreement have started under the auspices of the United Nations Framework Convention on Climate Change (UNFCCC) and its Kyoto Protocol. Signatories to the UNFCCC met in Poznan, Poland in December 2008.

The first draft of a concrete negotiating text will be available at a UNFCCC gathering in Bonn, Germany in June 2009. The goal is to enter into a new, binding global climate change agreement at the 15th Conference of the Parties to the UNFCCC in Copenhagen, Denmark in December 2009. At Poznan, the Kyoto Protocol's Adaptation Fund was finalized. The money is to be used to finance adaptation projects and programs in developing countries that are Parties to the Kyoto Protocol.

The UN expects the Adaptation Fund to grow to about US$300 million by 2012. There is recognition that this is only a fraction of what is needed. 19 Despite the current global financial crisis, the international community appears willing to make the necessary hard decisions when it comes to climate change. The United Kingdom, host of the April 2nd, 2009 G-20 Leaders Summit, is keen on keeping the momentum going towards an ambitious deal at Copenhagen. UK Secretary of State for Energy and Climate Change, Ed Milliband stated: "The start of 2009 is a crossroads moment on climate change."

"To stay on the path to a deal, 2009 must be a year of negotiation not discussion, and we all need to raise our game. Morally, we know the scale of the threat of a changing climate. Economically, we know that the costs of not acting outweigh the costs of acting, and the costs grow the longer we wait." The U.S. Department of State has appointed Todd Stern as its Special Envoy for Climate Change. He will serve as a principal advisor on international climate policy and strategy, and the Administration's chief climate negotiator. On a recent trip to Asia, he, and Secretary of State, Hillary Clinton, opened dialogue with China, Indonesia, Japan and South Korea on common approaches to the challenges facing the international community, including climate change.

In early February 2009, China's Ambassador to the United States, Zhou Wenzhong, stated that his government would welcome co-operation on energy and climate change with the United States. The April G-20 Leaders Summit offers an opportunity to develop a conceptual framework of ideas for the successor agreement to the Kyoto Protocol at Copenhagen-an agreement that includes all major economies and major greenhouse gas emitters, including the United States, China and India.

ENERGY SECURITY

Energy security, like climate change, is a complex issue with global reach, requiring global cooperation. The energy challenges are massive. The global population is expected to grow from over six billion today to more than 8 billion by 2030. The world will need at least 50 percent more energy in 2030 than it uses today. Energy is a driver of growth and development around the world. Greater competition for finite supplies will put pressure on prices, disproportionately affecting developing economies. The globalised nature of oil markets, and increasingly integrated natural gas market, imply that natural and geopolitical disruptions in one country can have major repercussion in other countries.

The upcoming G-20 Leaders Summit offers an opportunity to collaborate on developing a full range of short-term and long-term strategies to enhance global energy security, and foster economic growth and development. Such a strategy should include a focus on: ensuring stable and growing energy supplies through diversification; diversifying modes and routes of transit to lessen the impact of supply disruptions; better integrating electric, oil and gas transmission infrastructure systems; reducing energy demand by improving energy efficiency; accommodating rising demand from emerging market economies, like China and India; protecting pipelines, refineries, and shipping channels from terrorist aggression; promoting a gradual transition to market prices in the economies of the developing world to encourage more efficient utilization of limited world energy supplies; developing new technologies for cleaner, cheaper, and more reliable energy sources; and promoting energy security policies in developing countries.

AID AND GLOBAL POVERTY

In the long-term, global stability depends very much on reducing poverty. Recognizing this, the IMF and the World Bank collaborate closely with each other in the area of poverty reduction and helping countries draw up poverty reduction strategies. Both institutions routinely exchange information on country assistance. The OECD has issued a call to the world's main aid donor countries to stand by their development pledges, despite the economic downturn. History has shown that cutting back on aid during a recession has material negative consequences for developing countries' agricultural production, infrastructure investment, social welfare, and political stability. OECD Secretary-General Angel Gurría warned that the financial crisis is quickly turning into a social crisis.

According to the World Bank, almost 40 percent of 107 developing countries are highly exposed to the poverty effects of the crisis, and the remainder moderately exposed. World

Bank Group President, Robert B. Zoellick, said: "the global economic crisis threatens to become a human crisis in many developing countries unless they can take targeted measures to protect vulnerable people in their communities." He urged developed countries to allocate 0.7 percent of their fiscal stimulus packages to help poorer countries. For Canada, this would mean approximately $2.8 billion over the next two years. The economic downturn has systematically spread to developing countries.

It is expected that G-20 Leaders will acknowledge that sufficient, predictable, and effective flows of aid are more important than ever, pledging to do more. As a small, open, and export-dependent economy, it is in Canada's interest to ensure a well-functioning global governance architecture that promotes stable and sustainable economic growth, a sound financial system, and open and transparent trade and investment policies. At the April 2nd, 2009 G-20 Leaders Summit, Canada can lead by supporting dramatic and lasting change in global governance, including a permanent and more inclusive global steering committee-a Leaders 20 group-that reflects the economic and political realities of the 21st century.

Canada can also contribute ideas to reform multilateral institutions, and address global challenges and opportunities. Canada is well positioned to take a leadership role. We are a model for much of the world. Our financial sector has been recognized as being the strongest in the world thanks to effective regulatory and prudent practices. We were the first and chief proponent for a G-20 Leaders forum. We have a reputation as the world's leading multinational nation. Our fiscal and regulatory positions are healthier than most other nations. Canada has gained the world's respect for its significant efforts in debt reduction, and its aggressive debt cancellation policies.

Canada has taken a leadership role in establishing and financially contributing to the Global Health Fund to fight HIV/AIDS, malaria, and tubercsulosis. It has a great peacekeeping heritage, and it is making a difference on the ground in Afghanistan. As a multicultural nation, we understand the world. This is political capital for Canada in the international community. Let's put it to great use by recommending reforms and presenting solutions to address today's challenges and tomorrow's opportunities that serve our own interests and the global community at large in a balanced way.

For Canada, demonstrating greater leadership at the G-20 Leadership Summit and explicitly committing to making the G-20 Leaders group a permanent global steering committee is critically important for another reason-Canada risks finding itself no longer part of the G-7/8. The G-7 represents six of the seven largest economies by nominal GDP. In 2007, Canada was overtaken by China and Spain in terms of nominal GDP and was the world's ninth largest economy. In 2008, it was the world's 11th largest economy overtaken by China, Russia, Spain and Brazil.

The stakes are high. While we are proud of our accomplishments, a major rebalancing of global economic power is taking place. Canada must be prepared to take on a greater leadership role and to focus on what it does best-use of persuasive tools, negotiating, advocating for freer international trade and more representative organizations-to maintain its influence, protect and promote its interests, and increase its international competitiveness. New governance structures are needed to effectively manage knowledge based societies. In a knowledge society, knowledge is the key resource for development. To achieve its full impact, this knowledge must be widely accessible to all members of society.

These two important factors change our basic assumptions about power, privilege and influence within society. Building productive knowledge societies must start with these new assumptions and find ways to reorganize in order to make better use of knowledge. The challenge is to assure that all individuals, communities and nations gain access to and are able to use effectively, the knowledge they need to address their development challenges and improve their lives. Aim of Transforming Governance The concept of governance is complex and subjective. One definition of governance is "the process through which ... institutions, businesses and citizen's groups articulate their interests, exercise their rights and obligations, allocate human choices and opportunities, and mediate their differences".

Less formally, governance is characterized as "the process by which a society or organization steers itself". The aim of the Transforming Governance track will be to help the Global Knowledge Partnership (GKP) develop an understanding of new governance requirements and possibilities brought on by the information age. The track will examine the relationship between different levels of governance - including local, national, regional and global levels. It will attempt to improve our understanding of knowledge societies and the need for shared sovereignty concepts.

The governance track will identify possible approaches to strengthen civic participation in the governance process at all levels and help develop better social, economic, and political frameworks to support effective governance. The track will examine methods by which all partners (government, the private sector and civil society) can take part in the process of governance. It will examine how ICTs can broaden individual participation in society, especially by those previously without access to the governance structure. In sum, it will attempt to answer two related questions:

1. What is and should be different about governance in knowledge societies; and
2. What impacts should this new governance approach have on GKP partners and their programmes?

The Goal The goal is to create a shared framework for transforming governance that will provide a common language and a guide for prioritized action. A new framework will support a common view of the goals, purpose, and procedures of governance in knowledge societies. It will address the mounting development challenge for governance brought on by new technologies and examine how to create space for new non-state actors. It will attempt to alter the roles of government, the private sector, and civil society and examine more inclusive ways of governing. To achieve its goals the Transforming Governance working group will: develop frameworks on transforming governance, learn from ongoing examples of what has worked and what has not, work with Partners on new pilot schemes, and build a strong GKP governance network to share and develop learning on governance in the information age.

The Approach New governance issues will be examined as part of a learning process. This process involves a conceptual focus as well as one which addresses practical development issues within socio- economic-political dimensions. The proposed transforming governance issues will include:

a. An integrated approach: the creation of frameworks on transforming governance that will include a learning and evaluation system and a system for communicating new ideas;
b. A social focus: examine issues related to building capacity for inclusive, equitable and effective participation in society;
c. A political focus: examine sovereignty issues and the participatory decision-making processes required for productive and fair knowledge societies; and
d. An economic focus: examine issues related to governance and the market.

The Transforming Governance track must be focussed and practical, yet at the same time address the vast spectrum of key governance issues in the information age. Our input will be strategic in nature rather than involve significant financial and programming inputs. In order to develop a broader understanding of the issue, innovative models of governance in knowledge societies will be evaluated for lessons learned. Through this process, we hope to gain a better understanding of what new governance issues are a priority and how to best govern them. This new understanding would help shape partners' actions and programs.

The transforming governance working group will address its development issues by creating:

a. Issue Frameworks: Each issues item will have a framework that will be based on the Global Knowledge concepts of greater partnerships. The framework will examine closer state collaboration with civil society and the private sector and will focus on knowledge as a key input to security/ prosperity for the individual and society. It will focus on the specific issue items, and create a conceptual framework within which specific action items can be undertaken.

b. A Learning and Evaluation System: Each issues item must have a research and learning component, within which ongoing activities would be analysed within the parameters of the new framework to gain a better understanding of governance in the Information Age.
c. Communicating Ideas: The issue items must develop an awareness program with key stakeholders on the new framework and its implications for development in the Information Age.
d. Creation of Governance Networks: Each issue item should develop specific governance networks of interested partners to examine different roles to address the action items of transforming governance.

Four Issue Items of the Transforming Governance Track Following is the list of four Issue Items and possible action items the Transforming Governance working group is proposing for discussion at the GKP Action Summit:

Integrated Governance Approach New technologies and the creation of knowledge based societies have increased the connection between economic, social and political issues surrounding governance.

For example, what previously had been simple trade issues are now becoming complex issues dealing with the environment, labour, sovereignty and a range of other factors. New approaches are required to bring together all key stakeholders, especially those previously excluded from the process, around shared goals and objectives. The working group will develop an overarching framework to help consider these issues from a Global Knowledge perspective. It will incorporate and create cohesion between the work being done on the three issue items concerning the social, political and economic dimensions of development.

The framework will serve as a basis on which learning will occur and priorities will be identified. Possible action items: Creation of Theoretical Framework to Discuss Development and Governance in the Information Age.

Sovereignty in the Information Age: Concepts and Instruments (political dimension) Under the old international system, governance was predominantly guided by the state.

Through the use of new technologies, governance structures increasingly transcend the state by collaborating with sub-national and transnational private sectors and civil society. While governments can produce a conducive political, economic and legal environment, it is civil society that can facilitate political and social interaction and mobilize groups to take part in economic, social and political activities. New technologies are changing the way we interact with government by increasing the "horizontalisation" of the governance structure. The breakdown of the vertical structures in our societies leads to increased horizontal interaction where a multitude of individual decisions are taken.

The transfer of power and sovereignty from the state is occurring in three directions - upwards to global markets, downwards to sub-national groups and horizontally through interdependence. In knowledge societies many of the old rules of sovereignty no longer apply. Actions within one sovereign state increasingly have an immediate and direct impact on other sovereign states. This raises issues surrounding national sovereignty and legitimacy. Individuals and non-state actors are increasingly questioning governments' authority for actions influencing their lives. Faced with new ICTs, increased democracy, changes in the global political milieu, and social/ economic/environmental problems without boundaries, good governance is central to directing the prosperity of all individuals.

The new forms of governance must be holistic and more widely participatory. They must balance the various levels of local and regional governance with the needs and interests of their local and regional societies. The need to create a harmony between local and global governance offers new opportunities for development activities in forms that are quite different from current international development practice. Possible action items:

- Global Taxation
- Governance of Legal Systems
- Governance of the Financial Markets
- Asymmetrical Governance Structures
- Multilateral Processes
- Urban Governance

BUILDING CAPACITY FOR EQUITABLE AND EFFECTIVE PARTICIPATION IN SOCIETY

The presence of a diverse and active civil society is central to the notion of governance in all cultures. The concept of good governance conveys to people and institutions the need to recognize rights, assume roles, accept responsibilities and nurture relationships premised upon mutual trust and respect. Good governance empowers citizens and creates an enabling environment to yield a better quality of life, eradicate poverty, and ensure sustainable development. It hinges on equal partnership, collective wisdom, co-operation and responsible action on the part of all actors in governance and society.

Enabling conditions such as freedom of association, laws and regulations that create a space for citizen participation, a supportive tax code, and freedom of the press and of expression, is important ingredients for the growth and formation of a healthy civil society. The new citizens of the information age now have the tools needed to assist their debut onto the world stage. The central ingredient to the creation of knowledge societies is to increase the individual access and ability to use the new tools to better their lives.

The goal of the Governance track is to ensure that the new global citizen not only has access to these tools, but also a space within which they can articulate their concerns and reach their full potential. These major changes require a broad consensus and a shared framework created in partnership with civil society and traditional governance institutions. The framework must focus on improving the welfare of the individual to allow them a place within their local governance structure. As the communities and perspectives that make up civil society become more numerous and diverse, the process of constructing shared frameworks across boundaries becomes increasingly important and difficult.

To govern effectively in the information age, the need to create a community of discourse among people with different perspectives, languages and interests is increasingly apparent. Possible action items:

- Expanding participation in decision making for those previously excluded from the process
- Building an enabling policy environment for expanded access to knowledge
- Bottom-up versus top-down approaches in governance
- Open space for contentious criticism and advocacy as a means to empower citizens

Governance and the Market (economic dimension) Governance structures are necessary to ensure that through the use of ICTs, the fruits of development are equitably distributed. Responses to these challenges reside in the areas of: policy and regulatory frameworks; public and private investment in infrastructure; incentives and institutions to foster change; and training and capacity building. These responses are interrelated and each nation and community must create an approach that is appropriate to their needs within their own social and cultural context. These new tri-sectoral partnerships (government-private sector-civil society) require innovative forms of governance.

In some cases self-regulation by the private sector will provide the appropriate measures, while in others, civil society organizations and the state apparatus will continue to play a role. Countries can address governance issues in the information age with new international agreements, global institutions and standards, and with user-fees on commercial exploitation of the global commons. More research is needed into the developmental and ethical impacts of ICTs and global markets on copyright and other contract laws. Structures should be implemented to protect vulnerable financial markets from defective information. ICTs may also give rise to new types of countervailing powers, such as globally active NGOs drawing on the Internet's capability to instantly broadcast information world-wide and the ability to harmonize their lobbying campaigns.

If world-wide (technical) standards for the ICT industry are set by market players or by governments, then new institutions may be needed to cope with this governance issue. Possible action items:

- Governance of Intellectual Property Rights.
- Governance of the Internet.
- Legal and regulatory frameworks for the liberalization of markets and privatization the telecommunication industry.
- Corporate Governance & Governance of Transnational Corporations.
- Self-Governance and transparency by Market Challenges and Opportunities.

In the wake of the demonstrations that accompanied the Third Ministerial Meeting of the World Trade Organization in Seattle, the World Economic Forum Meeting at Davos, and the 10th UN Conference on Trade and Development in this city, more and more questions are being asked about the path that globalisation is taking, doubts are being raised about the wisdom of that path, and calls are being made-both in developed and developing countries — for reform by some, and for abolition by others, of the WTO, which has become the main symbol of a globalizing world.

As parliamentarians, you are in a unique position to participate in the debate and contribute to its clarification and to its resolution, both in your own countries and in official international forums. Three possible outcomes are possible, depending on how issues are resolved: a world where unhampered market forces overwhelm state institutions and indigenous social cultures, a managed globalisation where equity is at least as strong a driving force as efficiency, or a protectionist world where flows of trade, investment and information are obstructed in the name of nationalism. Obviously, the stakes are high. This chapter hopes to provide the participants of this conference an overview of globalisation and the issues surrounding it. We start, in the next section, by attempting to define globalisation, providing illustrations of what it is all about.

There is no use reinventing the wheel. Most of the materials presented in this overview are drawn from the 1997 and 1999 Human Development Reports (HDR) of the UNDP, which in turn draw from several commissioned background papers and special contributions as well as a very rich lode of research done on different aspects of globalisation.

The 1999 HDR deals entirely with globalisation, while the 1997 HDR devotes one chapter to it. They are highly recommended as reading material, as are the other HDR's, which have been published yearly since 1990. Needless to say, the responsibility for any errors made in my attempts to summarize and reformat the information for this conference. Globalisation may be defined in several ways, and from different perspectives. One can talk about globalisation as the widening and deepening of international flows of trade, finance and information in a single, integrated global market. An alternative would be to describe it as the increasing linkages between the world's people (including the international spread of cultures...as well as diseases and crime) as natural and artificial barriers fall.

Or, one can refer to it as the transformation (shrinking) of the world into a global village, as borders disappear, distances shrink, and time shortens. The fall of natural barriers, the shrinking of space and time, can be illustrated by the trend in sea and air transport costs as well as the costs of communication. Average ocean freight and port charges per ton fell by more than two-thirds between 1920 and 1990, from US$95 (in 1990 US$) to $29. Air transport costs have decreased even more, and travel times have also been shortened.

Average revenue per passenger mile fell by more than 80% between 1930 and 1990, from US$0.68 to US$0.11. In 1950, it took four days to fly from Manila to New York. It now takes under a day. The largest cost and time reductions have occurred in communications. The cost of a 3-minute international call between New York and London fell from US$245 (in 1930) to US$32 in 1970 to US$3 in 1990. At present, it costs less than US$0.10. Documents can now be transmitted by fax in a matter of minutes, and by e-mail instantaneously, compared to days, weeks, and even months half a century ago.

The cost of computers in 1960 was 125 times what they were in 1990, which in turn were more than double what they cost now. Artificial or man-made barriers to trade such as tariffs and quotas have also been brought down. Other artificial barriers of a more political and social nature, such as the cold war and apartheid have likewise been toppled. In 1947, average tariffs on manufactured imports were 47%, but by 1980 they were down to 6%, and by the time the Uruguay Round is fully implemented, they will go down to 3%. At the same time, controls over the flows of capital have been lifted, particularly after the Bretton Woods system of fixed exchange rates broke down in 1971, with developed countries leading the way, and developing countries following, encouraged in no small degree by the Bretton Woods institutions and the OECD.

The same trend is observable with regard to foreign exchange flows. It must be pointed out, however, that globalisation is not a new phenomenon. It has happened before, probably even on a larger scale, as was the case over a century ago. Towards the end of the nineteenth century, trade flows were roughly the same proportion of national income as they are today, while capital transfers were relatively even larger, and movements of people far greater than they are today, when immigration is much more restricted. What is different about the current globalisation is not so much the scale of flows, but their character.

While it has become a dominant force in the last decade of the twentieth century as it was in the last decade of the nineteenth, it has new features: new markets (e.g., globally linked financial markets working around the clock with new instruments, global consumer markets with global brands, e-commerce), new actors (e.g., multinational corporations, the World Trade Organization, proliferation of international NGO's, regional blocs, policy coordination groups), new rules (multilateral agreements in trade, conventions on human rights, on global environment), and new tools of communication (e.g., cell phones, faxes, e-mail).

IMPACT OF GLOBALISATION

Globalisation has many positive, innovative and dynamic aspects, all related to the increased market access, increased access to capital, and increased access to technology and information which have led to greater income and employment opportunities. There is no dearth of examples: The world as a whole is definitely more prosperous and more healthy, with average per capita incomes tripling in the last fifty years, child mortality rates halving and life expectancy increasing by ten years since 1965.

Trade flows also increased 12-fold in the past fifty years as a result of the removal of natural and artificial barriers. Exports are now US$7 trillion a year, with more than a fifth of the world's goods and services being traded. Capital flows expanded even faster, with Foreign Direct Investment amounting to US$400 billion in 1997, seven times its real level in the 1970's and portfolio and other short-term capital flows amounted to US$2 trillion in gross terms, three times what they were in the '80's.

These in turn pale in comparison with what has happened in the foreign exchange markets, where volumes increased over a hundred times between the mid-70's and the mid-90's, with a US$1.5 trillion daily turnover in 1998. At the same time, international bank lending grew more than sixteen times, from US$265 million in 1973 to US$4.2 trillion in 1994. The Uruguay Round of the General Agreement on Tariffs and Trade (GATT), which has given globalisation greater impetus in the last decade, is expected to increase global income by an estimated US$212-US$510 billion (from trade and efficiency gains and higher rates of return on capital) by 2001. Movements of people have also increased.

Tourism more than doubled between 1980 and 1996, from 260 million to 590 million travellers a year. Despite tight restrictions, international migration continues to grow, and workers' remittances amounted to US$58 billion in 1996. In the information and communications area, time spent on international telephone calls more than doubled between the first and second half of the last decade-from 33 billion minutes in 1990 to 70 billion minutes in 1996. At the same time, travel, the internet and the media have stimulated an exponential growth in the exchange of ideas and information: 28,000 international NGO's in 1993 where there were less than 600 in 1964.

As of mid-1998, there were an estimated 139 million internet users, with the number of new subscribers doubling every year. The revolution in information and communication technology, for example, have allowed people in the remotest villages access to the most modern medical advice, while the potential for education is tremendous.

The Disturbing News

While the world as a whole has benefited from globalisation, there are negative and marginalizing aspects of globalisation. These are what have led to a backlash, as reflected to a certain extent in the demonstrations by civil society accompanying recent international conferences, and by increasing expressions of dissatisfaction at the governmental level.

Unbalanced Distribution of Benefits

The first negative aspect of globalisation is that its gains are not equally distributed, both between and within countries. Examples of the badly skewed distribution among countries of the benefits of globalisation can be gleaned from the following data from the period1980 to 1997: While world per capita income increased, per capita income contracted in fifty nine countries, widening income disparities. Exports of goods and services grew at less than 5% annually in 46 countries, and at less than 1% a year in 9 countries.

Insofar as financial flows are concerned, the majority (58%) of flows of foreign direct investment in the '90's went to developed countries. 85% of the FDI that went to developing and transition economies went to only 20 countries, with the bottom sixteen of these receiving less than what the top two got. And for nine countries, the flows have been negative. The distribution of portfolio and other short-term flows is even worse: 94% of these went to only 20 countries in 1997, with the bottom 13 of these countries receiving less in total than the top two. Finally, only twenty-five developing countries have access to private markets for bonds, commercial bank loans and portfolio equity.

The benefits from the Uruguay Round are also expected to be unbalanced, with 70% accruing to the developed countries and 30% to the developing countries. Among developing countries, China is expected to get the lion's share (27% of the 30%). The most excluded from the benefits of globalisation are the Least Developed Countries (LDCs) and Sub-Saharan Africa. They are actually expected to lose as things stand-US$600 million and US$1.2 billion a year respectively. What all these mean is that while the world has shrunk into a global village, the gap between the rich and the poor in that village is widening. Hundreds of millions of people are being excluded from the benefits of globalisation.

The information and communication technology revolution, which is regarded as the newest sinew of globalisation, has created a gap of its own-the so-called digital divide. The exponential growth of internet users adverted to earlier masks tremendous disparities: In 1998, industrial countries accounting for 15% of the world's population had 88 per cent of internet users. In contrast, South Asia, home to 20% of that population, had less than one per cent of the internet users, while Sub-Saharan Africa, with 9.7% of the world's people, had only 0.1 per cent connected to the internet.

Unbalanced distribution of benefits

The benefits of globalisation are also badly skewed within countries, both developing and developed. Income inequality is rising in many countries, particularly in the OECD countries. Worse, job and income insecurity is increasing, particularly for unskilled labor, although corporate restructuring has also meant job insecurity for professionals. Within developing countries, the increased world agricultural prices expected to result from the Uruguay Round should benefit those in agriculture.

The urban poor will suffer when food prices rise, but will gain from employment in new export industries. Young women hired by multinationals are likely to benefit most-their incomes increase, with a concomitant increase in their household status. Consumers also gain from the reduction in local prices due to increased competition from abroad.

Financial Volatility

Unbalanced benefit flows are not the only negative aspects of globalisation. Globally integrated markets have financial volatility as a permanent feature, the frequency of financial crises increasing with the growth in international capital flows. The human costs of such financial volatility can be very high, as shown by the effects of the Asian crisis-bankruptcies, poverty increase, rising unemployment, reduced schooling, reduced public services, and increased social stress and fragmentation-in short, a reversal in human development.

Contagion

The closer linkages that characterize globalisation also allow for contagion and worldwide recession, or at least slowdown. The Asian crisis had repercussions everywhere — in South America, Russia, Africa, the Middle East-which were affected either directly or indirectly. More human insecurity: crime, disease, and loss of cultural identity. Unfortunately, the many opportunities opened up by the widening and deepening of information flows and contacts among the world's people also include increasing opportunities for crime (trafficking in drugs, weapons, women, international syndicates), for the spread of HIV/AIDS as well as ideas, and for the flow of culture and cultural products which may lead to cultural homogenisation, which, while considered enriching by some, is considered as a loss of cultural identity by others.

IMPACT ON WOMEN

The impact of globalisation on women is also mixed. As adverted to earlier, greater trade openness increases women's share of paid employment, as firms producing for export (including multinationals) employ more female workers. This is a worldwide pattern, and is particularly evident in Asia. However, women are also among the first to lose their employment when economic crunches occur, such as those resulting from financial volatility discussed above. Women also predominate in informal subcontracting, which is on the rise under globalisation-but this is associated with low wages and poor conditions.

Globalisation is also associated with homework, part-time work, and tele-work, where women again predominate. The upside here, is that this accommodates women's family care obligations, but the downside is that the jobs are precarious and poorly paid.

FACTORS CONTRIBUTING TO THE UNBALANCED IMPACT OF GLOBALISATION

While there are several reasons to which the skewed flows of globalisation's benefits can be attributed, they can be grouped under three main headings: Bad Policy, Bad Terms, and Bad Rules. The first has to do with national policy failures, and the other two are the result of international forces.

Bad Policy

Trade and investment flows to countries are impeded by poor macroeconomic policy that leads to chronically large fiscal deficits, which creates instability. Investors, as well as exporters, are also discouraged by policies that lead to an overvalued currency, and by policies that overprotect local producers for long periods, with their concomitant bureaucratic procedures (leading to delays and corruption) and lack of incentive to gear up for international competition. Additionally, policies that lack transparency or consistency make for unpredictability and uncertainty, which lead foreign investors and local businesspersons to adopt a wait-and-see attitude, a state of suspended animation.

Neglecting investments in human capital as reflected in the low priorities given to basic health and education (low human priority expenditure ratio) in the government budget is a sin of omission which has large negative implications: without basic skills, people cannot take advantage of changing market conditions, apply, much less create new technology, or shift to more sophisticated exports. Likewise, neglect of investment in infrastructure-transport and communication-again makes it difficult to access global opportunities.

Lack of farm to market roads constrains exports; lack of communication facilities isolates a country and its people from the benefits of the revolution in information and communication technology. It is well to note that these bad policies, which really indicate poor governance, would hamper a country's development in any case, with or without globalisation. Globalisation merely exacerbates the effects of bad policy, just as it would tend to increase the rewards of good policy.

Bad Terms

The responsibility for the limited or negative benefits of globalisation cannot all be laid on the shoulders of the developing country governments. The terms under which trade and finance take place often are very unfavorable. Between 1980 and 1990, for example, real commodity prices fell by 45%, as a result of which developing countries as a whole suffered cumulative terms-of-trade losses amounting to US$291 billion. The terms of trade for developing countries' manufactured goods also fell by 35% between 1970 and 1991 Terms of finance are also unfavorable for poor countries. They generally have to pay higher interest rates than the rich countries do, if they can access credit at all.

This makes debt servicing much more difficult, and limit the resources available for trade and investment. Seventeen years after the onset of the international debt crisis, the problem of highly indebted poor countries has not yet been resolved. Recently, because of the disastrous floods that have wiped out the development gains of a poor country like Mozambique, its official creditors (Paris Club) decided to postpone its payments-until June of this year. Which doesn't really help Mozambique's situation?

To make matters worse, even flows of people from developing countries can be on unfavorable terms. Developed countries prefer those who are highly skilled, contributing to the brain drain problems of the developing world. Refugees are admitted rather grudgingly, but facto if those with capital to invest are welcome with open arms.

Bad Rules

De facto if not *de jure*, the rules of the game are stacked against developing countries, and the Uruguay Round (UR), which created the rules-based World Trade Organization, has not changed the situation very much. Most of the protection for industry and agriculture in industrial countries was left intact. Part of the dissatisfaction with the WTO is the perception that the issues it addresses are those which concern the developed countries, brushing aside those of interest to the developing world. Moreover, there remains a very large scope for evading the spirit, if not the letter of the UR agreements.

Some examples: Tariff reductions for goods from industrial countries were greater (45%) than those coming from developing countries (20-25%). Tariff escalation-setting higher tariffs on processed goods than on raw materials-which discourages developing countries from adding value to their exports, is still very much in practice. Non-tariff barriers, particularly anti-dumping measures have been used as an excuse for protection by developed countries, who have take advantage of the vague rules about what constitutes dumping, and have applied them to a wide range of developing country exports.

The enforcement of Intellectual Property Rights (IPR) have increased the cost of technology transfers to developing countries, which, in an increasingly knowledge-intensive global economy, reduces their ability to take advantage of opportunities that globalisation offers. At the same time, the provisions on special and differential treatment in favor of developing countries have not yet been fully implemented and operationalised, and labor markets have not been opened to the same extent as capital markets. Moreover, tariffs remain high on goods with the greatest potential for the poorest countries, as in textiles and agricultural commodities.

MAKING THE MOST OUT OF GLOBALISATION

The Choices: Given this picture of globalisation, warts and all, is it worth keeping? What is to be done? As mentioned at the outset, there are three alternatives: one is to maintain the status quo-that is to say, the present situation is to continue, a globalisation that is exclusive and marginalizing, that increases human insecurity and vulnerability, even as it opens tremendous opportunities. Judging from the increasing volume of protests heard around the world, this alternative is becoming more and more unacceptable.

A second alternative would be to move the clock back, as it were, at least to pre-WTO, and even pre-Uruguay Round era – that is to say, to abolish the WTO, which has become the symbol of globalisation. Those who favor this alternative argue that WTO is too powerful and has encroached upon the sovereignty of different countries by forcing them, for example, to accept free-trade rules over other legitimate concerns such as food safety; Or they argue that WTO was completely dominated by industrialized countries and therefore beyond repair.

Those who are attracted to this alternative, however, will probably be brought up short when they realize that flawed as it is, the WTO still represents a rule-based system with a system of dispute settlements that has been successfully used, albeit infrequently, by small countries against larger, more powerful ones. They will be giving this up for one which is based on old-style power politics in trade negotiations, with very little means of redress for the poorer players — where the golden rule is that "he who has the gold, rules".

Clearly, if the present situation is beginning to result in a backlash, but the alternative of switching back the clock may put the world in a worse situation than before, the only truly acceptable alternative is to manage globalisation better, so that its downside-inequality, instability, insecurity, can be minimized, and its benefits maximized. Fortunately, the negative trends are not inevitable. They can be reversed.

Governance is the Key

A closer look at the downside of globalisation strongly suggests that underlying all these negative results is a failure of governance-either at the national level, or at the global level, or both. By governance is meant not mere government, but the framework of rules, institutions and established practices that set limits and give incentives for the behavior of individuals, organizations, and firms. It is the lack of good governance at the national level that contributes to bad policy. It is the lack of good governance at the international level that has contributed to bad terms and bad rules.

And finally, it is the lack of good governance at both levels that has contributed to financial volatility which has led to contagion, and in some cases, civil conflict, the international spread of crime and disease, and the rise of other forms of human insecurity. This is not a surprising conclusion. Basic economics teaches us that the magic of the market — the most efficient allocation of resources — works only under very stringent conditions: pure competition, no externalities, mobility, and information.

Absent any of these, market failures occur. Government's role is to correct those market failures. But even without market failures (which is not the case in global markets) , even with the most efficient outcomes-the magic of the market gives no assurance of equity, stability, and growth, which are at least equally important goals. Government must use its visible hand to ensure that these objectives are met. Good government, that is, because there is danger of government failure as well. At present, while there are no formal institutional arrangements, the current de facto situation is that a few developed country governments (G-7 and even G-1) directly and through multilateral institutions controlled by them (e.g., the World

Bank, the IMF, the Bank of International Settlements), have the reins of international economic governance firmly in their hands.

It is this governance that has failed to get the most from the opportunities and avoiding the pitfalls of globalisation, because of the paucity and inadequacy of institutions, norms of conduct, and regulatory frameworks to address issues of inequity, instability, and responsibility in the international economy. The challenge lies in reforming global governance so that global competition and free market approaches can be harmonized with human development and human rights in all countries. Always acknowledging, of course, that even with good global governance, lack of good local governance a developing country will still find itself excluded and marginalized from the benefits of globalisation. In brief, good global and national governance go hand in hand, with both placing people, not just profits, squarely in the center of policy and action.

Agenda for Action

There is no dearth of "solutions" to the problems of globalisation, requiring either national or international action or a combination of both. While they may differ from country to country depending on the cultural and historical contexts in which they take place, certain key elements common to all can be highlighted: At the national level, appropriate economic and social policies are needed to capture global opportunities trade, capital flows and migration, and to protect people against the vulnerabilities that globalisation creates.

For example, national governments can manage trade and capital flows more carefully; invest in human capital and in more flexible sets of workers skills, which are of prime importance; foster small enterprises-these will contribute to job-creating growth; manage new technology; and provide safety nets. It must be noted that this already tall order is made more difficult because governments are faced with a resource squeeze: they collect less revenues because of lower tariffs and import duties, tax competition with other countries, the globalisation of the tax base (increasing transnational operations) and the growth of the informal economy.

At the same time, they are faced with greater demands on public resources. At both the national and global level, the governance challenge is to reduce the threats of financial volatility, which have become increasingly common, and all their human costs. The costs of governance failures in this arena are very much larger than generally perceived. The East Asian crisis and its global repercussions resulted in output losses (over a three-year period) estimated at nearly US$2 trillion, while the human costs include civil conflict, rising unemployment and declining school attendance, erosion of the social fabric, more crime, more violence in the home.

At the national level, emphasis should be given to liberalizing the capital accounts more carefully, subjecting financial institutions to greater transparency and accountability, integrating macroeconomic management and social policies. At the international level, the focus should be on strengthening international action to regulate and supervise banking systems, developing better systems of early warning and crisis management, and establishing an international lender of last resort.

At the global level, stronger action must be taken to tackle global threats to human security (crime, disease, environmental degradation), reverse the marginalization of poor, small countries, remedy the imbalances in the structure of global governance with new efforts to create a more inclusive system, and build a more coherent and democratic architecture for global governance in the 21st century. Again, it must be noted that the difficulties of reinventing or reforming global governance is extremely difficult, because it involves changing the status quo, which tends to meet with stiff opposition from those (in this case, the wealthy countries) who benefit from the status quo.

ROLE OF PARLIAMENTARIANS

As mentioned in the beginning of this chapter , parliamentarians are in a unique position to contribute to the successful management of globalisation, particularly in reinventing national and global governance. Their role can be divided into three different, but inter-related areas of information, identification and alliance building. Their role in the information area involves participation in activities that would raise the capacity of civil society groups as well as government groups (including themselves-this conference is a first step) to analyze and participate in the process of globalisation and to transform their economies to minimize risk and maximize benefits.

These could include parliamentary inquiries on the kind of national machinery in place to deal with globalisation, and seeing to it that they have the flexibility, technical expertise, institutional memory and political clout to handle the complexities of globalisation. These could also include seminars and forums on different aspects of globalisation (e.g., agriculture, textiles, intellectual property rights, biotechnology, labor), where the views of the stakeholders are heard, and their fears (or hopes) dealt with. In short, any activity that would help the nation as well as local communities understand the developments and be ahead instead of behind them, and help them be active and informed participants in whatever decisions need to be made. This is, after all, part of empowering the people.

There are areas of key interest that have to be identified, and hard choices that have to made. The question of the trade-off between protecting culture and a traditional valued way of life, and global integration, must be debated and resolved. Several slices of this major topic immediately suggest themselves: how fast should trade and capital flows be liberalized? Should multinationals be welcomed with open arms, or viewed with hostility and suspicion? Are they threat or opportunity? What is the tradeoff between the foreign exchange generated by overseas workers and the possible brain drain and erosion of the social fabric? Between efficiency and equity, between profits and people, what should be the priority? What are the next steps? Parliamentarians must encourage, and be part of this debate.

Decisions about development strategy must be an open, participatory and transparent process, if they are to be "owned" by the people. Without social consensus, as multilateral institutions have learned, no change can be sustainable. Whether at the national or at the international level, the creation and reform of institutions, norms of conduct, and regulatory frameworks-in other words, the strengthening or reinvention of governance-will require strong alliances both within and between countries to help overcome the forces that are content with the status quo.

For peaceful, sustained reform to take place-alliances, partnerships and negotiated compromises are the key-and parliamentarians, to my mind, have a comparative advantage, or at least better experience than most in winning broad and diverse support. A clear, shared vision of the future that hopefully is the result of the information and identification processes described above, is the first step in mobilizing alliances and partnerships. A second step would be to find or create common interests among the stakeholders: between employers and employees, between beneficiaries and providers, between urban and rural poor. This is a particular challenge to the parliamentarians, and again, the information and identification processes will help in the search.

At the same time, there is a need to exploit differences among the powerful countries, who may have different interests at different times. Here, parliamentarians can touch base with organizations such as UNCTAD and UNDP for help in creating negotiating strategies. But in intellectually and politically empowering the people, identifying priorities, and pushing the right buttons to achieve the common goals, parliamentarians must not forget their basic responsibility-they must keep their eye on the ball, so to speak: and that is to ensure that at all times, the state machinery, which they in part run, is an enabling one, acting in the common interest or in the interest of poor people, rather than a disabling one, which runs counter to those interests.

The 1990s have been marked by the global spread of democratic ideals and the globalisation of the market economy. Indeed, alternative models of political organization and modes of economic management have been nearly supplanted by the hegemony of the neo-liberal precepts underpinning the so-called" Washington consensus,' which advocates deregulation, liberalization, fiscal discipline, monetary rigor and trade liberalization. A principal challenge for the new century is to build modes of global governance that are both adequate and adaptive to the changing nature of world affairs.

International security, conflict management, economic and social justice, sustainable development, poverty alleviation and reduction, democratization œ all these issues require global frameworks, especially given the inadequacy of local, national and regional regulatory mechanisms for addressing them. Moreover, a myriad of new actors (inter-, non- and state actors operating at the sub-, infra-, supra- or trans-national level) have become involved in global affairs, challenging the traditional role of the state and, indeed, the underpinnings of the Westphalian system as a whole.

Furthermore, existing global governance arrangements have been found lacking with respect to efficiency, equity and democracy. As a result, alternative approaches and innovative solutions are needed to reform the institutions, norms and practices of global governance. During individual presentations and group workshops, participants considered the global challenges of managing conflict, pursuing economic prosperity and ecological sustainability, and ensuring human rights, global health, democratic governance and effective security.

One concern was central to all these discussions: the need to achieve modes of global governance that can mediate the differentiated processes associated with globalisation and the inequities that tend to ensue from such processes. An interceding influence, it was argued, is essential to ensuring equitable and sustainable development, the protection of human rights, the promotion of human health, and the preservation of the global commons. It is also required to infuse globalised interactions with increased transparency, accountability and representation of the needs, beliefs and values of those people who are marginalized despite œ and sometimes because of globalisation.

In general, participants agreed that the solution for managing global governance lies not in the establishment of a rigid supra-national governance framework. Rather, they focused on exploring innovations in agendas, concepts, institutions, instruments and analytical methods designed to more effectively address global issues through flexible, multi-layered and dynamic mechanisms. Many rich and novel ideas emerged during the workshop.

These insights can be captured in six main categories of innovations: refinements in the agenda of global governance; novel concepts and discourses relating to global governance; creative institutional mechanisms of global governance; improved tactics for shaping global governance; new reconstructions of the deeper social structures that underlie global governance; and more effective methods for the study of global governance.

INNOVATIONS IN GLOBAL GOVERNANCE

The following paragraphs attempt to capture and synthesize the main conclusions and recommendations.

1. *Nuclear Non-proliferation*: The Kargil conflict between India and Pakistan of May-July 1998 demonstrated the ineffectiveness and even failure of international nonproliferation regimes such as the Comprehensive Nuclear Test Ban Treaty (CTBT) and the Nuclear Nonproliferation Treaty (NPT). This blatant breach of the international norm against the horizontal spread of nuclear weapons demonstrates that it is not as strong as the norm against the use of these weapons. The international community's attitude toward India and Pakistan proves that the proliferation issue has been subsumed by other concerns such as economic cooperation in the case of India, and international terrorism in the case of Pakistan. Until the norm against the spread of nuclear weapons becomes as strong as the norm against their use, the world is destined to live with de facto nuclear powers like India and Pakistan.
2. *Transnational Security Threats*. Governments have identified the unique nature of transnational security threats like

drug smuggling, but there is a clear disconnect between the nature of these threats and the state-centric manner in which governments have responded to them. The tendency of governments to focus on the security challenge posed, rather than the transnational nature of the threat, precludes the consideration of less state-centric responses. Study of international responses to transnational threats outside the traditional security realm, such as those posed by substandard international shipping, can inform more effective responses to emerging transnational security threats.

3. *The Role of the United Nations*. Within the United Nations system, innovations in the global governance agenda include a shift away from traditional definitions of [national?] security towards an enlarged concept of human security. This notion is characterized by an increasing emphasis on conflict prevention as well as attempts to define criteria for humanitarian intervention and to establish guidelines for corporations in zones of conflict.

   The assumption behind these policy innovations is that the UN has the capabilities necessary to construct a universal doctrine of human security œ one that would be considered legitimate not only by all states, but also by all peoples. Nevertheless, the new human security agenda runs the risk of reinforcing the already serious North-South divide. The lack of participation both by developing nations and by populations affected by conflicts in UN decision-making structures remains a major obstacle to the possibility of the UN constructing a consistent and legitimate basis for a universally accepted doctrine of human security.

4. *National Human Rights Institutions* (NHRIs), which have proliferated since the 1990s, both provide an opportunity to embed international norms in domestic structures and present a series of intertwined challenges. In order to be effective, NHRIs must be granted political, organizational and financial independence from governments. Moreover, in designing NHRIs, international standards should be tailored to match the local context. In addition, it would

be adequate to devote resources to strengthening, and not just creating, NHRIs. Furthermore, closer links among transnational networks of NHRIs ought to be forged and, finally, new international rules devised for accommodating emerging actors like NHRIs.

5. *Protecting Civilians during Conflict*. One of the most disturbing characteristics of contemporary internal armed conflicts is the consistent and intentional violation of the customary distinction made between combatant and civilian. International humanitarian legal norms are responsible for both producing and protecting this distinction in times of war. Consequently, they have acquired a new prominence in international efforts to mediate and adjudicate current internal armed conflicts. Yet, international humanitarian law provides scant and imprecise means for distinguishing between combatant and civilian. Evidence suggests that it is informal, contextual understandings that inform the meaning and, in turn, the implementation of this distinction. These understandings must be considered in the formulation of policy.
6. *Resettlement of Refugees and Internally Displaced Persons*. The settlement of returning refugees and internally displaced persons (IDPs) is a central aspect of post-conflict reconstruction, especially in Sub-Saharan Africa. As UN agencies assist local governments in this task, they must acknowledge the deep political and social impact of resettlement strategies if they are to avoid reproducing conditions that are likely to lead to violent conflict in the future. UN agencies acknowledge that refugees and IDPs are not only objects of policy, but full-fledged actors and agents of social and political change, who must take part in making the decisions that affect their future. In addition, policy-makers must recognize that resettlement is not an unproblematic end to the experience of displacement: it shapes the lives of refugees and IDPs, their perception of themselves and their relationship with other groups and the state.
7. *Promoting Democracy*. Complex peacekeeping operations in the post-cold war era included the support for

institutional reforms and the promotion of democratization. These projects privileged political rights and modernization of state institutions; while other aspects of democratization such as citizens participation, development and economic rights were often set aside. The UN should re-assess the viability and implications of its democratization efforts, and consider ways of promoting more inclusive approaches.

8. *Strengthening Indigenous Institutions*. Current initiatives by the international community to promote post-conflict reconstruction need to recognize the social and political capital that domestic communities have for constructing viable mechanisms and institutions for good governance based on their indigenous heritage. Externally imposed notions of what democracy is, or is not, and what it entails often undermine efforts to build political institutions that the local population can respect and internalize. In the interests of building a culture of democracy that genuinely enhances broad participation and effective accountability, post-conflict reconstruction efforts must carefully examine how their initiatives can be enhanced by indigenous structures of governance. Effective consultative mechanisms for indigenous populations are necessary at all stages of the post-conflict reconstruction process in order to determine the most appropriate institutions of governance that, ultimately, they will have to live with.
9. *Administering Territories*. In Bosnia, Kosovo and East Timor, international organizations perform an unusual activity: administering territory. By governing territories, conducting foreign relations, creating structures of government and promoting a certain domestic political culture, international organizations move beyond their usual role of performing discrete activities and assisting with or monitoring state activities, to performing state activities directly. The nature of this new role suggests that a significant reorientation of policy regarding the functions and accountability of those organizations involved is necessary.
10. *Disease Control*. The transboundary spread of diseases fueled

by globalisation of travel, commerce, tourism and refugee movements has diluted the erstwhile distinction between national and international health. Indeed, globalisation has offered an opportunity for infectious diseases and pathogenic microbes to infect populations globally with unprecedented speed. Transboundary infectious disease threats constitute a global crisis requiring multilateral cooperation. Given the current financial inability of multilateral institutions such as the World Health Organization to face the challenges of transboundary spread of diseases, private-public sector partnerships may be desirable. Indeed, the WHO has already undertaken joint ventures with private organizations such as the Bill & Melinda Gates Foundation and the Rockefeller Foundation with respect to its Roll-Back Malaria Project. However, in carrying out such initiatives, care must be taken to integrate traditional medical practices and beliefs of local communities into global policy as a guard against globalism-from-above.

11. *Global Public-Private Partnerships* (GPPPs) are emerging as popular vehicles for global governance and for the provision of global public goods. A review of a sample of these partnerships in the health sector reveals that the institutional arrangements governing these collaborations fail to conform to principles of good governance - i.e., legitimacy, representation, accountability and transparency. The proliferation of GPPPs (as currently constituted) may therefore further exacerbate problems associated with health sector governance at all levels. These developments suggest the need to develop best-practice guidelines for GPPPs as well as implementing mechanisms that assure adherence to the former. Further research is therefore warranted in order to guide the development of, and compliance with, such guidelines so as to promote more democratic governance through public-private collaboration.

12. *Multilateral Environmental Treaty-making*. The UN-sponsored series of world summits throughout the 1990s was an important innovation in global governance. The first of

these, the 1992 UN Conference on Environment and Development (UNCED), provided an unprecedented forum for focusing worldwide attention and action on sustainable development. UNCED also served as a crucial incentive for concluding two treaties: the Convention on Biological Diversity and the Framework Convention on Climate Change. The contemporary framework-protocol approach to multilateral environmental treaty-making has proven effective in operationalising the often ambiguous and soft legal content of sustainable development conventions into more precise and binding provisions. However, rather than resolving the political tensions inherent in the original UNCED agreements, the development of sub-agreements (or protocols) have at times reinforced these. Consequently, additional avenues œ which address political as well legal concerns œ for implementing global environmental treaties should be explored.

13. *Shared Compact*. Multilateral treaties have emerged as a legal mechanism for responding to transnational environmental harm. Developing nations argue they are entitled to resources and technologies to implement these treaties without compromising possibilities for their own economic development and industrialization. These arguments have been somewhat successful and are giving rise to an innovative concept in international environmental management: a shared compact, a common but differentiated responsibility, between the developed and developing world. There are important questions to be answered regarding the effectiveness of the shared compact as a tool in promoting treaty compliance as well as the depth of the developed world's commitment to redistribution.

14. *The World Bank and Good Governance*. In recent years, the World Bank -and international financial institutions in general - has significantly stretched its policy frontier by endorsing good governance as a core element of its development strategy. However, the contours of good governance remain ambiguous, leading not only to a proliferation of definitions and performance indicators for

assessing the quality of governance in developing countries, but also to a growing sense of "Washington confusion.' Ultimately, the quality of governance is attributable to its democratic content. Consequently, for the World Bank to substantially improve good governance in borrowing countries - and reinvent itself in the process - it will need to cross the Rubicon of politics and explicitly address issues of power, politics and democracy. The governance of multilateral financial institutions undoubtedly deserves greater scrutiny and reform.

15. *North-South Aid Relations*. Northern donor agencies and non-governmental organizations (NGOs) limited knowledge of the poor tends to affect the accuracy of their decision-making and, ultimately, the effectiveness of aid. The policies of Irish aid agencies toward Bangladeshi NGOs provide an illustration of this phenomenon. Although Irish NGOs think of Bangladeshi NGOs as their partners, a relationship of dependency remains the dominant reality for the Bangladeshis. The Irish official aid agency provides aid to Bangladeshi NGOs through Irish NGOs. A more suitable approach would be to send funds directly to Southern NGOs, bearing in mind that, because local capacities are limited, procedures for disbursing funds, monitoring progress and evaluating impact need to be simplified. More fundamentally, aid relationships should strive for an idea of partnership (rather than dependency) that has local purchase. The governance of aid needs to be revisited accordingly.
16. *Multinational Corporations and Global Governance.* Previously, states were concerned above all with issues of sovereignty and security, while multinational corporations (MNCs) focused on productivity and profits for shareholders. Nowadays, states are expected mainly to provide welfare, while MNCs face increasing demands from stakeholders to deliver goods in an economically profitable, ecologically sustainable and socially responsible way. When the state is weak, MNCs may find themselves assuming welfare-provision roles. The introduction of best practices in corporate governance - insofar as these ensure wider

representation and the recognition of stakeholder rights, transparency and accountability in top-level decision-making - may serve to partly remedy the democratic deficit of MNCs participation in local and global governance.

17. *The NAFTA Environment Debate*. There is a general expectation that a Global Civil Society (GCS) is emerging and that this trend will contribute to democratization. The NAFTA environment debate has highlighted several key features of this process. First, the emergence of a GCS is neither an automatic nor a linear process. Second, the national background of non-governmental organizations (NGOs) importantly affects their transnational role. Third, cross-border NGO activities have only a limited democratizing effect.

Democratisation should thus continue to be a major goal of national and global policy agendas. Living in an interdependent world Since the 1970s, trade in goods and services between countries and continents has almost tripled. The rise in foreign direct investment has risen dramatically, reaching an annual level of more than US$800 billion. This degree of international financial market integration is unprecedented in history. Growth in trade and foreign direct investment has substantially outperformed growth of world output. This provides evidence of an ever-growing international division of labour and of a deepening interdependence of the world economy.

Globalisation has become a widely used term to describe the ongoing process of increasing global economic interaction. It is spurred by impressive technological progress especially in the fields of information, communication and transport, as well as by political decisions to open up and deregulate markets, and further enhanced by international competition. Although initially facilitated by intentional political decisions, it would seem that the trend towards deepening global interdependence is virtually irreversible.

This process brings about fundamental change to the organisation of our economies. It creates new opportunities for all people around the globe, including the developing countries. It is inevitable, however, that in the context of this transformation, new pressures of adjustment arise in both the industrialised and the developing world. Greater economic integration may not always bring the anticipated benefits. Furthermore, as economic and financial interdependence intensifies between countries, the risk of contagion tends to increase and can transform the failure of one actor into a systemic crisis.

Global governance is key to ensuring that the positive impacts of globalisation are enhanced and its potentially negative effects are adequately balanced and mitigated. The post-world war period has witnessed unprecedented economic growth around the globe. Average living standards have improved across the world, life expectancy has risen, access to health care has improved, infant and child mortality has fallen, school enrolment has increased and the gap between girls and boys in school enrolment is narrowing. However, notwithstanding the remarkable success of the world economy, at the dawn of the 21st century the vicious circle of stagnation and poverty in the poorest countries remains unbroken.

Despite a decline in the proportion of people living in extreme poverty since the early 1990s, about one fifth of the world's population continues to live on US$1 or less per day, and a further quarter lives on less than US$2 a day. Poverty is particularly serious in Africa, where nearly half the population lives on less than US$1 per day. The international community is entering the new millennium with the largest difference ever recorded between rich and poor countries. Whilst some countries experienced strong economic progress, economic growth in others remained moderate, stagnated or even declined.

In a large number of poor countries during the last 25-30 years the per capita income did not rise but fell in absolute terms. Today, the per capita income of the richest 20 countries is almost 40 times higher than that of the poorest 20 countries. Forty years ago it was less than 20 times higher. At the same time, the gap between the rich and poor is increasing within many countries and regions. In all countries it is the less skilled who are more likely to be in poverty rather than those with the required education and skills. Growing inequality is both a result of existing poverty trends and an impediment to poverty reduction. Overall, it threatens the cohesiveness of local and regional communities and could ultimately lead to upheaval, political instability and violent conflicts within and between countries and regions.

Sharp differences in income levels are also a major reason for migration, which can further dampen the development potential in the country of outward migration. A just and balanced form of global governance may help to prevent such an outcome. Poverty is a multifaceted phenomenon that is best characterised by a lack of freedom, which leads to a lack of access to opportunities: access to sufficient nutrition, to decent clothing and housing, to basic health services and education, to transport and communication, to credit and insurance against natural disaster. The Human Development Report of the United Nations Development Program (UNDP) notes that some 90 million school-age children in the developing world are denied the chance to go to primary school.

The consequences of the lack of access to adequate health services combined with poor disease prevention are particularly serious and severely threat the development perspectives for many countries. By the end of 1999, nearly 34 million people were infected with HIV, 23 million in Sub-Saharan Africa. Approximately 5 million die annually from the three major communicable diseases: AIDS/HIV, tuberculosis and malaria. Access to markets also plays an important role: The potential gains from liberalising trade for developing countries are estimated to be far greater than today's volume of official development aid. Only recently have steps been taken by the European Union to open its markets and abolish tariffs and quotas for the least developed countries.

It is the prime responsibility of every country to ensure sound economic, social and environmental conditions and to put in place domestic policies aimed at effective poverty reduction. Poor domestic management, overburdened and inefficient administrative systems, outright corruption, and more generally the lack of the rule of law are among the reasons why in the past indigenous development has frequently remained disappointing, and why official development aid has often not fulfillled its expectations. Despite rising GNP levels in the industrialised countries during the 1990s, total official development aid (ODA) has continued to decline. Far from reaching the objective of 0.7 per cent of GNP, ODA has decreased over the last decades on average to a mere 0.2 percent.

While the growing role of private financial capital flows renders it imperative to ensure sound domestic policy conditions, the multitude of challenges faced by the poorest countries cannot be met without continued support from the international community. Private capital flows, including foreign direct investment, today account for approximately 80 - 90 per cent of total resource flows to developing countries. But the lion's share of these private flows has so far bypassed the poorest countries. According to the World Bank, all of sub-Saharan Africa received only 1,2 per cent of international financial flows to developing countries in 1998. These are the countries most vulnerable to diminishing aid budgets.

Based on the outcome of various UN conferences, the international community has set itself a number of international goals for global development, such as the objective to halve the number of people living in extreme poverty by 2015 compared to 1990 levels. Current trends are not encouraging. In a world characterised by rapid population growth in the South, the achievement of these goals can only be realised if underpinned by appropriate international support and a clear commitment to enhanced efforts for poverty reduction both domestically and internationally. Better global governance is necessary to identify priorities and to ensure that the challenge of poverty reduction is addressed effectively through a coherent and comprehensive approach.

The interdependence among states in a globalised world has drawn attention to the need to protect the environment for the sake of all nations. Scientific research indicates that our planet is increasingly threatened by a severe degradation of the environment. Whilst in some respects significant progress has been made in industrialised states, the developing states show alarming signs of ecological deterioration rather than advance. On the other hand, recent decades have witnessed growing awareness of these new environmental issues, which are truly global in nature.

The global climate is changing as a consequence of the so-called greenhouse effect. The Framework Convention on Climate Change and the Kyoto Protocol are the first, limited international steps to reduce the emission of greenhouse gases on a worldwide scale. However, more effort is required and the final success of these endeavours will depend on political will and the successful outcome of future negotiations. The depletion of the ozone layer is another global environmental concern. The Convention for the Protection of the Ozone Layer, together with the Montreal Protocol, has proved to be one of the most successful international environmental agreements.

The conservation of biological diversity has also been recognised as a common concern of humanity. So far, however, the Convention on Biological Diversity has not effectively provided protection for endangered species. Biological diversity is linked to the protection of our forests, which are also endangered, but so far lack a coherent framework for international action. Furthermore, desertification and drought have been recognised as problems with a global dimension. Finally, water quality degradation and overexploitation of marine resources threaten international waters. In many regions of the world, fresh drinking water is a scarce resource. A sustainable form of global governance is urgently needed to solve global environmental problems.

Worldwide economic integration and new ways of communication have brought people closer to one another. This is clearly a positive development but, in concrete terms, people around the world sometimes fear the possible loss of their national identity through the demise of their culture and its value systems as they are submerged by global homogenisation. However, the maintenance of a culture is dependent on the will and commitment of its people to protect the customs, traditions, language and values against the tide of one global cultural movement. Realistically, any system of global governance can only provide limited help in this respect.

Though it should provide a means to defend cultural diversity, global governance itself depends on a fundamental set of values and principles that must be accepted universally. It is clear that international institutions and national governments can support cultures, but global institutions cannot generate them. A realistic form of global governance must be sustained by a fundamental set of values and principles, which people all around the world - from a great variety of cultures and creeds - could accept. It is evident that global problems need global solutions.

The present lack of coherence in international economic, social and environmental decision-making is a significant obstacle to more and better global governance. The efficiency of the international institutional family is severely hampered by the lack of coherent mandates and a sometimes-inadequate degree of complementarity and co-operation between individual institutions. A pertinent example became evident during the November 1999 World Trade Organization (WTO) ministerial meeting in Seattle. On the one hand, there were far-reaching decisions taken by governments - in the framework of the twin Bretton Woods institutions (International Monetary Fund (IMF) and the World Bank) - to reduce significantly the debt of 41 heavily indebted poor countries.

On the other hand, these same governments failed only two months later - through the structure of the WTO - to launch a new trade round which would have attempted to eliminate trade barriers to exports from developing countries, which is a key precondition to any sustainable reduction of poverty. A failure to revive the trade talks in the near future would make a mockery of the debt initiative. In more general terms, the fragmented institutional architecture of the international economic system makes it virtually impossible to address the issue of interdependence in an effective and coherent manner.

Calls for closer co-operation between institutions are not a new phenomenon, nor are complaints about overlap and duplication. They can be interpreted as symptoms of the lack of an effective overarching framework to ensure coherence and a complementary division of labour. One reason for this lack of coherence in dealing with global challenges can be found at the domestic level, where different sections of national administrations are not always aware of international engagements, which are the responsibility of other departments. Therefore, if more coherence and convergence is needed at the global level, this is also true at the national level.

Global governance does not mean global government in the form of a centralised body that holds exclusive world power and controls global economic flows and information. Rather, it would provide the capacity for effective and legitimate political decision- making at the global level through international institutions and structures of co-operation, co-ordination and perhaps even shared sovereignty. Global governance implies that nation states pay more attention to the international impact of their domestic policies, respect their global obligations and accept the basic principles of multilateralism. International institutions themselves have to learn to co-operate in a more coherent and structured way.

Global governance will also require the emergence of public opinion with a more global view, in order to promote, develop and enforce globally agreed behaviour. Such global public opinion will be assisted in its formation by transnational businesses and labour unions, non-governmental organisations and private foundations, and by politicians. The Churches and other world religions will also have to play their role. This development has to be supported by the media, their plurality and independence being essential.

The 1991 papal encyclical *Centesimus Annus* outlines the Catholic Church's thinking on global governance: "The increasing internationalisation of the economy ought to be accompanied by effective international agencies which will oversee and direct the economy to the common good, something that an individual State, even if it were the most powerful on earth, would not be in a position to do. In order to achieve this result, it is necessary that in evaluating the consequences of their decisions, these agencies always give sufficient support and consideration to peoples and countries which have little weight in the international market, but which are burdened by the most acute and desperate needs, and are thus more dependent on support for their development."

It will not be necessary to build a new system of institutions and organisations from scratch to achieve global governance. The existing international system of organisations can be adapted. Improvement is required, not replacement. Major decision-making will still come from consensus among the nation states, which will continue to be the basic unit, at least for the foreseeable future, as they adapt to new global changes. Global governance is currently characterised at best as an intergovernmental as opposed to a supranational arrangement like the European Union. The latter will perhaps inspire further advances over time. However, even the current intergovernmentalism will not function without a basic set of core values and principles that are universally accepted.

No real progress in global governance is possible without a values system that is jointly embraced and respected. In this regard too, the social teaching of the Church offers its insights "to all men and women of good will". In the light of these teachings, the reality of the life of the Church and the world unfolds. The Church offers her social teaching as a definition of values and principles for a system of global governance. Human dignity is the core value of Christian social teaching, which must be respected and pursued in all human activity. This value has already been embraced by the full membership of the United Nations.

In the preamble of the UN Charter we read: "We, the people of the United Nations, determined ... to reaffirm faith in fundamental human rights, in the dignity and worth of the human person ... have resolved to combine our efforts to accomplish these aims." Admittedly, universal respect for human dignity is far from being a global reality, but it is a goal, an orientation for global policies. This innate dignity confers on human beings a set of fundamental rights, as expressed in numerous human rights declarations. Exercising one's fundamental rights goes together with obligations towards others and the community as a whole, as has been expressed again, for example, in the preamble of the Charter of Fundamental Rights of the European Union.

Enjoying one's fundamental rights and assuming obligations towards others are necessary if we wish to improve the human condition in both material and spiritual ways. Truthfulness is a clear obligation that derives from human dignity. Honesty is essential for the respect of human dignity and produces real consequences for the economy and public life. For instance, there has been a multiplication of tax havens in various parts of the globe over the last decades that have encouraged tax evasion. For the sake of the community it is vital that everyone pays their taxes in full; tax havens encourage cheating, which is unacceptable.

Allied to respect for personal human dignity, a sense of responsibility for the global common good is indispensable. In particular we have to face the challenges that are posed by the management of the world economy. Responsibility is a key aspect of Christian anthropology and ethics. Pope Paul VI, in his 1971 Apostolic Letter *Octogesima Adveniens*, put it this way:

"To take politics seriously at its different levels-local, regional, national and world-wide-is to affirm the duty of man, of every man, to recognise the concrete reality and the value of the freedom of choice that is offered to him to seek to bring about both the good of the city and of the nation and of mankind". At decisive turning points in history, this responsibility has taken on a variety of forms and challenges.

The consequences of globalisation, the persistence of poverty, the growth of inequality and the increase of environmental stress on a global scale call for a renewal of the human sense of responsibility in at least three respects:

- The responsibility of each country - large or small - for the world at large;
- The responsibility of the world community to put in place an ethically-grounded new development paradigm;
- The responsibility of all actors in society - and not just governments - to play their part in the direction the world takes to reach the above-mentioned goals and to espouse the idea of world citizenship.

The responsibility of each country: Due to the intricate relationships between countries in a globalised world, economic events in one country can have an unintentional effect elsewhere. Thus, when Thailand defaulted on its debt payments in 1997, the confidence of global financial markets in developing economies was severely shaken. The Thailand crisis provoked a string of subsequent shocks in Korea, Indonesia, Russia and Brazil, even though they had limited or no real relationship with the Thai economy.

This is just one example of the series of financial crises the world experienced during the last decade of the last century. It demonstrates that today, whether a country is large or small, any crisis can become systemic through contagion in the globalised market. Domestic economic policy therefore must, now more than ever, take into account its potential worldwide impact. A duty of universal responsibility is incumbent upon all. All countries and not just the strongest ones are responsible for the stability and quality of world growth. This adds a new dimension to the duties required of every government in the management of its economy.

The responsibility of the world community: The world community as a whole must assume responsibility for putting in place a new ethically-based development paradigm, where the international rules for trade and investment, together with the integrity of international monetary and financial management on the one hand and policies to reduce poverty on the other hand, form a two-way relationship. All countries must be encouraged not only to seek balanced books, but also to discover and realize what their global responsibilities imply.

This of course includes obligations relating to prudence in domestic policies. In this context the monitoring by the International Monetary Fund (IMF) is particularly important. Poverty reduction will not be achieved without sound economic policy; equally, economic policy is not ultimately sustainable if patent inequality and poverty are left unaddressed. The necessary popular support for a stable economy and reform efforts cannot be guaranteed unless the whole population, including the poorest, is able to have its say in the formulation of the policies adopted, and of course to benefit from them. This two-way relationship is part of an emerging and more comprehensive development paradigm in which moral values are an integral part. The new paradigm also tries to take into account different cultural and social models and to follow a more pragmatic country-by- country approach.

The responsibility of all actors in society: By suggesting a contribution from all actors, the third aspect of responsibility becomes apparent. To care about the direction that the world community takes is no longer the sole responsibility of governments, politicians and international or regional organisations. Other actors must take part: companies, financial institutions, labour unions and non- governmental organisations, as well as Churches. Every person must play a role in the success of the newly emerging development paradigm and thus become a global citizen. In other words, what is needed is a stronger sense of world citizenship.

The growing relevance of non-governmental organisations, which spearheaded many important initiatives in recent years, shows that the concept of world citizenship is becoming more and more a reality. However, NGOs should refine what has always been central to their achievements: patient and non-violent efforts to seek the truth in order to help public opinion become more aware and enlightened. NGOs must above all respect the democratic political process and act accordingly.

Many people lack a sense of the universal. It has not been possible for them to integrate the impact of the rapid developments in economics, finance and information. Their sense of the universal has been undone by these changes. They feel cut off from the universal, just as after the Treaty of Versailles in the 1920s Europeans did not have a sense of identification with Europe. The potential of the 21st century will not come to fruition if a new generation of opinion leaders does not deliberately accept the responsibility for giving public opinion a global conscience. A new kind of citizenship must be created, one that is not simply a vague cosmopolitanism, but a genuine citizenship, and rich in the appreciation of our affiliations at all levels: local, national, regional and global.

To combat poverty and to deal with widespread corruption, crime, money laundering and threats to the environment, more solidarity is needed. The pursuit of solidarity is essential for effective global governance. When José Angel Gurria, the Finance Minister of Mexico, spoke about poverty at the outset of the Asian crisis as the "ultimate systemic threat", his reference to the health of the system of global finance echoed the remarks of Pope John Paul II in his encyclical letter Sollicitudo Rei Socialis: "Either development becomes shared in common by every part of the world, or it undergoes a process of regression even in zones marked by constant progress".

While active solidarity is necessary to help the poorest, it also provides safeguards for the future generations of rich countries. Active solidarity is therefore also in the enlightened self-interest of the more wealthy societies. Solidarity is not only about generosity. It calls for the appropriate participation of every person in society and of every country in the world economy. Even in pragmatic terms, it is now widely recognised that ownership of economic and social policy by public opinion is a necessary condition for their success. The slogan "Globalisation without marginalisation" can be restated as: global justice as participation. Social justice is essentially participation in society. Justice as participation means strengthening a rule-based world system that allows for market participation.

Solidarity is central to organising and strengthening the very fabric of a world economy, which is now 'one' in a real sense. For industrialised countries, global solidarity does not simply mean sacrifice of the superfluous; it means dealing with vested interests and entrenched power structures, with life-styles and models of consumption. The change needed for genuine human development involves equally radical reforms in the South. In both the North and the South, it is a matter "of orienting the instruments of social organisation according to an adequate notion of the common good in relation to the whole human family".

The principle of subsidiarity occupies an important place among the core principles for global governance. Unless we pay due respect to this principle, which Catholic social teaching has long advocated, organising change will be difficult if not impossible. In fact, a major factor behind the resistance to change stems from the fear that national sovereignty might be handed over to anonymous and distant institutions that are not accountable to any democratic control. As Pope John XXIII clearly states in his encyclical letter Pacem in Terris, it is "necessary that the relationship that exists between the world-wide public authority and the public authority of individual nations be governed by the same principle (of subsidiarity).

This means that a worldwide public authority must tackle and solve problems of an economic, social, political or cultural character, which are posed by the universal common good. Indeed because of the vastness, complexity and urgency of those problems, the public authorities of the individual states are not in a position to tackle them with any hope of a positive solution. The worldwide public authority is not intended to reduce the sphere of action of the public authority of the individual states, much less to take its place. On the contrary, its purpose is to create, on a world basis, an environment in which the public authorities of each state, its citizens and intermediate associations, can carry out their tasks, fulfill their duties and exercise their rights with greater security".

The teaching of the Church on subsidiarity is formulated by considering "the way God acts in governing the world, which bears witness to such great regard for human freedom". This suggests that the more we see the need to consolidate or to grant new responsibilities to world bodies, the more it is also necessary to recognize the limits of their contribution. It should be clearly understood that nothing can be accomplished at the global level unless it has been taken up at the grassroots level and supported by the entire institutional chain, in which non-governmental organisations can play an ever-greater role. Responsible citizenship at all levels is a key to the global challenges of the 21st century.

Greater coherence, transparency and accountability of international organisations to the public should equally apply to the core principles of global governance. Too often, international institutions are portrayed as unaccountable and technocratic. The truth is that they are in fact responsible and accountable to their member governments. The problem is that they are not perceived as such. One reason for this lack of transparency is that governments have an interest in obfuscating their role in decision-making on the international level. On the one hand, they tend to refer to the imperative logic of the international regime to justify measures that are unpopular at home. On the other hand, they claim the positive achievements for themselves.

This contributes to an often-distorted perception of international organisations by the public. As a result, international organisations are often primary targets of public outrage about the deplorable state of global living conditions and the focal point of fears about the consequences of unleashed globalisation. In order to enhance global governance, national governments must voice their unequivocal support for the positions taken in the executive bodies of these institutions.

If the above-mentioned values and principles are to become the foundation of a system of global governance, it will be a task that must involve everybody who can contribute, for it can offer a response to the search for a sense of purpose in peoples' lives, especially among the world's youth. Vaclav Havel, the President of the Czech Republic, admirably suggested this in September 2000, when he delivered a speech to Ministers of Finance, Central Bank Governors and other bankers from around the world on the occasion of the annual meeting of the IMF and the World Bank in Prague. He said: "We often hear about the need to restructure the economies of the developing or the poorer countries and about the wealthier nations being duty-bound to help to accomplish this.

If this is done in a sensitive manner against a backdrop of sound knowledge of the specific environment and its unique interest and needs it is certainly a worthy and much needed effort. But I deem it even more important that we should begin to also think about another restructuring - a restructuring of the entire system of values which forms the basis of our civilization today. This, indeed, is a common task for all. And I would even say that it is of greater urgency for those who are better off in material terms..." There is little chance that this will happen unless it becomes possible to connect these values to something that lies beyond the horizon of immediate personal or group interest. So, how can this new value system be achieved without the recognition of the significance of the spiritual dimension of human existence?

Values and principles for global governance must be acceptable to non-believers and believers alike. They are not the exclusive concern of the world's religions. It is noteworthy to observe that the values and principles which Christians have been given by Christian social teaching - human dignity, responsibility, solidarity, global citizenship, justice, participation, subsidiarity, coherence, transparency and accountability - are values and principles shared by many people of good will around the world. They can therefore offer a basis for a more human system of global governance.

Bibliography

Andrews, Peggy. *Sisters Listening to Sisters: Women of the World Share Stories of Personal Empowerment.* Bergin and Garvey, 1996.

Awkward, Michael. *Negotiating Difference: Race, Gender, and the Politics of Positionality.* University of Chicago Press, 1995.

Bannerji, Himani. *Thinking Through: Essays on Feminism, Marxism, and Anti-Racism.* Women's Press, 1995.

Basu, Amrita, ed. *The Challenge of Local Feminisms: Women's Movements in Global Perspective.* Westview Press, 1995.

Butler, Judith and Joan W. Scott, ed. *Feminists Theorize the Political.* Routledge, 1992.

Carver, Terrell and Veronique Mottier, ed. *Politics of Sexuality.* NY: Routledge, 1998.

Chapman, Jennifer. *Politics, Feminism and the Reformation of Gender.* Routledge, 1992.

Chapman, Jenny. *Politics, Feminism and the Reformation of Gender.* Routledge, 1993.

Cocks, Joan. *The Oppositional Imagination: Feminism, Critique, and PoliticalTheory.* (out of print)

Elshtain, Jean Bethke. *Meditations on Modern Political Thought: Masculine/Feminine Themes from Luther to Arendt.* Penn State Univ. Press, 1992.

Fowlkes, Diane L. *White Political Women: Paths from Privilege to Empowerment.* Univ. of Tennessee Press, 1992.

Fraser, Nancy. *Justice Interruptus: Critical Reflections on the "Postsocialist" Condition.* Routledge, 1997.

Gottfried, Heidi, ed. *Feminism and Social Change: Bridging Theory and Practice.* Univ. of Illinois Press, 1996.

Hughes-Freeland, Felicia and Nickie Charles, ed. *Practising Feminism: Identity, Difference and Power.* Routledge, 1996.

Jones, Kathleen B., ed. *Citizenship in Feminism: Identity, Action, and Locale.* Indiana University Press, 1998.

Kenney, Sally J. and Helen Kinsella, ed. *Politics and Feminist Standpoint Theories.* Haworth Press, 1997.

King, Katie. *Theory in Its Feminist Travels: Conversations in U.S. Women's Movements.* Indiana Univ. Press, 1994.

Meehan, Elizabeth and Selma Sevenhuijsen, ed. *Equality Politics and Gender.* Sage, 1991.

Meyers, Diana Tietjens, ed. *Feminist Social Thought: A Reader.* Routledge, 1997.

Naples, Nancy A., ed. *Community Activism and Feminist Politics: Organizing Across Race, Class, and Gender.* Routledge, 1997

Okin, Susan Moller. *Women in Western Political Thought.* Princeton Univ. Press, 1992.

Pascall, Gillian. *Social Policy: A New Feminist Analysis.* 1997.

Pateman, Carole and Elizabeth Gross, ed. *Feminist Challenges: Social and Political Theory.* Northeastern Univ. Press, 1987.

Phillips, Anne. *Engendering Democracy.* Penn State Univ. Press, 1991.

Phillips, Anne. *Feminism and Politics.* Oxford, 1998.

Randall, Vicky and Georgina Waylen, ed. *Gender, Politics and the State.* NY: Routledge, 1998.

Rocheleau, Dianne, Barbara Thomas-Slayter, and Esther Wangari, ed. *Femininst Political Ecology: Global Issues and Local Experiences.* 1996.

Sapiro, Virginia. *A Vindication of Political Virtue: The Political Theory of Mary Wollstonecraft.* Univ. of Chicago Press, 1992.

Simon, Sherry. *Gender in Translation: Cultural Identity and the Politics of Transmission.* Routledge, 1996.

Sunstein, Cass R., ed. *Feminism and Political Theory.* Univ. of Chicago Press, 1990.

Thomas, Sue and Clyde Wilcox, ed. *Women and Elective Office.* Oxford, 1997.

Waring, Wendy, ed. *By, For and About: Feminist Cultural Politics.* Women's Press, 1994.

Warren, Karen J. and Duane L. Cady, ed. *Bringing Peace Home: Feminism, Violence, and Nature.* Indiana Univ. Press, 1996.

Wolf, Naomi. *Fire with Fire: The New Female Power and How It Will Change the 21st Century.* Fawcett Books, 1993.

Young, Iris Marion. *Justice and the Politics of Difference.* Princeton, 1998.

Young, Stacey. *Changing the wor(l)d: Discourse, Politics, and the Feminist Movement.* Routledge, 1997.

Zack, Naomi, ed. *American Mixed Race: The Culture of Microdiversity.* Rowman and Littlefield, 1995

Index

I

L

M

N

O